Statewide
Coordination
of Higher Education

.

STATEWIDE COORDINATION OF HIGHER EDUCATION

by Robert O. Berdahl

*with the assistance of Jane Graham
and Don R. Piper*

AMERICAN COUNCIL ON EDUCATION · WASHINGTON, D.C.

Library of Congress Catalog Card Number: 73-153667
© 1971 by the American Council on Education
Printed in the United States of America
ISBN 0-8268-1383-6

The issue of university autonomy will never be finally solved. It can only be lived with.

John Gardner

Autonomy does not depend upon financial independence, for in these days, no university . . . is financially independent. Nor does it depend upon isolation from politics, which at best is nervous and unreal, for every university these days must engage in constant conversations with those who have been elected to public office. Academic autonomy really depends on a broad social assumption that, despite the exigencies of the moment, we must not make decisions on inadequate information.

Claude Bissell

Contents

List of Tables

Foreword

Ten years ago in a paper on the organization of American higher education, prepared for USIA distribution, I related the autonomy of our colleges and universities to their freedom from unified control by any political, religious, or other centralized national agency. I described the largely voluntary associations of individuals and institutions comprising a "system" of higher education, where leadership has come mainly from within, rather than being imposed from without.

I did make passing mention of trustee roles, and included a single sentence which stated, "Institutions within a state system likewise have their activities influenced in varying degree by politically appointed or elected agencies such as legislatures, governors, state budget offices, statewide commissions, 'super boards,' and so on." In light of subsequent concerns, I would now remark, "What an understatement!"

Robert O. Berdahl's *Statewide Coordination of Higher Education* should heighten our awareness of a drastic change that has taken place in the governance of many institutions during recent decades. Among the fifty American states in 1969, only two had no politically named coordinating agency and only two continued to rely on voluntary association to perform the coordinating function. Considering the attention paid to intramural changes in academic governance, it is astonishing how little popular notice has been given to the kind and number of decisions that have been shifting to an extramural locus. And this locus, as Dr. Berdahl points out, is often a statewide coordinating agency.

Because the future of American higher education, and more especially its public sector, is likely to be heavily influenced by the actions of such agencies, it is important to understand their structures and functions. The main purpose of this book, *Statewide Coordination of Higher Education*, is to further such an understanding. Berdahl's overview is by no means the first, but it is the most comprehensive, and one of the few to venture beyond description and exposition.

In his opening chapter, the author asserts that "A major source of current friction [in the area of coordination] is that many academics are trying to protect too much, and many persons in state government are trying to claim too much." He then goes on to draw a needed distinction between academic freedom and university autonomy, with a careful re-examination of the substantive and procedural aspects of autonomy. In ten subsequent chapters, he attempts to develop the thesis that a "climate of mutual trust and respect" between higher education and state government can be promoted best through the wise use of statewide coordinating agencies.

The evolution of various agency forms is set forth. Agency structures, functions, and relationships are delineated in chapters on membership and staff, planning, budget review, program review, and agency roles as intermediaries between government and institutions. In Part Three, Dr. Berdahl explores problems and issues, and in Part Four, he comes to grips with the nettlesome subject of evaluation. The appendixes give two examples of formula budgeting and two dissenting opinions regarding the author's conclusions and recommendations.

Various readers will doubtless have their own dissenting opinions about some of the author's views, but there should be no disputing the usefulness of this inquiry. It combines original research with a judicious application of findings from other studies. Unlike many of those studies, however, this one does not hesitate to judge alternatives and to evaluate outcomes. Dr. Berdahl has correctly noted that his conclusions and recommendations are his own and do not imply endorsement by the American Council on Education. Whether or not we are persuaded by them, he has, in my judgment, rendered a valuable service in bringing together significant facts and analyzing them objectively; he has arrived at some conclusions and recommendations which the decision makers in and for American higher education need to note with care and concern.

LOGAN WILSON, President
American Council on Education

Preface

John Gardner was undoubtedly correct when he observed, "The issue of university autonomy will never be finally solved. It can only be lived with." It is the assumption of this study that the issue can be lived with more successfully if the persons concerned make periodic efforts to re-examine and bring up to date their thinking about the meaning of the central terms.

This means that, for our purposes, the concept of autonomy as it applies to relations between higher education and state government had to be carefully analyzed. In our interviews with persons from both spheres, we found confirmation of the comment in a 1967 staff paper of the Education Commission of the States that "while the two groups generally can reach agreement *in principle,* . . . this apparent agreement shows rather clearly divergent viewpoints when applied *in operation.*" Our aim in this study is to try to narrow this gap somewhat and to reduce confusions by offering the following sequence of analysis:

1. a set of definitions distinguishing academic freedom from university autonomy and, within the latter category, substantive autonomy from procedural autonomy (chapter 1).

2. a brief description of the evolution of state coordinating bodies dealing with substantive developments in higher education and an explanation of the methods used in our research on their operations (chapters 2 and 3).

3. an extended analysis of the structures, functions, and relationships of the various types of state coordinating agencies (chapters 4–8).

4. an examination of certain related issues: e.g., relations between the state and private higher education; the impact of Federal programs on state coordination; and relations between higher education and the public school system (chapters 9 and 10).

5. a set of normative conclusions based on my own evaluation of most of the issues analyzed and a look at variables that may affect university-state relations in the future (chapter 11).

Most of the field research for the study was done in 1966–67; however, much of the analysis covers changes up to 1969. In general, events during the 1969–70 academic year have not been covered.

In the report, the pronoun *we* is used to indicate a staff effort; however, in chapters 1, 3, and 11, where my own personal opinions are advanced, the first-person singular is used. The staff included Jane Graham, who wrote the first draft of chapter 4 and who was a tireless companion on many fatiguing field trips, and Donald Piper, who shared field assignments and who drafted an invaluable background paper on recent developments in state governments. Otis Singletary and Richard Knoller also undertook brief field trips. Not "staff members" but "cooperating scholars" is the appropriate term for Samuel Gove, James Heck, and Charles H. White, who agreed to study, under ACE sponsorship, certain states not covered by our staff, and for Frank B. Brouillet and James G. Paltridge who generously made available to us the results of their own independent studies of still other states. There is also a long list of persons who were especially helpful to this study: Harry S. Allen, Lanier Cox, Kent Halstead, Emanuel Hurwitz, Jr., Eugene C. Lee, Lionel J. Livesey, Jr., Lewis B. Mayhew, James L. Miller, Jr., David W. Minar, Ernest Palola, Emogene Pliner, John M. Smart, and Michael D. Usdan. To all these colleagues, I would like to express my appreciation, at the same time relieving them of any responsibility for conclusions and recommendations that are my own.

To the American Council on Education, in general, and to President Logan Wilson and successive Vice-Presidents Allan Cartter, Otis Singletary, and Kenneth Roose, in particular, go special thanks for generating the idea of the study, giving it generous support, demonstrating much patience, and bestowing complete freedom of action. In addition, I am happy to acknowledge the counsel of the Advisory Committee to the study (listed elsewhere). Neither the Advisory Committee nor the American Council on Education, however, should be assumed to endorse the findings or opinions offered herein (see Appendix B).

It is impossible to express adequately our debt of gratitude to all the hundreds of people whom we interviewed in the field. They gave generously of their time and often of their confidences; but since we assured them that their comments would not be specifically identified, we can render only a blanket thanks. Charmian Black and Charles Andersen also gave willing and welcome assistance, and to them we express our deep appreciation.

Finally, I want to acknowledge the crucial assistance of two other persons almost as close to the manuscript as I: my wife, Ann, who has cheerfully suffered through the many months of seeing the study completed and put into print, and Laura Kent, the editor, who has lent her considerable skill to bringing more clarity and logic to the presentations.

ROBERT O. BERDAHL

Buffalo, New York
September 1970

PART ONE

INTRODUCTION TO THE PROBLEM

ONE

Autonomy and the public interest

This study of emerging relations between higher education and state governments has been undertaken at a time when soaring costs and campus militancy bring higher education increasingly to the attention of those in state government, and when state fiscal controls and occasional political interferences have convinced some academics that university freedoms are rapidly disappearing.

Clearly, the nerves of all parties are on edge, and it may not seem the best time to attempt a dispassionate examination of the topic. Indeed, Chancellor Samuel B. Gould, of the State University of New York, issued a general warning to this effect in 1966:

> full and unreserved public discussion of the relations between a university and state government could have the effect of straining and weakening the very elements such a discussion is intended to strengthen. . . . the whole subject is surrounded by a sense of fear and hesitancy that tends to becloud the realities.[1]

As if to confirm Gould's observations, two major figures in American higher education—one the head of a state coordinating board and the other a university president—warned me that a study such as this one would inevitably be biased, but their warnings were mutually contradictory. The former feared a bias toward universities, with resultant damage to the public interest; the latter, a bias toward state government, with university autonomy suffering in consequence.

No one concerned with the values both of the public interest and of university autonomy can lightly dismiss such advice, and I did not. But

1. "The University and State Government: Fears and Realities," *Campus and Capitol*, ed. W. John Minter (Boulder, Colo.: Western Interstate Commission for Higher Education, November 1966), p. 3.

after careful reflection and considerable work in the field, I was convinced that the time had come to grasp this nettle firmly and attempt a thorough analysis of the delicate relations between higher education and state government. It remains for others to decide whether the consequences are destructive or beneficial.

Why State Government?

In view of predictions by authorities like Clark Kerr and Alan Pifer that the Federal government will play an increasingly important and perhaps ultimately dominant role in the financing of higher education, it might be asked why this study limits its focus to the state level of government.

This question admits of several answers. The most obvious is that a study of the relations between higher education and *all* levels of government would be either too big to handle or too superficial to be useful. But quite apart from that, there are other good reasons under present conditions for concentrating on the state role. First, increased Federal aid notwithstanding, state governments will continue to be the major source of funds for all public institutions of higher education, except for a handful of prestigious research universities; and for the forseeable future even they will depend heavily upon state subsidies to remain fiscally viable. Furthermore, it is likely that state support for private as well as public higher education will increase in some states.

Second, even if Federal aid to higher education grows by a large percentage, it does not necessarily mean a proportionate decrease in state influence. For it has not yet been determined whether such Federal aid would go directly to the institutions, directly to the students, or directly to the states, to be channeled through them. If Federal block grants are given to the states, the latter will have even wider influence over higher education than they presently exercise.[2]

Third, even if the state role in financing higher education were to diminish markedly, all institutions—public and private—would still have to function in a context of state law and state sovereignty. Thus, state policies and procedures in the areas of educational planning and institutional governance and coordination would still be of great interest to all higher education.

Finally, there is considerable evidence that the misunderstanding which occasionally divides the general public and the academic world is

2. The potential impact of Federal aid to higher education on state coordination and planning is examined further in chapter 10.

reflected more immediately and more intensely at the state level of government than at the national. This is certainly true in several states at the present time. In short, relations between the campus and the statehouse may be more strained than those between the campus and the nation's capital.

The two most recent works to examine comprehensively the relationship between higher education and state government were both published in 1959,[3] and since that time, higher education has continued to grow in size, complexity, and cost; state programs and budgets have expanded proportionately; and state after state has created new, or altered existing, mechanisms for the planning and coordination of higher education. Thus the time seems ripe for a reexamination of this relationship and a reassessment of the related twin concerns of institutional autonomy and the public interest.

On Academic Freedom and University Autonomy

A major source of current friction is that many academics are trying to protect too much, and many persons in state government are trying to claim too much. A fundamental cause of this confusion is the failure of persons on both sides to recognize that academic freedom and university autonomy, though related, are not synonymous and that university-state relations in the one area may quite properly differ from those in the other.

Happily, academic freedom as a centuries-old tradition has been widely and often astutely treated as a subject for research.[4] Our task, then, is to define it and to make the crucial distinction between it and university autonomy.

Academic freedom has been defined as

that freedom of members of the academic community, assembled

---

3. Lyman A. Glenny, *Autonomy of Public Colleges*, (New York: McGraw-Hill Book Co., 1959); Malcolm Moos and Frank Rourke, *The Campus and the State* (Baltimore: Johns Hopkins Press, 1959).

4. The best-known works in this country are: Richard Hofstader and Walter Metzger, *The Development of Academic Freedom in the United States* (New York: Columbia University Press, 1955); and Robert M. MacIver, *Academic Freedom in Our Time* (New York: Columbia University Press, 1955). Also helpful are: Hans W. Baade and Robinson O. Everett, eds., *Academic Freedom: The Scholar's Place in Modern Society* (Dobbs Ferry, N.Y.: Oceana Publications, 1964); and Russell Kirk, *Academic Freedom: An Essay in Definition* (Chicago: H. Regnery, 1955). The *Bulletin* of the American Association of University Professors frequently has articles on the subject. Sir Eric Ashby's comparative study *Universities: British, Indian, African* (Cambridge, Mass.: Harvard University Press, 1966) has an excellent chapter on this topic.

in colleges and universities, which underlies the effective performance of their functions of teaching, learning, practice of the
arts, and research. The right . . . is not sought as a personal privi-
lege . . . [but] in order to enable faculty members and students to
carry on their roles.[5] (Order transposed.)

At its strongest, this freedom embraces security of tenure for those
faculty members who have been judged by their senior colleagues to meet
the standards of competence established by the academic profession. Protected by this security, a professor can defend margarine in a dairy state,
attack cigarettes in a tobacco state, sponsor poetry readings or plays
deemed obscene by some, or criticize American institutions from the Left
or Right, and usually survive. Though more vulnerable, junior faculty
without tenure, and even students, have profited to some extent from the
tradition of the campus as a privileged sanctuary for the whole spectrum
of ideas. Richard Hofstader and Walter Metzger describe this concept as
a composite one, taking

> from modern science . . . the notion of a continuing search for
> new truths, fostered by freedom of inquiry, verified by objective
> processes, and judged by those who are competent; from com-
> merce . . . the concept of a free competition among ideas—hence
> the suggestive metaphor of a free market in thought; from the
> politics of the liberal state . . . the ideas of free speech and a free
> press and an appreciation of the multitudes of perspectives in a
> pluralist society; from religious liberalism and the long historical
> development which led to the taming of the sectarian animus
> . . . the ideas of toleration and religious liberty.[6]

But this ideal has been realized only imperfectly on most campuses.
Attacks have been launched on the ostensible neutrality of the Academy
from both sides of the political fence. At the height of Cold War tensions,
conservative critics asserted that many campuses had fallen under Marxist
influence. More recently, the New Left has charged that American campuses act as agents for the Establishment on such matters as Vietnam and
racism. From each side have come demands that the universities and colleges refuse to consort any longer with "evil"; and currently, the radical

5. Ralph Fuchs, "Academic Freedom: Its Basic Philosophy, Function, and History,"
Academic Freedom: The Scholar's Place in Modern Society, eds. Baade and Robinson,
p. 1.
6. *The Development of Academic Freedom in the United States,* p. 61.

Left is using its power base of a militant minority on campus to try to force the rejection of "immoral tolerance."

But to abandon the concept of the university as a haven for *all* ideas is to play into the hands of political demagogues who are quick to spot a sensitive issue in higher education and who find it easy to arouse public resentment of the special freedom claimed in its name. Governors and legislators who do understand the concept of the privileged sanctuary find the task of defending it increasingly difficult, for they must survive politically in a world that is hypersensitive to adverse public opinion.

Actually, given the subtlety of the arguments for granting universities and their scholars these special freedoms, it is not surprising that some government authorities have tried to ensure the orthodoxy of the ideas transmitted within universities. Although most people would regard the connections between free science, technological improvements, and economic prosperity as obvious enough to justify unhindered inquiry, it requires considerable sophistication to understand the paradox that the university sometimes serves society best in social, economic, and political spheres by acting as a shield for its critics—even its severe critics. The Supreme Court has described the sensitive, probing function of the university very well:

> No field of education is so thoroughly comprehended by man that new discoveries cannot yet be made. Particularly is that true in the social sciences, where few, if any, principles are accepted as absolutes. Scholarship cannot flourish in an atmosphere of suspicion and distrust. Teachers and students must always remain free to inquire, to study and evaluate, to gain new maturity and understanding; otherwise our civilization will stagnate and die.[7]

Assuming that academic freedom is of absolutely central importance to a university's proper functioning, and recognizing that it is difficult to maintain in the face of limited public understanding, this report argues that the cause of academic freedom will be strengthened if it is disengaged somewhat from the question of university autonomy. Academic freedom must be firmly defended wherever and however it is threatened; but institutional autonomy has necessarily and legitimately been reduced by state

---

7. *Sweezy v. New Hampshire*, 354 U.S. 250, as quoted by Fuchs, "Academic Freedom: Its Basic Philosophy, Function, and History," p. 13.

actions over the past two decades in ways not fully grasped by many people, and here the defense must be much more discriminating.

By *autonomy* here is meant the power of a university or college (whether as a single institution or a multicampus system) to govern itself without outside controls. James A. Perkins has noted that "autonomy for the university surely has its strongest case in its role as protector of intellectual freedom,"[8] and obviously autonomy is related to academic freedom in that the latter is more likely to flourish in the autonomous institution. But, as Sir Eric Ashby has pointed out, the connection is not a necessary one: 19th century Oxford and Cambridge were autonomous institutions which themselves denied academic freedom to some of their scholars, whereas academic freedom thrived in 19th century German universities which, under the control of their respective governments, lacked autonomy.[9]

Yet the temptation remains for persons both in higher education and in government to link the two concepts closely together, albeit for very different reasons. For instance, the academicians who dominated the distinguished Committee on Government and Higher Education argued forcefully in their 1959 report, *The Efficiency of Freedom*, that

> intellectual freedom and institutional independence can hardly be separated. . . . Intellectual freedom may suffer seriously if public colleges and universities are subjected to the same controls as other state activities. Conversely, *protecting the authority of boards of lay trustees from interference by the state is every bit as vital to the freedom of the university as is the preservation of freedom for teaching and research.*[10] (Emphasis added.)

From the perspective of this report, such an analysis is dangerous. It is understandable that institutional presidents and trustees would want to preserve to themselves maximum freedom of action. But unless the phrase "interference by the state" is defined so narrowly as to mean only crude political interventions (e.g., a call from the statehouse urging that a particular building contractor be used for university construction), this position would deny the state its legitimate interest in many university policies and procedures (e.g., a request that university administrators clear

---

8. *The University in Transition* (Princeton, N.J.: Princeton University Press, 1966), p. 14.
9. *Universities: British, Indian, African*, p. 290.
10. Baltimore: Johns Hopkins Press, 1959, p. 6.

plans for a new medical school with appropriate state officials). The real issue with respect to autonomy, then, is not whether there will be interference by the state but rather whether the inevitable interference will be confined to the proper topics and expressed through a suitably sensitive mechanism.

Those academicians in public higher education who weld autonomy and academic freedom together in equal importance and who refuse to yield any of either to the state are unwittingly issuing a convenient invitation for politicians to act similarly: that is, to refuse to distinguish the one concept from the other and to push state power legitimate in the area of autonomy into the area of academic freedom, where it would be disastrous.

Ashby has elaborated further on the distinction between academic freedom and university autonomy:

> There is a very strong case for asserting that [academic freedom] cannot vary with latitude, race, politics, or creed. A country where political doctrine or commitment to a religious creed interferes with academic freedom cannot have free scholarship or good universities. By contrast university autonomy does not always and everywhere assume the same pattern.[11]

> One example, generally acknowledged to be a feature of autonomy, will suffice to illustrate this: the procedure for appointing professors. [Sir Eric then describes the significant variations in this practice at three British universities and goes on to contrast the French, German, and American variations.] . . . the amount and nature of the freedom allowed by these different practices are very diverse: yet none of the practices is regarded as inimical to autonomy in the countries where they occur.[12]

According to this analysis, academic freedom as a concept is universal and absolute, whereas autonomy is of necessity parochial and relative, with the specific powers of governments and universities varying not only from place to place but also from time to time. This qualification in no way detracts from the importance of autonomy as an essential aspect of university life; it merely emphasizes the urgency of keeping its definition relevant to changing conditions.

11. *Universities: British, Indian, African,* p. 321.
12. Ibid., p. 293.

Autonomy Reexamined: Substantive and Procedural

Autonomy is, in a public college or university, obviously limited at the very least by the need to seek funds from the state government. But normally the state's interest goes far beyond merely deciding on the gross amount of tax support to be provided; it can extend to the substantive goals, policies, and programs that an institution has chosen to pursue, to the procedural techniques selected to achieve the chosen goals, or to both. The problem is to determine which interferences by the state constitute *necessary* safeguards of the public interest, which constitute *marginal* safeguards of the public interest, and which constitute actual threats to the essential ingredients of autonomy, perhaps best described as "the portion of our institutional life and development which is not within the bailiwick of anyone else to prescribe or control or even touch."[13]

Faced with the imposing task of trying to categorize the various types of state interventions in higher education, we early decided to bypass most of those involving essentially procedural controls and to concentrate on those relevant to substantive autonomy. This decision seemed justified for several reasons. Like academic freedom (and unlike substantive autonomy), procedural autonomy has already been thoroughly investigated by other persons.[14] Moreover, we found ourselves in basic agreement with their verdict that most state procedural controls are more a hindrance to good management and good higher education than a necessary safeguard of the public interest. We did not agree, however, with the claim that such state controls threaten the essential ingredients of autonomy. It was our belief that procedural controls are of only marginal importance to either side, and on these grounds, we omitted them from detailed consideration.

These points need some elaboration: Most critics of state procedural controls propose that, beyond the required postaudit of appropriated funds, controls be limited to those demonstrably necessary for good state budget practices: e.g., establishing common categories for reporting

13. Gould, "The University and State Government: Fears and Realities," p. 5.
14. State procedural controls are the central theme of the Committee on Government and Higher Education's *The Efficiency of Freedom* and a major theme of the accompanying staff report by Moos and Rourke, *The Campus and the State*. Other works that include material on the topic are: James L. Miller, *State Budgeting for Higher Education: The Use of Formulas and Cost Analysis*, Michigan Governmental Studies no. 45, University of Michigan (Ann Arbor: Institute of Public Administration, 1964); Glenny, *Autonomy of Public Colleges*; and M. M. Chambers, *Chance and Choice in Higher Education* (Danville, Ill.: Interstate Printers and Publishers, 1962).

budget data; formulating common definitions of terms like *full-time-equivalent students*, and *faculty/student ratio*; and applying common standards to measure space utilization and so forth. M. M. Chambers points out that those public universities which are usually regarded as the best (e.g., California, Michigan, Minnesota) have all been granted constitutional autonomy which allows them considerable freedom of internal administration.[15] According to modern theories of good administrative practices, the officials responsible should be delegated maximum power and resources to carry out policies and then held strictly accountable after the fact. If such broad administrative discretion leads to an occasional instance of institutional mismanagement, the answer (the critics continue) is not to abrogate the discretion but to replace the administrators. Presidents have no tenure and trustees have limited terms. But (they conclude) the higher quality of the administrator—and perhaps of the faculty member—attracted by an institution which has been given room for "creative administration" will more than compensate for the isolated case of mismanagement. Though difficult to prove, it is nonetheless true that the state stands to lose far more through the diminished creativity and attenuated vitality of an overly controlled institution than through the relatively small sums that might be saved through the imposition of a tight preaudit of expenditures.

Yet our research team found many legislators and some governors who were very reluctant to exempt higher education from the state procedural controls which normally accompany the expenditure of public funds: e.g., line-item budgets with tight control over transfers from one item to another; preaudits of authorized expenditures, sometimes for propriety as well as for legality; central controls over all nonacademic personnel; central controls over capital outlay programs, sometimes including design; central purchasing of supplies and equipment; and central controls over various administrative routines such as approval of out-of-state travel.

It should be obvious by now that I disagree with state officials who maintain that these controls are *necessary* safeguards of the public interest. *Marginal* safeguards, perhaps, but usually purchased at too high a price. On the other hand, I do not concur with those academicians (both administrators and faculty) who complained during the interviews (indeed, some we could hardly get off the subject) that such controls would drain the very lifeblood of their institutions. Surely, unless the full pano-

15. *Freedom and Repression in Higher Education* (Bloomington, Ind.: Bloomcraft Press, 1965), p. 119.

ply of controls is applied with incredible heavy-handedness, the verdict must be that the controls are highly irritating and probably even counterproductive—but hardly so serious as to merit the shrill note of outrage which should be sounded for state assaults upon academic freedom or upon the really essential ingredients of autonomy. One must not shout, "Wolf, wolf!" too often or the cry will lose its effectiveness. In this report, we wish to save our major concern for the issues, so far rather neglected in the literature, involving substantive autonomy.

One final paradox concerning procedural autonomy should be noted. The Committee on Government and Higher Education warned that "intervention of state agencies into ostensibly nonacademic areas can quickly penetrate to educational policy." [16] Granting that matters of academic administration cannot easily be separated from policy issues and that state procedural controls which intrude into policy matters are undesirable, we feel it is imperative to point out that they are undesirable not because the state has no business concerning itself with higher education policies, but because when it is expressing its legitimate interests in substantive issues, the "penetration" should take place at the front door, as a conscious act of state sovereignty. In short, the state should participate through a suitably sensitive mechanism for dealing with educational policies rather than as an incidental result of administrative controls being applied by persons only modestly (if at all) conversant with the special problems of higher education.

The State–Higher Education Partnership

A major implication of the view expressed here is that a state's willingness to recognize the claims of academic freedom and procedural autonomy may be reinforced by the institutions' equal willingness to recognize the state's right to participate in some of the decisions regarding the substantive development of public higher education. The questions that must next be answered are: (1) which decisions? and (2) by what form of participation?

The nature of the decisions

To keep the issue of state partnership in perspective, one must realize that by far the majority of the decisions involved will pertain to new

16. *The Efficiency of Freedom*, p. 7.

developments, from establishing campuses to creating degree programs. Normally, the agenda will center on questions as to which of the institutions' proposed programs are compatible with state interest, and which of the state's requests for assistance are compatible with the institutions' definition of their own purposes. Only rarely will ongoing programs be jeopardized in any way, beyond suffering the standstill budgetary consequence of being given low priority for expansion and improvement. In a few instances, states have empowered agencies to recommend the elimination of existing programs found to result in wasteful duplication, but given the current need for expansion of both the number and types of programs, the probable state role is that of traffic cop for new programs rather than destroyer of existing ones. Of course, there is always the danger that, under conditions like those in the depression-ridden 1930s, states may again react by forcing severe cutbacks in current programs. Perhaps if more careful procedures for establishing new programs are instituted now, it will be less necessary in the future to engage in brutal wholesale retrenchments. This is especially true for new graduate programs where the dangers of overproduction have already become obvious.

The state plays an obviously minimal role in the approval of new programs by agreeing to fund them. But with the increase in the quantity, complexity, and costs of requested new programs, most states are no longer willing to confine themselves to ad hoc fiscal answers. They want to know which of the requested new programs represent genuine state needs, whether the basic mission and particular characteristics of the requesting institution make it the proper one for the program in question, whether the state has the resources to fund all new programs that make it over these two hurdles, and if not, what order of priority should be accorded those deemed eligible. This, then, is the rationale for widespread state involvement in institutional requests for new programs.

Proposals for new programs can come from the state to the institutions as well as from the opposite direction. Naturally enough, state officials tend to want universities and colleges to prove their utility by serving practical state needs in a variety of ways. Since institutions of higher education belong to a national—and, in some cases, to an international—community of scholarship which honors "excellence" more than it does utility, there will often be a tug of war with, on the one side, powerful forces in the university pulling for program packages to improve quality (e.g., initiating prestigious new degree programs, research institutes, and so forth; attracting top scholars through higher salaries, lighter teaching loads, better sabbatical arrangements, and so forth; improving library facilities) and, on the other, powerful outside forces pulling for greater institutional sensitivity to the state interest (e.g., giving priority to local, regional, and state needs when establishing new courses or undertaking research or public service activities; cutting costs by using modern instructional techniques and by operating on a year-round basis).

Since the demands for utility are backed by the financial power of the state, most public institutions are in greater danger of becoming service stations than of remaining ivory towers. Logan Wilson has described this dilemma very well:

> If we saddle universities with responsibilities they cannot effectively discharge, or if we shift to them burdens more logically belonging to other agencies, we run the risk of distorting their basic purposes and splintering their effectiveness. In serving society, colleges and universities must not become subservient to it. Their highest utility is in their distinctive functions, and if they become unduly enmeshed as agencies of social welfare, these functions will be eroded.[17]

The delineation of which substantive decisions are appropriate for state participation is, then, no minor problem. A state may honor academic freedom, impose few procedural controls, and still threaten the long-run health of its universities and colleges by displacing their aspirations for excellence and substituting its demands for utility.

Of course, the two sets of goals are not incompatible, and it becomes the duty of well-disposed persons on both sides to determine the form and content of the partnership. In some decisions, the state must have the primary voice (e.g., determining the overall level of state support); in others, the institutions must be dominant (e.g., establishing new courses; setting academic standards); and in still others, the state and the institutions must work closely together (e.g., master planning the future of higher education; deciding on new professional schools). If one accepts the thesis that autonomy is a parochial and relative concept, then in each state of the union, representatives of higher education and government officials must come together to discuss their respective roles in substantive decision making.

17. "The Abuses of the University" (Commencement Address, Michigan State University, March 10, 1968), p. 5.

The "suitably sensitive mechanism"

But because the particular concordats (as Ashby calls them) between governments and higher education may vary not only from place to place but also over time in the same place, it is important to have a *continuing* vehicle for transmitting the state's wishes to higher education and higher education's needs to the state. This is the "suitably sensitive mechanism" which has already been mentioned.

It is possible, of course—particularly in a small state with a limited number of public institutions—for these delicate continuing relationships to be conducted purely on a personal basis. In such cases, formal mechanisms, whether created by state statute or voluntarily established by the institutions, may be irrelevant or unnecessary. Indeed, Gould, whose admonitory remarks about "unreserved public discussion of the relations between a university and state government" opened this chapter, suggests that even in a state as large as New York, it is "the more subtle personal contacts which are the warp and woof of the fabric of this relationship" and that such contacts "defy rules and definitions and formulas." He continues:

> they are the true means by which the delicate balance of authority, responsibility, and interdependence existing between the university and state government is maintained, or, when matters go awry, is upset. They represent the interplay of personalities, the development of attitudes on the part of these personalities reflecting a clear understanding of respective roles and motivations, and most of all the creation of a climate of mutual trust and respect.[18]

In the face of such a judgment from so knowledgeable an observer, it may seem an exercise in futility to ring the changes on the apparent strengths and weaknesses of the different state structures set up to deal with substantive developments in higher education. But surely the answer is not to deny the importance of personalities but rather to point out that structures create the context in which personalities meet and interact. Harold Enarson noted some years ago that:

> The growth of . . . cooperation [between higher education and government] will be dependent on two things: first, the "climate of opinion" . . .; second, the availability of practical machinery to encourage cooperation. [It] rarely "just happens." The climate

18. "The University and State Government: Fears and Realities," p. 4.

of opinion . . . may change faster than we think, largely because of the availability of practical machinery.[19]

My own personal experience serving on a commission to study Canadian university government taught me that Enarson's observation is true. To a surprising extent, many faculty, administrators, and trustees—displaying a certain potential for either antagonistic or cooperative attitudes—ultimately displayed the one or the other depending on whether the formal structure brought them together as adversaries or as partners of some sort in a joint venture.

I do not mean to take the sweetness-and-light view that proper structures will soothe all the wild beasts but rather to suggest that it is worthwhile to examine the various types of structures and at the same time to hope that men of good will and top stature will be elected or appointed to the relevant offices in both state government and higher education.

Many people would deny that there is any single "proper form" for state participation in decision making in higher education. Here again, one can agree and still insist that a careful survey of the varieties of existing forms, along with some assessment of the strengths and weaknesses of each, may serve a valuable purpose. Over forty-six states now have some kind of formal mechanism for dealing with higher education and twenty-seven of these have altered their structures in the past fifteen years.[20] While a state's decisions about the powers, membership, and staffing of the agency in question are probably more highly influenced by its own particular history, needs, and resources than by abstract theories of administration, nevertheless it is possible that some unfortunate mistakes could be avoided if more were known about the advantages and disadvantages of certain kinds of choices.

Finally, one must reply to those cynics who point out that, even given benevolent personalities working together in admirable administrative structures, the improvements possible are limited by other variables. For example, in Oklahoma we were told that "tinkering with the system would have a very modest effect—you would simply run into the value system of the state and the problem of economic scarcity." Presumably this means that in a state where there are heavy demands on limited resources and where public opinion is unenthusiastic about changing

19. "Cooperative Planning to Meet the Needs of Increased Enrollments," *Current Issues in Higher Education,* ed. G. Kerry Smith (Washington: Association for Higher Education, National Education Association, 1956), p. 321.
20. See chapter 2 for a detailed description of these developments.

state priorities or increasing the tax rate, it is foolish to expect too much from mere administrative reforms. But if such reforms can teach universities to work cooperatively with each other and with the state, it is at least conceivable that the needs of higher education will be granted a higher priority in the allocation of existing state resources or, less probably, that politicians, growing more confident about the universities' sensitivity to the public interest, will agree to tax increases. This report is dedicated to helping to create "the climate of mutual trust and respect" between state government and higher education that might make such developments possible.

TWO

The types and evolution of state-wide coordinating agencies

The last chapter argued that state governments have a legitimate partnership role in making some of the decisions concerning substantive developments in higher education and that this role is best expressed through a specialized agency developed with particular sensitivity for its complex task as intermediary between higher education and state government.

This chapter will describe the major types of such state coordinating agencies and discuss briefly the patterns by which they emerged.

Types of Agencies

For purposes of this study, the states have been divided into four categories,[1] on the basis of the degree of centralized coordinating authority exercised over all senior public institutions within the state. The categories are:

I States which have neither a single coordinating agency created by statute nor a voluntary association performing a significant statewide coordinating function.

II States in which voluntary statewide coordination is performed by the institutions themselves operating with some degree of formality.

III States which have a statewide coordinating board created by statute but not superseding institutional or segmental governing boards. This category is divided into the following subtypes:

1. The basic typology, modified to meet our definitions, and much of the material in Table 3, was derived from James G. Paltridge, "Organizational Forms Which Characterize Statewide Coordination of Higher Education" (MS, Berkeley, Center for Research and Development in Higher Education, University of California, 1965).

    a. A board composed in the majority of institutional representatives[2] and having essentially advisory powers.

    b. A board composed entirely or in the majority of public members and having essentially advisory powers.

    c. A board composed entirely or in the majority of public members and having regulatory powers in certain areas without, however, having governing responsibility for the institutions under its jurisdiction.

IV States which have a single governing board, whether functioning as the governing body for the only public senior institution in the state or as a consolidated governing board for multiple institutions, with no local or segmental governing bodies.

To avoid confusion in referring to these categories, the term *coordinating agency* will be used to signify a board in *any* of categories II, III, or IV, the term *voluntary association* will be used for category II, the term *coordinating board* will be used for category III, and the term *governing board* will be used for category IV.

Categories II and IV are not further divided into subtypes because all voluntary associations tend to have institutional members and advisory powers, and all governing boards to have public members and regulatory powers. Table 1 lists the states within the different categories and gives information concerning the titles, membership, and year of creation of their agencies.

Membership

Chapter 4 deals with the topic of agency membership in detail. Here we will merely mention a few basic points.

First, the term *public member* refers to someone appointed to represent the general public. Some institutions which have publicly elected trustees would claim this status for those of their trustees who serve on coordinating agencies; but in this report, lay trustees chosen because of their connection with a university or college are regarded as institutional representatives.

Two other types of appointment raise problems. Some persons would classify gubernatorial appointments from private institutions of higher

---

2. The terms *institutional representative* and *public member* are explained in the next section of this chapter.

TABLE 1

TYPES OF STATE COORDINATING AGENCIES

CATEGORY AND STATE	TITLE OF PRESENT AGENCY	YEAR FIRST CREATED	MEMBERSHIP	
			Public	Institutional
I. *No state agency: 2*				
Delaware				
Vermont				
II. *Voluntary association: 2*				
Indiana	Inter-institutional Study Committee	1951	0	4
Nebraska	Coordinating Council Steering Committee	1966	0	10
III. *Coordinating board: 27*				
a. *Institutional Majority Advisory Powers: 2*				
California	Coordinating Council for Higher Education	1960	6	12 (3 priv.)
Minnesota	Higher Education Coordinating Commission	1965	8	10 (2 priv.)
b. *Public Majority Advisory Powers: 11*				
Alabama	Commission on Higher Education	1969	9	0
Arkansas	Commission on Coordination of Higher Education Finance	1961	10	0
Kentucky	Council on Public Higher Education	1934	9	6[a]
Maryland	Council for Higher Education	1962	9	4 (1 priv.)
Michigan	State Board of Education	1963	8	0
Missouri	Commission on Higher Education	1963	6	4 (1 priv.)
Pennsylvania	State Board of Education	1963	15	2[b]
South Carolina	State Advisory Commission on Higher Education	1962	7	6
Virginia	State Council for Higher Education	1956	10	0
Washington	Higher Education Coordinating Commission	1969	15[c]	10[c] (2 priv.)
Wyoming	Higher Education Council	1969	10	0
c. *Public Majority Regulatory Powers: 14*				
Colorado	Commission on Higher Education	1965	7	0
Connecticut	Commission for Higher Education	1965	12	4 (1 priv.)
Illinois	Board of Higher Education	1957	8	5
Louisiana	Coordinating Council for Higher Education	1969	13	2
Massachusetts	Board of Higher Education[d]	1965	6	5 (1 priv.)
New Jersey	Board of Higher Education[d]	1965	9	6 (1 priv.)
New Mexico	Board of Educational Finance	1951	11	0
New York	Board of Regents[e]	1784	9	0
North Carolina	Board of Higher Education	1955	15	7
Ohio	Board of Regents	1963	11	0
Oklahoma	State Regents for Higher Education	1941	9	0

TABLE 1—*continued*

CATEGORY AND STATE	TITLE OF PRESENT AGENCY	YEAR FIRST CREATED	MEMBERSHIP Public	MEMBERSHIP Insti- tutional
Tennessee	Higher Education Commission	1967	9	0
Texas	Coordinating Board, Texas College and University System	1955	18	0
Wisconsin	Coordinating Council for Higher Education	1955	9	8
IV. *Consolidated governing board: 19*				
Alaska	Board of Regents	1935	8	0
Arizona	Board of Regents	1945	10	0
Florida	Board of Regents[f]	1905	9	0
Georgia	Board of Regents[d]	1931	15	0
Hawaii	Board of Regents	1907	10	1
Idaho	State Board of Education	1912	9	0
Iowa	State Board of Regents	1909	9	0
Kansas	Board of Regents	1913	9	0
Maine	Board of Trustees of the University of Maine	1968	15[g]	0
Mississippi	Board of Trustees of State Institutions of Higher Learning	1910	13	0
Montana	State Board of Education	1889	11	0
Nevada	Board of Regents	1864	9	0
New Hampshire	Board of Trustees	1963	15	9[g]
North Dakota	State Board of Higher Education	1911	9	0
Oregon	State Board of Higher Education[d]	1929	9	0
Rhode Island	Board of Regents[h]	1969	9	0
South Dakota	Board of Regents	1897	7	0
Utah	State Board of Higher Education	1969	15	0
West Virginia	Board of Regents	1969	10	0

[a] Six institutional presidents sit on the board as nonvoting members.

[b] Pennsylvania law permits, but does not require, the appointment of up to two persons from educational institutions, from either the public or the private sector or both.

[c] In Washington, six of the public members (four from the legislature and two from the governor's office) and all ten of the institutional members are nonvoting.

[d] Georgia, Massachusetts, New Jersey, and Oregon have all created loose educational planning bodies to try to integrate the work of their coordinating agency for higher education and their state board of education. These bodies are discussed in Chapter 10.

[e] Because the Board of Regents' coordinating authority over public higher education was largely unexercised until 1961, at which time legislation reemphasized its statewide planning function, the Board of Trustees of the State University of New York, which was created in 1947 and has power to govern the many institutions in SUNY and to coordinate some state-contract colleges administered by private institutions, is designated by some observers as the centralized coordinating agency. But we have chosen to regard the Regents as the statewide agency because they have planning jurisdiction over SUNY, the City University of New York, and private institutions.

[f] The Board of Regents governs the senior institutions in Florida but is itself ultimately responsible to the Board of Education, which is composed of the six elected statewide political officers of the state (who also constitute the cabinet, the Budget Commission, and other executive bodies).

[g] In merging their state college and state university governing systems, New Hampshire in 1963 and Maine in 1968 both attempted to give legal guarantees that the separate boards being eliminated would be represented on the consolidated board being established. In Maine, this was done by requiring that some of the *initial* appointments to the new board be from members of the outgoing boards. But because the governor was left free to make subsequent appointments from the public at large, all members are classified as public members. In contrast, the New Hampshire law bestows upon the alumni of the merged institutions *continuing* legal rights to elect a certain number of trustees to the consolidated board. These trustees are therefore called institutional representatives. In addition, three institutional presidents sit ex officio on the New Hampshire board.

[h] The Rhode Island Board of Regents has just been established, with jurisdiction running from kindergarten to doctoral programs. It has the power to delegate governance of elementary-secondary education, higher education, or both, or neither to subboards, but as of April 1970 had not yet decided to do so.

education as public members since they represent institutions which may have no direct material interest in agency deliberations; but we consider such appointees to be institutional representatives. For one thing, it is their institutional affiliation that has led to their being appointed to the agency. For another, since many agencies are now administering Federal programs which include the private sector and since a few states are beginning to render direct or indirect state aid to the private sector, it seems somewhat naive to disregard the institutional interests which members from the private sector would naturally want to safeguard.

Finally, some classifications designate state superintendents of education as professional educators and therefore not public members. But we regard such appointments or ex officio memberships as public members unless the superintendent is acting as executive officer of some subsystem (junior colleges, state colleges) which is itself being coordinated by the broader agency. In these cases, he is regarded as an institutional representative.

The types of membership in each category of agency are summarized in Table 2.

TABLE 2

TYPES OF MEMBERSHIP IN EACH CATEGORY OF COORDINATING AGENCY

Category of Agency	All-Institutional	Institutional Majority	Public Majority	All-Public	Total
II. Voluntary association	2	0	0	0	2
IIIa. Coordinating board	0	2	0	0	2
IIIb. Coordinating board	0	0	6	5	11
IIIc. Coordinating board	0	0	7	7	14
IV. Consolidated governing board	0	0	1	18	19
Total	2	2	14	30	48

Of the nineteen agencies having institutional representatives, eight—all of them coordinating boards—include one or more representatives from the private sector.

Jurisdiction

Of the forty-eight existing agencies, forty-one have jurisdiction over all or nearly all public higher education. In seven states—one with a coordinating board (North Carolina) and six with governing boards (Arizona, Florida, Iowa, Kansas, Mississippi, and Oregon)—the junior colleges are coordinated separately; and where post-high school vocational-technical education is handled outside the junior colleges or university branch campuses, it is usually not under agency jurisdiction. In six states—three with coordinating boards (Michigan, New York, and Pennsylvania) and three with governing boards (Idaho, Montana, and Rhode Island)—the State Board of Education has been designated as the coordinating agency, and its jurisdiction encompasses not only higher education but also the public school system. The problem of coordinating agency liaison with separate systems of junior colleges, vocational-technical institutions, and public schools is briefly discussed in chapter 10.

As later chapters will reveal, more agencies are attempting to incorporate the private sector of higher education in their planning efforts. But as a matter of law, only the State Board of Regents in New York has jurisdiction over the private sector with respect to program approval. In Connecticut, Minnesota, and Missouri, the coordinating boards are empowered by law to request information from private institutions and to make planning recommendations which include the private sector. And, as will be made clear subsequently, Federal programs administered by state coordinating agencies are willy-nilly bringing those institutions in the private sector which participate in such programs under agency jurisdiction in those limited areas.

Powers

Only two states have given constitutional status to their coordinating agencies: Oklahoma in 1941 to its coordinating board and Georgia in 1943 to its consolidated governing board. In both cases, highly controversial political intervention in higher education had occurred, and constitutional autonomy for the agency, linked with the power of lump sum appropriations, was considered to be at least a partial solution.

The other forty-four coordinating and governing boards were created by regular state statutes, most of which can be found, in digest form, in Robert L. Williams's *Legal Bases for Coordinating Boards in Thirty-Eight States.*[3] The voluntary associations, by contrast, were all created by agreements among the institutions, with no force of law. In Indiana, a

---

3. Chicago: Council of State Governments, 1967.

legislative rider, attached to the 1949 Appropriations Act and repeated each biennium until 1967, called for the four state universities to cooperate in working out a common budget formula. Since the universities were left entirely free to determine the mode and degree of their collaboration, however, it seems legitimate to classify the Indiana system as voluntary.

As mentioned earlier, it is relatively simple to designate the powers of voluntary associations as advisory and those of the governing boards as regulatory. It is much more difficult to decide whether a coordinating board has advisory or regulatory powers. The task is complicated by at least three factors:

1. Board functions extend over a wide range of possible activities—planning, budget review, program approval, capital outlay review, administration of Federal programs, to name only the major ones—and board powers may be advisory in some areas and regulatory in others.

2. There may be significant discrepancies between the de jure existence of powers and their de facto exercise.

3. The de facto exercise of powers may vary over time as the board confronts changing conditions in state government, higher education, or both.

It is widely recognized that a power which exists in law may not, for a variety of reasons, be exercised; conversely, powers which do not exist in law may be exercised by other means. The failure to exercise existing powers may be traced to factors operating from either the political or the educational side. As an example of the former, a college president in Oklahoma told us that their State Regents for Higher Education—one of the strongest coordinating bodies in the country in that it has constitutional status and is granted lump sum appropriations—were "essentially powerless to deal with some of the major issues in the state. In theory they have the power, but in practical politics they do not."

A classic case of the nonexercise of legal powers because of educational factors can be found in the operations of the Wisconsin Coordinating Committee for Higher Education between 1955, when it was established, and 1965, when its membership and staffing procedures were altered. James G. Paltridge, in an intensive analysis of the Wisconsin scene, notes a basic irony. After defining the three potential roles which a coordinating agency may fill—(1) advocate for the interests of higher education; (2) administrative agency for the state; and (3) intermediate mechanism for interpreting the interests, needs, and goals of each side to the other—he observes that the Wisconsin board was intended to act in the third role, that its legal charge read as though it would play the second role, but that in actuality it functioned in the first role. Strong powers were not exercised because the board, which had a majority of institutional representatives and lacked an independent professional staff, chose not to exercise them.[4]

To illustrate the opposite principle—the de facto exercise of "non-powers"—the Illinois coordinating board was granted the power to make only budget recommendations; but since its recommendations were always accepted virtually intact by the state government, the institutions soon began to take this fact into account, and any evaluation of board powers should recognize this psychological reality.

In addition, missing powers can sometimes be supplied by judicious interpretation and application of granted powers. For instance, the early New Mexico board used its power of budget review to influence the adoption of new programs, and the Ohio board has "helped" the institutions to determine their home and branch campus ratios of lower division, upper division, and graduate enrollments by deliberately setting budget formulas which make some categories more attractive than others.

The problem of assessing de facto powers is complicated even more by the fact that these powers vary not only from one state to another but also within a given state at different periods of time. Lyman A. Glenny has noted: "Coordination may mean one thing when the agency first attempts to bring order among the state institutions and a different thing when a system has been established, cooperative attitudes developed, and certain procedures routinized."[5] Our research staff found that the phenomenon of changing attitudes works both ways: Some persons who were at first hostile to the concept of coordination may, as the agency operates through time, be converted to the belief that it should be given stronger powers. But others—whether politicians or educators—whose initially favorable expectations were not fulfilled, may subsequently try to weaken or even eliminate the agency.

In short, generalization is difficult, since a variety of subtle historical, educational, and political factors determine what particular set of powers will actually be operating in a given state at a given time. To make judg-

4. James G. Paltridge, *Conflict and Coordination in Higher Education: The Wisconsin Experience* (Berkeley: Center for Research and Development in Higher Education, University of California, 1968), p. 45.
5. *Autonomy of Public Colleges* (New York: McGraw-Hill Book Co., 1959), p. 61.

ments concerning agency powers, therefore, our research staff drew on data from a number of recent studies, most of them giving rather general descriptions of the powers granted and, unfortunately, not always agreeing among themselves on either categories or classifications.[6] In cases where agencies were granted advisory powers in some areas and regulatory powers in others, we looked to program review as the key area. Thus, if an agency has been given the power to reject an institution's proposed new educational program, it is classified as regulatory; if it can only recommend, it is called advisory. This criterion is consistent with our emphasis on the role of the agency vis-à-vis substantive autonomy and avoids the confusions that surround the various degrees of agency powers in other areas such as budget and capital outlay review.

The Evolution of Statewide Coordinating Agencies

Table 1 shows the present status of the states but gives no indication of how these patterns emerged through time. According to Pliner, the development of statewide coordinating systems in higher education can be divided into four major periods, some of them overlapping but each manifesting a dominant trend:[7]

1. Complete autonomy of institutions lasting from colonial days to the late 19th century;

2. Creation of single statewide governing boards beginning in the late 19th century, reaching a peak in the first two decades of this century, and currently undergoing a slight revival;

3. Creation of voluntary arrangements gaining impetus in the 1940s and 1950s; and

4. Creation of statewide coordinating boards beginning in the 1950s and still continuing.

These periods are correlated rather closely with the growth patterns of American universities and colleges. During the first period, the state

6. See Lewis B. Mayhew, *Long Range Planning for Higher Education* (Washington: Academy for Educational Development, 1969); Williams, *Legal Bases for Coordinating Boards in Thirty-Eight States*; Emogene Pliner, *Coordination and Planning* (Baton Rouge: Public Affairs Research Council of Louisiana, 1966); Paltridge, "Organizational Forms Which Characterize Statewide Coordination of Higher Education"; Sebastian V. Martorana and Ernest Hollis, *State Boards Responsible for Higher Education* (Washington: U.S. Department of Health, Education, and Welfare, Circular no. 619, 1960).

7. *Coordination and Planning.*

universities adopted the lay governing board pattern of the private institutions. It was assumed that a governing board, whose members had no direct material interests in the institutions, would not only protect the university's autonomy but would also see that it was run in the public interest. The same governing pattern was extended to the new state land-grant institutions created by the Morrill Act of 1862 (though in some cases, of course, land-grant functions were simply assumed by the existing state university).

The second half of the 19th century saw the widespread establishment of state normal schools to meet the rapidly growing need for public school teachers. Many of these institutions were administered by the state boards of education, under whose auspices they gradually broadened their curricula to become teachers colleges or state colleges; later, some even became state universities with their own governing boards.

During this period of rapid growth, state governments learned that the assumption that lay governing boards would protect the public interest was only partially correct. Although the lay trustees usually worked conscientiously to avoid wasting public funds, they were also understandably ambitious for their institutions. Thus they sometimes advanced proposals for expansion and for new programs which, taken by themselves, may have been legitimate but which, viewed in connection with similar proposals from other institutions, constituted a set of financial demands and a plethora of program offerings going beyond the state's resources or needs.

Between 1864 and 1945, thirteen states—generally those with fewer institutions, slower growth rates, and more limited fiscal resources—decided to control such premature expansion and proliferation by creating one single consolidated board for higher education and, at the same time, abolishing any existing local governing boards where necessary. Some of these consolidated boards—particularly in Georgia, Iowa, and Oregon—moved aggressively to reduce program duplication; in Georgia, the agency founded in the depression year of 1931 eliminated ten institutions.

Up to World War II, however, most other states continued to deal separately with the various institutional governing boards. It is difficult to tell just what factors account for their restraint: the power of existing institutional boards to resist any moves toward centralization; the preference of the politically powerful to deal directly with the various institutional boards; or a genuine belief among the faster growing and richer states that the possible premature expansion of higher education was a lesser evil than reduction of the diversity and vitality which a more open system permitted.

Consequences of diversity and expansion

And diversity and vitality were certainly present in American higher education during the 20th century. Glenny has aptly described some of the developments which were taking place:

> Universities began extensive research programs in the physical and biological sciences; provided new services for the farmers, industries and other special-interest groups; added professional schools in new areas such as social work, public administration, industrial relations, and municipal management; further specialized in agriculture, medicine, and dentistry; and increased course offerings in almost all previously existing academic fields. Land-grant colleges began to extend their programs into academic and professional disciplines which had traditionally been offered only by the state university.[8]

In addition, as mentioned earlier, many of the normal schools were becoming state colleges and even universities and expanding their curricula accordingly. Along with these institutions came the flood of junior colleges, which extended the opportunity for some higher education to large new groups of young people: those who could not meet the entrance standards of some four-year institutions or those who lived in areas without four-year institutions and who could afford to attend college only if they lived at home.

This growth in the numbers and types of institutions and in the richness of their offerings reflected the tremendous postwar growth in student numbers and in turn led to a huge increase in state expenditures on higher education. Whereas in 1900, for example, only about 4 percent of the U.S. college-age population attended college, after 1945 the proportion mounted steadily to one-half, and this at a time when the "baby boom" was vastly increasing the basic pool from which this group was drawn. From an enrollment of under two million in the late 1940s, student numbers jumped to over six million by 1966, and are projected to reach twelve million by 1980. What is more relevant from

8. *Autonomy of Public Colleges*, p. 13.

the perspective of the states, the proportion educated in public institutions increased from about 50 percent in 1950 to 67 percent in 1965, with 77 percent projected for 1980. State expenditures on higher education rose from $500 million in 1950 to about $5 billion in 1967, and, unless Federal aid increases massively, they should reach $10 billion by 1980. Constituting about 7 percent of all state expenditures in 1950, higher education now consumes about 15 percent. Clearly, higher education has become a major concern of state governments.

At the same time, other state programs were also growing in size, complexity, and cost, and many new programs were being introduced in such fields as agriculture, highways, mental health, child care, conservation, prisons, and welfare; consequently, the organs of state government which usually handled higher education problems and finances in a more or less ad hoc manner were finding it increasingly difficult to do so. Many states during this period created Little Hoover Commissions to reorganize state government, and these commissions nearly always recommended, among other things, a stronger governor's office, which could use the executive budget as a chief tool for arranging various state programs into some set of priorities.

One state chief budget officer (himself a former professor) vividly described the difficulty of determining these statewide financial priorities:

> [The budget officer] is besieged for funds on all sides. The department of conservation wants 100 additional forest rangers and shouts that if it does not get them, there may be a conflagration which will destroy hundreds of thousands of trees, irreplaceable in our lifetime. The state police point to the mounting death toll on the highways and indicate the millions they must have to put an end to this holocaust. And the department of public health—to hear this department's well-intentioned representatives talk, we must forthwith construct a roof over the entire state, since all citizens are on the verge of nervous breakdowns and will need hospitalization. . . .
>
> Not only is higher education in severe competition with other governmental services, . . . but individual colleges and universities are in competition with each other for that portion of total funds to be allocated to higher education. . . .
>
> . . . In this highly competitive atmosphere, state budget officers, governors, and legislators are understandably asking more and more detailed questions about the management and

programs of public colleges and universities. [9] (Order transposed.)

Defenders and detractors of the various systems

In view of the need for more information, greater coherence, and less wasteful duplication, some of the states without formal coordinating agencies reopened the question of tighter coordination. Proponents of the consolidated governing board model claimed that only when the powers of coordination and of governance were combined could there be effective implementation of planning. Critics maintained that consolidation would lead to overcentralization and questioned whether such a board could successfully administer more than a modest number of institutions, particularly if they were of different types (e.g., two-year colleges, four-year colleges, universities). The critics also contended that, with such boards, "the important is sacrificed to the urgent," that planning, which should be given top priority, is usually subordinated to dealing with pressing administrative problems.

Defenders (and in our field work, we found this group to include most persons working under governing board systems) could point out that, in contrast to the rather hectic history of coordinating patterns in states with other systems, no state having adopted the consolidated governing board system has ever abandoned it. On the other hand, whether because of rejection in principle of the consolidated governing model or merely because of the political power of hostile institutional boards which would have been superseded by consolidation, only relatively small states (New Hampshire in 1963, Maine in 1968, and Utah and West Virginia in 1969) have adopted this model during the past twenty-five years.

During this same period, however, other types of coordinating agencies were established in some twenty-nine states. University and college presidents responded to increased state pressures for coordination by stepping up the tempo of interinstitutional voluntary coordination. In some states, these arrangements did not go beyond casual meetings and ad hoc agreements, but in at least eleven (Arkansas, California, Colorado, Illinois, Indiana, Michigan, Minnesota, Missouri, Nebraska, Ohio, and Washington), some degree of ongoing consultative apparatus was established. Although today only Indiana and Nebraska are still in the

9. Quoted in Malcolm Moos and Frank Rourke, *The Campus and the State* (Baltimore: Johns Hopkins Press, 1959), Appendix A.

voluntary category (and both are under strong political pressure to change to statutory coordination), some educators [10] insist that the voluntary form best permits the degree of institutional autonomy necessary for excellence, experimentation, and vitality. Christopher Jencks came across university presidents who feared that statutory boards would be

> too far removed from the subtleties and complexities of local situations to treat each institution with respect for its unique traditions, problems and clientele. If one wants to cope with diversity, . . . the only hope is to have many centers of authority and decision making, not one. This may lead to confusion, competition, and a certain amount of wasteful duplication among institutions, but it will be less wasteful and demoralizing than overcentralization. . . . What looks to an outsider like institutional nationalism and empire building looks to an insider like necessary and natural growth, and is the unavoidable price which must be paid for a dynamic institution.[11]

Other observers treat voluntary coordination less kindly. Lanier Cox points out that "its success is entirely dependent upon individual willingness to cooperate and the extent of that willingness has been directly related to the absence of competing interests."[12] Harry S. Allen, for five years Staff Director of the Colorado voluntary group before its demise, has noted that in circumstances where there are prolonged institutional disagreements over serious issues, "the demands placed upon the [agency research] staff . . . are virtually impossible to meet over the long haul." [13] And Glenny concluded that voluntary coordination tends to preserve the status quo and to lead to domination by the largest or oldest institution, gives inadequate representation to the public interest in policy making, and is ineffectual in coordinating large systems of institutions.[14]

Whatever the actual merits of the case, a majority of the legislators in nine of the states which had voluntary coordination obviously lost

10. See, for example, M. M. Chambers, *Voluntary Statewide Coordination in Public Higher Education* (Ann Arbor: University of Michigan, 1961).

11. "Diversity in Higher Education" (Consultant paper, White House Conference on Education, July 20–21, 1965), p. 58.

12. Cited by A. J. Brumbaugh, *State-wide Planning and Coordination of Higher Education* (Atlanta: Southern Regional Education Board, 1963), p. 31.

13. "Voluntary Coordination of Higher Education in Colorado" (MS, Office of Institutional Research, University of Nebraska, 1967), p. 55.

14. *Autonomy of Public Colleges*, p. 248.

faith in its effectiveness and, with their colleagues in some eighteen other states, opted for the establishment of a statutory coordinating board.

As a general model, the coordinating board has certain obvious advantages. In contrast to the consolidated governing board, it allows existing institutional boards to continue operation, thus satisfying the institutions and circumventing difficult political and constitutional issues which might otherwise trouble the legislators. In contrast to most voluntary systems, it usually recruits an independent staff which can, with board approval, produce research reports that reexamine the status quo as voluntary systems rarely do.

But the coordinating model also presents some acute problems: Because it stands between the institutions and state government in a way that neither the consolidated governing board nor the voluntary association does, it is more vulnerable to criticism from both sides. If its actions seem to identify it more closely with the institutions (as is sometimes the case with a board having only advisory powers, particularly if a majority of its members represent institutions), legislators who expect "instant coordination" are likely to become impatient and critical. One California legislator labeled his coordinating board "a voluntary system with a fig leaf, operating essentially to negotiate bargains among thieves." If such an attitude is common in state government circles, the board will not receive much support, whether the appraisal is justified or not.

Alternatively, if a board's actions seem to place it in the state government camp (as tends to be the case with a board having regulatory powers, particularly if it consists entirely of public members), universities and colleges complain bitterly that another layer of state bureaucracy has been thrust upon them. In Ohio, for example, we heard from a few quarters allegations that the coordinating board allowed the governor's office to intervene in higher education to an extent that would have been impossible before the board was created. If this belief is widely held in institutional circles, their necessary cooperation with the board may not be forthcoming.

It is not surprising, then, that even in the relatively brief lifetime of most coordinating boards, nearly half have had either their membership or their powers altered, at the behest sometimes of the universities and colleges and sometimes of the state capitol. Boards which originally had a majority of institutional representatives were changed to public majorities in Kentucky, Maryland, and Wisconsin; in California, the number of public members was increased from three out of fifteen to six out of eighteen. Conversely, some institutional representatives were added to the initially all-public boards in North Carolina and South Carolina. In Maryland, five years after institutional memberships had been eliminated, members from institutions were again included.

In the tug of war over powers, some boards have been strengthened, and some weakened. Because of political dissatisfaction over their apparent ineffectiveness, the boards in Illinois, Kentucky, and Wisconsin were made stronger. The North Carolina board, on the other hand, was reduced in power following strong criticism from the state university. In Virginia, institutional opposition resulted in a legislative rider (since removed) that enjoined the coordinating board from performing its assigned function in budget review. Finally, in Texas, following a change in government, the board was reorganized to have fewer budget powers but more authority in the areas of planning and program approval.

The instability of the voluntary association and the coordinating board models is indicated in Table 3, which shows the changes in coordinating patterns in each state over the last thirty years.

Table 4 is derived from the data in Table 3 and summarizes the national trends over time.

The present view

In view of the developments over the past three decades, the following observations seem justified.

1. Practically all states now have some type of formal coordination.

2. The trend toward voluntary coordination reached its peak in the 1950s but is now markedly receding.

3. Within the coordinating board category, the trend in membership is definitely toward public member majorities: twenty-five out of the twenty-seven boards now have this composition. But only thirteen of the twenty-five are composed entirely of public members.

4. Within the coordinating board category, it has recently become the trend to grant more regulatory powers, but thirteen boards out of twenty-seven must still be classified as essentially advisory.

5. The number of states with consolidated governing boards has increased only slightly, but no state adopting this system has changed it. (Wyoming, however, has created a IIIb-type board to coordinate the

TABLE 3

EVOLUTION OF COORDINATING PATTERNS WITHIN STATES

State	Prior to 1940	1940 to 1949	1950 to 1959	1960 to 1964	1965 to 1969
Alabama	I	I	I	I	IIIb
Alaska	IV	IV	IV	IV	IV
Arizona	I	IV	IV	IV	IV
Arkansas	I	I	II	IIIb	IIIb
California	I	II	II	IIIa	IIIa
Colorado	I	I	I	II	IIIc
Connecticut	I	I	I	I	IIIc
Delaware	I	I	I	I	I
Florida	IV	IV	IV	IV	IV
Georgia	IV	IV	IV	IV[1]	IV
Hawaii	IV	IV	IV	IV	IV
Idaho	IV	IV	IV	IV	IV
Illinois	I	II	IIIb	IIIc	IIIc
Indiana	I	I	II	II	II
Iowa	IV	IV	IV	IV	IV
Kansas	IV	IV	IV	IV	IV
Kentucky	IIIa[2]	IIIa	IIIa	IIIa	IIIb[3]
Louisiana	I	I[4]	I	I[5]	IIIc
Maine	I	I	I	I	IV
Maryland	I	I	I	IIIa (1962) IIIb (1963)	IIIb[6]
Massachusetts	I	I	I	I	IIIc[1]
Michigan	I	I	II	II (1961) IIIb (1964)	IIIb
Minnesota	I	I	II	II	IIIa
Mississippi	IV	IV	IV	IV	IV
Missouri	I	I	II	IIIb	IIIb
Montana	IV	IV	IV	IV	IV
Nebraska	I	I	I	I	II
Nevada	IV	IV	IV	IV	IV
New Hampshire	I	I	I	IV[7]	IV
New Jersey	I	I	I	I	IIIc[1]
New Mexico	I	I	IIIc	IIIc	IIIc
New York	IIIc	IIIc[8]	IIIc	IIIc	IIIc

NOTE: The categories are as follows:
I = No state agency
II = Voluntary association
IIIa= Coordinating board; institutional majority; advisory powers
IIIb= Coordinating board; public majority; advisory powers
IIIc= Coordinating board; public majority; regulatory powers
IV= Consolidated governing board

[1] A special liaison agency, linking higher education with the state department of education, was created. This arrangement is discussed in chapter 10.

[2] A coordinating board was formed in 1934 but was granted no state appropriations and remained largely inactive outside the field of teacher certification.

[3] Board membership was altered to nine lay members and six nonvoting institutional presidents.

[4] Coordinating board statute was passed in 1948, but no state funds were appropriated and no staff was hired.

[5] A voluntary coordinating body was created by Louisiana State University and the State Board of Education in 1961, but following a change in administration at LSU, the body ceased to function within six months.

[6] In 1968, four institutional representatives (three from public institutions, one from the private sector) were added to the nine lay members.

[7] In 1963, New Hampshire also created a Coordinating Board for Advanced Education and Accreditation, but its only authority over higher education is to recommend accreditation and to approve degree programs for institutions, public or private, created after 1963. The ongoing coordination of the state university and state colleges is handled by the consolidated University of New Hampshire Board of Trustees.

[8] New York in 1949 established a Board of Trustees to govern the various campuses of the State University of New York, but the Board of Regents retained its basic overall planning responsibility for SUNY, the City University of New York, and the private institutions of higher education.

TABLE 3—*continued*

State	Prior to 1940	1940 to 1949	1950 to 1959	1960 to 1964	1965 to 1969
North Carolina	I	I	IIIc[9]	IIIc	IIIc
North Dakota	IV	IV	IV	IV	IV
Ohio	I	II	II	IIIc	IIIc
Oklahoma	I	IIIc	IIIc	IIIc	IIIc
Oregon	IV	IV	IV	IV	IV[1]
Pennsylvania	I	I	I	IIIb	IIIb
Rhode Island	IV	IV	IV	IV	IV
South Carolina	I	I	I	IIIb	IIIb[10]
South Dakota	IV	IV	IV	IV	IV
Tennessee	I	I	I	I	IIIc
Texas	I	I	IIIc	IIIc	IIIc
Utah	I	I	IIIb	IIIb	IV
Vermont	I	I	I	I	I
Virginia	I	I	IIIb	IIIb	IIIb
Washington	I	I	I	II	IIIb
West Virginia	I	I	I	I[11]	IV
Wisconsin	I	I	IIIa	IIIa	IIIc
Wyoming	IV	IV	IV	IV	IV[12]
					IIIb (1969)

[1] A special liaison agency, linking higher education with the state department of education, was created. This arrangement is discussed in chapter 10.

[9] Coordinating board budget review powers were reduced by statute in 1959, but the board is still classified as a IIIc-type agency because it retained the power to approve new programs.

[10] Six institutional representatives were added to the seven-member lay board in 1967.

[11] Paltridge reports (in "Organizational Forms Which Characterize Statewide Coordination of Public Higher Education") that a voluntary committee was established in the early 1960s, but Pliner (*Coordination and Planning*), on the basis of questionnaire response, placed West Virginia in Category I.

[12] Wyoming has had only one senior institution whose governing board was classified until 1969 as being a Type IV agency. But in 1969, a coordinating council was established with jurisdiction over the university and the community colleges. It will administer Federal programs, develop plans for the location of new programs, and act as an advisory board. This new council does not cover elementary-secondary education and thus does not fit with recently established agencies in Georgia, Massachusetts, New Jersey, and Oregon (described in chapter 10).

TABLE 4

NUMBER OF STATES IN EACH CATEGORY OF COORDINATING AGENCY

Category	1939	1949	1959	1964	1969
I. No state agency	33	28	17	11	2
II. Voluntary association	0	3	7	4	2
IIIa. Coordinating board	1	1	2	3	2
IIIb. Coordinating board	0	0	3	8	11
IIIc. Coordinating board	1	2	5	7	14
IV. Consolidated governing board	15	16	16	17	19

activities of the university's consolidated governing board and the community college statewide board.)

A look to the future

What further changes are likely in the near future? Several states are currently considering possible changes in their coordinating patterns. Of the two states with no state agency, Vermont had a study commission

which recommended the establishment of a coordinating board of the IIIa model, whereas Delaware, which has only two four-year institutions, is currently examining its statewide coordination.

Of the two states in the voluntary category, in Indiana, legislation to create a coordinating board was recently vetoed by the governor, and in Nebraska, the issue is being studied. It is possible that both states will switch to some kind of statutory coordination within the next five years.

Finally, at least two states in the coordinating board category—California and Ohio—have been considering a change to a giant consolidated system with subboards that will coordinate by region rather than by type of institution. If this change is made in either or both states (and at this writing, the prospect seems doubtful), a new category of agency would have to be created.

THREE

Design of the study

Because state coordination of higher education has become so widespread and complex, and because it has undergone such rapid change, the limits of this study had to be carefully delineated. With the help of an advisory committee, the research staff made three major types of selection: geographic (which states to include), functional (which operations to analyze), and evaluative (what sorts of judgments to render).

This chapter discusses the decisions made in each of these areas, with particular attention to the last—that of evaluation—as it is related to the author's predispositions and perspective. The final section describes the research methods used in the study.

Selection of States

The available research staff being rather small, it was necessary to decide whether to study a large number of states superficially or a small number intensively. We chose the latter course, undertaking direct field research in some thirteen states. Four more states were studied by cooperating scholars working under subcontracts. Finally, we had access to independent studies recently undertaken in two other states. Although these nineteen states may not constitute an absolutely representative sample (assuming that a representative sample were possible, given such a small and diverse population), we nevertheless feel that we obtained a fairly broad selection with respect to coordinating categories, geographic regions, and maturity of agencies (see Table 5).

Selection of Functions to Be Analyzed

Even after the field research was narrowed to thirteen states, it was still necessary to select from among the myriad operations of coordinat-

TABLE 5

SOURCE OF RESEARCH BY TYPE OF COORDINATING AGENCY AND STATE

Category and State	Year Established	Source of Research
I. (No agency)		
Louisiana	n.a.[1]	ACE staff
II. (Voluntary association)		
Indiana	1951	ACE staff
Washington	n.a.[2]	Independent study by Frank B. Brouillet[3]
IIIa. (Coordinating board: institutional majority; advisory powers)		
California	1960	ACE staff
IIIb. (Coordinating board: public majority; advisory powers)		
Kentucky	1934	Subcontract to Charles H. White[4]
Maryland	1962	ACE staff
Pennsylvania	1963	ACE staff
Virginia	1956	ACE staff
IIIc. (Coordinating board: public majority; regulatory powers)		
Illinois	1957	Subcontract to James Heck[5]
Massachusetts	1965	Subcontract to Samuel Gove[6]
New Mexico	1951	ACE staff
North Carolina	1955	ACE staff
Ohio	1963	ACE staff
Oklahoma	1941	ACE staff
Texas	1955	ACE staff
Wisconsin	1955	Independent study by James G. Paltridge[7]
IV. (Consolidated governing board)		
Florida	1905	ACE staff
Georgia	1931	ACE staff
Oregon	1929	Subcontract to Samuel Gove[8]

[1] In 1969, Louisiana established a IIIc-type agency.

[2] In 1969, Washington established a IIIb-type agency.

[3] "An Analysis of State of Washington's Method for Coordinating Higher Education" (Ed.D. diss., University of Washington, 1968).

[4] "The Kentucky Council on Public Higher Education: Analysis of a Change in Structure" (Ph.D. diss., Ohio State University, 1967).

[5] "Coordination of Higher Education in Illinois" (MS, School of Education, University of Delaware, 1968).

[6] "The Massachusetts System of Higher Education in Transition" (MS, Department of Political Science, University of Illinois, 1967).

[7] *Conflict and Coordination in Higher Education: The Wisconsin Experience* (Berkeley: Center for Research and Development in Higher Education, University of California, 1968).

[8] "The Oregon State System of Higher Education" (MS, Department of Political Science, University of Illinois, 1967). Dr. Gove studied the Oregon State Board of Higher Education as a consolidated governing board for the public senior institutions. There is also an Education Coordinating Board (discussed in Chapter 10) which plans for both the State Board of Higher Education and the State Department of Education.

ing agencies those most relevant to our purposes. Chapter 1 has already made clear our primary interest in state decisions regarding substantive developments in higher education rather than in those relating to procedural controls or academic freedom. But even then, the scope of substantive decision making is so broad that further limitations are required.

In making our selection, we tried to take into account research that had already been done or that was being planned by others. Consequently, we called a conference of interested groups and individuals to discuss these matters, hoping thus to avoid the duplication of effort that is so exasperating to busy practitioners in the field (who already seem to be approaching the saturation point for questionnaires and interviews).

On the basis of our inventory of research, completed and planned, we made the following decisions:

1. That instead of going as deeply into the internal administrative procedures of coordinating boards as did Lyman A. Glenny,[1] into aspects of state government as did Malcolm Moos and Frank Rourke,[2] or into the impact on institutions of higher education as did Ernest Palola, Timothy Lehmann, and William R. Blischke,[3] we would attempt an overview of the three-cornered relationship, emphasizing the role of the coordinating board as intermediary.

2. That our study would concentrate on the functions of planning, budget review, and program approval, since these have the closest bearing on substantive developments in higher education. In examining statewide planning for higher education, we would bear in mind that aspects of this subject were also being studied by Lewis B. Mayhew,[4] Ernest Palola, and Kent Halstead.[5] Capital outlay review would receive comparatively little attention outside of its relation to planning and program review, because its technical aspects have already been thoroughly analyzed by Glenny.[6] The most important new development in the field—the increasing role of Federal funds—would be discussed in a separate section on the overall impact of Federal programs on state coordination (see chapter 10).

3. That in certain other areas, we would defer to, and profit from, studies being undertaken by other investigators:

   a) Technical details about agency membership, staffing, and powers (Emogene Pliner).[7]

1. *Autonomy of Public Colleges* (New York: McGraw-Hill Book Co., 1959).
2. *The Campus and the State* (Baltimore: Johns Hopkins Press, 1959).
3. *Higher Education By Design: The Sociology of Planning* (Berkeley: Center for Research and Development in Higher Education, University of California, 1970).
4. *Long Range Planning for Higher Education* (Washington: Academy for Educational Development, 1969).
5. *Handbook for Statewide Planning in Higher Education* (Washington: U.S. Office of Education, forthcoming).
6. *Autonomy of Public Colleges.*
7. *Coordination and Planning* (Baton Rouge: Public Affairs Research Council of Louisiana, 1966).

b) Relations between coordination agencies and state governments (John Marshall Smart).[8]

c) The impact of Federal programs in higher education on statewide coordinating agencies (Lanier Cox and Lester E. Harrell, Jr.).[9]

d) Relations between state governments and private higher education (Richard Knoller).[10]

e) Relations between elementary-secondary education and higher education (Michael D. Usdan, David W. Minar, and Emanuel Hurwitz, Jr.).[11]

Selection of Evaluative Criteria

Finally, having chosen the states and the specific topics for study, we had to decide on the framework for evaluation. In many ways, this presented the most difficult problem of all, for it raised the age-old issue of values. By what criteria does one judge whether statewide coordination of higher education is desirable and whether one type of coordination is better than another?

One searches the relevant literature in vain for objective canons of proof which would remove the subject from controversy, but one finds only unsubstantiated and contradictory arguments as to why coordination is "good" or "bad," or why this type is preferable to that.

M. M. Chambers's comments illustrate this dilemma:

South Dakota abolished institutional governing boards and set up one board in 1896 which now governs seven institutions. There have been sixty-four years of experience with this device. Who can prove, and by what techniques, that South Dakota's institutions of higher education are today any better (or any worse), or that the statewide system is any better or worse, than it would have been if separate governing boards had been continued, either in open rivalry, or with voluntary coordination, or with a compulsory coordinating agency?[12]

8. "Political Aspects of State Coordination of Higher Education: The Process of Influence" (Ph.D. diss., University of Southern California, 1968).
9. *The Impact of Federal Programs on State Planning and Coordination of Higher Education* (Atlanta: Southern Regional Education Board, 1969).
10. "An Overview of Issues and Ideas Relating to State Aid to Non-Public Institutions of Higher Education" (MS, Office of Institutional Studies, University of Vermont, 1969).
11. *Education and State Politics* (New York: Teachers College Press, Columbia University, 1969).
12. *Voluntary Statewide Coordination in Public Higher Education* (Ann Arbor: University of Michigan, 1961), p. 58.

It is tempting to bypass questions about the desirability of statewide coordination by stressing its apparent inevitability. But the problem of subjectivity and bias must be confronted. If bias cannot be eliminated, it can at least be somewhat neutralized by an early and explicit statement of the writer's private views, a statement which will permit readers to decide whether the subsequent selection and evaluation of material has been unduly influenced by such views.

My own predispositions, I should like to believe, balance each other out. On the one hand, as a practicing academic, I strongly agree with the view that universities and scholars work best when given maximum freedom; on the other, as a student of political science, I have long recognized that the democratic state may take measures to see that the entities operating under its protection work in the public interest. This position has probably made me more sympathetic to the claims for institutional autonomy than most state politicians are but at the same time more willing to concede the necessity for statewide coordination of higher education than most academics are.

Applying my judgment to the question of whether the gains to the public interest that result from statewide coordination could justify the inevitable diminution of institutional autonomy, I have come to the following conclusions (expanded in the final chapter):

1. Notwithstanding the impressive diversity and vitality of American higher education, qualities which are partly attributable to the lack of system and of centralized organization in the past, there is now a basic and inescapable need for the coordinating function to be performed at the state level.

2. There is no such thing as "no coordination." In cases where no coordinating agencies (either voluntary or statutory) were set up, normal state organs—the governor's office, the budget office, legislative committees, the state auditor, etc.—have made decisions (usually on an ad hoc basis) which explicitly or implicitly performed this function.

3. Rather than have coordination undertaken piecemeal by a variety of state offices, it is preferable from the standpoint both of autonomy and of the public interest that it be carried out by an agency specializing in higher education and planning on a comprehensive and long-range basis.

If one accepts coordination as desirable, it is then necessary to develop criteria for judging the relative merits of different types of agencies. Coordination can be viewed as the process of reconciling (as wisely and felicitously as possible) the numerous differences which exist within higher education and between higher education and the state. According to this definition, coordination is considered "good" if it results in "wise" policies and if it resolves conflicts with relative ease. But these criteria raise several problems.

First, and most obviously, there is no universal agreement as to what constitutes "wise policy." While most people would tend to accept such general goals as "efficient and effective use of resources" or "maximum quality of higher education consonant with relatively open access," when it comes to embodying such policies in specific forms, preferences differ greatly, not only from state to state but also from group to group within a state and even from person to person within a group. For instance, a governor, the chairman of a legislative finance committee, a university president, a state college executive, a community college chief, and the director of a coordinating agency may give widely divergent answers to such policy questions as: Should we expand existing institutions or create new ones? Should we establish more community colleges or open university branch campuses? Should doctoral programs be strictly limited to certain institutions? While one's own common sense may indicate that some of the suggested answers are more in the public interest than others, there is no way of proving this definitively, and one must concede that so-called common sense is highly vulnerable to subjectivity.

Second, to evaluate coordinating agencies by the relative ease with which they resolve conflicts may avoid the problem of what constitutes wise policy, but the use of this criterion requires that certain important distinctions be made. In view of the widespread disagreement over policies, one cannot realistically expect an agency to operate free of controversy. A "peaceful" agency may well be an agency that is dodging the tough but important issues. It is one thing, however, for an agency to be involved in continuing policy disagreements and quite another for it to be charged with consistently ignoring either the point of view of the state as a whole or that of the institutions. Policy disagreements we regard as certainly inevitable and probably healthy; procedural quarrels, on the other hand, are probably avoidable and certainly unhealthy.

Ease of conflict resolution refers, then, not to total consensus about emerging policies but to general agreement that an agency's policy-making procedures are fair. The term *fair* may be as value-laden as the term *wise*, but we felt far better able to judge whether complaints about agency decision making were genuine or reflected merely the understandable tendency of parties whose views have been rejected to claim that they were not given a fair hearing. We also learned to distinguish between the pro forma appearance of consultation and participation and the slower, more exasperating version of the real thing.

Thus, to sum up, we decided to focus this study on the sensitivity of the agency to its role as intermediary between the state and higher education, examining in particular the decision-making procedures that relate to planning, budget review, and program approval in the selected states. It is our basic thesis that both the public interest and the substantive autonomy of academic institutions will be better protected in the long run by the essential fairness of agency procedures than by an insistence on the rightness or wrongness of any given policy.

Research Methods

Having chosen the states, the topics, and the evaluative criteria, and having read extensively the relevant documentation, we visited each of the thirteen selected states for at least one week, conducting confidential interviews with some twenty to forty persons, most of them from the state government, the coordinating agency, and the higher educational institutions. Usually our spread included some or all of the following categories: the governor; past governors; state budget officers; chairmen or members of the finance, appropriations, and education committees of the legislature; staff of the legislative research council; directors, staff, and members of coordinating agencies; university, college, and community college presidents, administrative officers, trustees, and occasionally faculty and student leaders. We also spoke with the heads of some private institutions in each state and with a few other persons informed about higher education (e.g., newspapermen and civic leaders).

We decided to put a rather small number of open-ended questions to our interviewees rather than a long list of narrow ones. While the latter technique would have allowed for easier quantification of responses, it was our experience that by far the most significant and candid information came out of less structured situations. We encouraged each person to discuss the key issues in higher education from his own perspective, sometimes hearing very different versions of the same issues.

The following analyses and interpretations, then, have emerged from our reading of state coordinating documents and other relevant literature, from widespread interviewing in the field, and from the findings of other studies.

PART TWO

AGENCY STRUCTURES, FUNCTIONS, AND RELATIONSHIPS

FOUR

Membership and staffing

It is a truism that the ultimate effectiveness of any enterprise depends on the quality of the people engaged in it. Students of statewide coordination and planning have emphasized repeatedly the importance of "personalities" and the need, in such a new and delicate enterprise, for coordinating agency members and staff to be people of high perception and good will. Certainly, even the most careful structuring of a policy-making board cannot prevent its ultimate effectiveness from depending, in the last resort, on the abilities and other personal characteristics of its members and staff. But the composition of a coordinating agency and the organization of its staff are themselves structural factors, intimately related to the sort of coordination an agency exercises, the powers it has, and its effectiveness in establishing successful relations with two formidable communities—higher education and the central public policy authorities of the governor and the state legislature.

The history of statewide coordination illustrates repeatedly the close relationship between an agency's composition and the powers it exercises. In instances where voluntary coordinating groups composed wholly of institutional representatives have been replaced by legislatively established agencies, at least some persons representing the general public have at the same time been added. And virtually all consolidated governing boards, legally the most powerful kind of coordinating agency, have been composed wholly of laymen.[1]

The relationship between composition and powers has been noted by Lyman A. Glenny:

> The amount of legal power the board will have over the institutions will be determined primarily by the composition of the

1. The two exceptions are New Hampshire, for reasons explained in footnote g of Table 1 (chapter 2), and Hawaii, which has one institutional representative: the president of the University.

board, whether it is composed of a majority of public members or a majority of members with a direct stake in collegiate institutions. Boards controlled by public members tend to have final authority over important educational policies; those controlled by collegiate members tend to have advisory powers only.[2]

In Glenny's view the composition of the coordinating agency determines not only its powers but also what he calls its "mode of coordination." "One mode is that of the coordinating agency which looks upon itself as a mediator or arbitrator among the conflicting forces at work on higher education, and thereby assumes the role of a broker in the political market." The other mode "provides leadership in planning for all major aspects of higher education development." Both the brokerage and the leadership mode may be found in legally established agencies, but boards having a clear majority of public members are more likely to exercise a forceful leadership.[3]

Other studies of coordination have demonstrated that state government authorities, who were originally responsible for stimulating the establishment of coordinating and planning mechanisms, are unwilling to give substantial powers to an agency composed of a majority of college presidents or trustees. In the state government view, such powers should be exercised by a board consisting of a substantial number of members who represent the public interest.

The relationship between an agency's membership and its powers may be more of a chicken-or-egg question than Glenny suggests. Not all coordinating agencies with a majority of public members have been delegated wide powers. Moreover, some all-citizen boards appear to practice the brokerage mode of coordination. But many governors and legislators seem to be convinced that a coordinating agency with strong powers over institutions of higher education will not use them if it is composed mainly or wholly of college presidents and trustees.

In recent years, then, as pointed out in chapter 2, state governments have tended not only to replace voluntary systems with statutory agencies but also to stipulate that these agencies have at least a majority of mem-

2. "State Systems and Plans for Higher Education," *Emerging Patterns in American Higher Education,* ed. Logan Wilson (Washington: American Council on Higher Education, 1965), p. 92.

3. "Politics and Current Patterns in Coordinating Higher Education," *Campus and Capitol,* ed. W. John Minter (Boulder, Colo.: Western Interstate Commission for Higher Education, 1966), pp. 33-35.

bers who represent the general public. Even if state government officials are not looking for the vigor and initiative that characterize the leadership mode of coordination, their past experiences with college presidents and alumni associations often disillusion them about the ability of a predominantly institutional board to rationalize expenditures or to lessen the pressures of higher education on state government.

But higher education—that other powerful community with which a statutory coordinating agency must identify—views with skepticism and even hostility the exercise of educational decision making by agencies on which educators either do not have a commanding voice or, except as advisors, have no formal voice at all. The prospect of vigorous leadership by a board of noneducators stirs up the fear that political interference will increase and institutional autonomy will be lost. Educators have a third major anxiety, which has been expressed as follows:

> Issues in higher education are too vital a concern of the public at large to be settled by professional educators alone, of course; yet it would be the height of folly to remove front-line leaders from the foreground of decision making and replace them with politically constituted committees, commissions, and other agencies remote from the real scenes of action.[4]

The structure of the coordinating body largely defines the means by which expert educational advice is piped into the decision-making process. In a voluntary system, the decision makers are professional educators. They can talk to one another as experts and do not have to educate or influence outsiders. But statutory coordinating agencies, as they are currently structured, are made up in all but two cases of at least a majority of nonexperts. Here, professional advice can be channeled into the deliberations by a variety of means: by administrators or trustees from public institutions sitting as a minority of the board; by educators from private institutions sitting on the board; by the board's professional staff; by advisory bodies composed of institutional administrators, trustees, or faculty; and by special consultants. Which of these channels are actually used will be determined partly by the abilities and good will of the board members, staff, and educational experts involved. But

4. Logan Wilson, "State Coordination of Higher Education" (Speech to the Association for Higher Education of the Washington Education Association, Seattle, December 2, 1966).

the choice of means, and the extent and effectiveness of their use, also depend upon board structure and organization.

Even in states where the principle of coordination is no longer highly controversial, the questions of how to structure the agency's membership and how to organize the board and the staff continue to be disputed. States with long-established consolidated governing boards are not exempt from this problem, especially as the boards' planning responsibilities become more significant. The membership and staffing of voluntary systems are such major problems that they have often proved fatal to the system. In the few states which previously had no formal coordinating mechanism and which are now investigating the possibilities, the type of board and its composition remain matters of controversy even among those who agree on the need for coordination.

In the many states with some sort of coordinating agency, alterations in board or staffing arrangements are frequent. Dissatisfaction with board operations accounts for some of these changes, but not all. Additional delegation of power from the legislature or governor, changes in the pattern of institutional governing boards, or the pressures of new educational issues—such as the future of private institutions or the administration of Federal higher education programs—may also make such changes necessary.

In short, both higher education and state government have a strong stake in the nature of coordinating agency membership. And our interviews confirm that the significance of membership is generally understood by both communities.

The rest of this chapter describes the membership and staffing of various types of coordinating organizations. The first part deals with the composition of existing agencies, some of the considerations that affect the selection of members, the problems presented by either an all-public board or one with institutional representatives, and current practices in board organization. The second part discusses problems and practices in staffing.[5]

5. Aside from the data collected in the course of this study, most of the factual information on membership, and a considerable amount of the information on staffing, was derived from Emogene Pliner's *Coordination and Planning* (Baton Rouge: Public Affairs Research Council of Louisiana, 1966). The Smart questionnaire, to which reference is frequently made, was shared with us by the author and was undertaken as part of his study "Political Aspects of State Coordination of Higher Education: The Process of Influence" (Ph.D. diss., University of Southern California, 1968). Our material in this chapter does not cover all the changes that have occurred since 1969.

Membership

Existing coordinating agencies range in composition from those having only institutional representatives to those made up wholly of public (or "lay" or "citizen") members.

Voluntary associations, of course, are by their nature composed solely of institutional members, even when the existence of the organization is recognized in law, as in Indiana. Usually, voluntary groups have been composed of the presidents of the institutions, sometimes joined by members of the boards of trustees (as was the case with the Ohio Inter-University Council) or, occasionally, by business officers (as in Indiana). The most recently formed voluntary organization, in Nebraska, is composed of both presidents and trustees and is chaired by a University of Nebraska regent.

Consolidated governing boards, by way of contrast, are nearly always exclusively public in membership, reflecting the American tradition of lay trustees for governing institutions of higher education.

With respect to the coordinating board category, the membership pattern is fairly diverse, an indication of their uneasy role in "the middle": They may be wholly public, or they may include institutional representatives. Some of the oldest (e.g., Oklahoma) and some of the newest (e.g., Ohio) are entirely public. But a slight majority include some members who are selected as representatives of the public institutions.

Some boards also have one or more representatives of private institutions among their membership. Insofar as private institutions are affected by the deliberations of a coordinating council and have a stake (likely to increase) in its policy making, these representatives (often presidents) may be regarded as institutional members. But it is questionable whether they can speak for the private sector with the same authority that public college presidents and trustees command from their sector. And, in fact, the private college representatives—who, like the lay members, are usually appointed by the governor—may see themselves as lay members. For instance, according to James G. Paltridge, the three private institutional representatives on the California Coordinating Council have usually functioned as individuals who "defined their role" as "primarily that of representing the interests of the public and the 'best interests' of higher education."[6]

6. *California's Coordinating Council for Higher Education: A Study of Organizational Growth and Change* (Berkeley: Center for Research and Development in Higher Education, University of California, 1966), p. 48.

Moreover, even when the members from the private sector see themselves as institutional representatives, their interests do not always coincide with those of representatives from the public sector. To illustrate this divergence: In California, a recommendation was made in 1967 to increase faculty salaries in the public institutions 5 percent over and above the figure strictly justified by quantitative parity with comparable institutions elsewhere in the United States, the argument being that such an increase would offer an additional incentive for faculty to move to the Far West. The Coordinating Council rejected the recommendation by a nine-to-nine vote, with all three private institution members voting with the six public members against the nine representatives from public institutions. The private college representatives openly stated their fear that such an increase would make them unable to compete, a position which evoked resentment from faculty at the public institutions.

Only two existing coordinating boards have a majority of institutional representatives, if the persons appointed to these agencies from private higher education are regarded as institutional rather than public members. The California Coordinating Council has six members representing the public and three each from the university, the state college system, the public junior colleges, and the private institutions. The Minnesota Commission has eight public members; two from the private institutions; two each from the university, the state colleges, and the junior colleges; and two from the State Board of Education.

On all the other coordinating boards, the public members are in a clear majority. A variation is the Kentucky agency, on which the presidents of the state university and of the five regional universities sit as nonvoting members along with nine voting public members. Representatives of higher education are allowed to vote in all other cases except Washington.[7] Coordinating boards, like consolidated governing boards, occasionally include the superintendent of public instruction as an ex officio member.

The three state boards of education that have coordinating responsibilities over higher education make no formal provision for institutional representation, but persons from universities and colleges may get elected to the board in Michigan or appointed in New York and Pennsylvania. The Pennsylvania structure is unique: seven members are appointed to the Council of Higher Education and seven to the Council of Basic

7. See footnote d, Table 1 (chapter 2).

Education, and these two councils in joint meeting plus three additional members at large constitute the Board. No more than two members of either council may be employed by an educational institution.

In the recent past, several boards with mixed membership have been altered to increase the public representation. For example, in 1966, the California Coordinating Council's public membership was increased from three to six, and in 1964 enough lay members were added to the Wisconsin board to outnumber the institutional members, who previously had been in the majority.

In a few instances, all-public boards have been reconstituted to provide for some minority institutional representation. A recent example was the Maryland Council for Higher Education, which for several years was an all-public group. In 1968, following a recommendation from a governor's commission on organization of the executive branch, legislation was passed adding three representatives from public higher education and one from the private sector to the nine citizen members.

Selection of members

The public members of formal coordinating agencies are nearly always appointed by the governor, usually with the consent of the state senate. Nevada's Board of Regents, a Type-IV agency (for a description of the various types, see Table 1, pp. 20–21), and Michigan's State Board of Education (Type IIIb) are elected by the people, the candidates in Michigan being selected by the state's party conventions. Members of the New York State Regents are elected by the legislature. Under Utah's new law creating a consolidated governing board, the leader of each legislative house is responsible for naming three members, and the governor for naming nine.

Representatives of the public institutions take their seats by virtue of their positions as presidents or trustees, predominantly the latter. Only in Kentucky and Missouri do presidents alone sit on the council, while in California and Minnesota, both presidents and trustees constitute the institutional representation. Trustees may be selected by their boards, as in California. In Illinois and some other states, the institutional membership consists of the chairman of each governing board of an institution or group of institutions.

Typically, the membership of voluntary associations has been small, partly because voluntary coordination has worked only in states with few institutions. Coordinating boards and consolidated governing boards range in size from seven to twenty-six, with around half of them having nine, ten, or eleven members. Coordinating councils tend to be larger than governing boards, often because they include institutional representatives.

The laws establishing statutory agencies contain a number of restrictions on the governor's choice of lay appointees, although perhaps not as many as one would expect, given the delicacy of the coordinating task and the presumption that formal coordination is intended to depoliticize higher education. The citizen members of all coordinating boards and consolidated governing boards serve staggered terms—the conventional device for preventing a policy-making board from coming under the control of any single governor. The length of terms for lay members ranges from four to fifteen years but is typically from six to nine years. Although a relatively long term may be an important factor in making the board member independent of political authorities, like so many other mechanisms, its blessings are mixed. It is true that longer terms—say, nine years or so—can give an agency continuity of direction and permit members to develop expertise and to ride out unpopular decisions. On the other hand, long terms may make it difficult for the agency to cultivate fresh viewpoints or accommodate to the changing climate of the educational world.

In some states, a single governor can—if he is in office long enough and if the number of vacancies and the terms of the members break right—appoint a majority of the agency. And, of course, when a new board is established or an existing one dissolved and reorganized, a governor can name an entire board to his liking. He may pay some price for this freedom, however; in Ohio, which created a IIIc-type agency in 1963, and in Texas, where the IIIc agency was restructured in 1965, two colorful and politically expert governors were able to appoint all the new members, with the result that some persons in both higher education and state government complained nervously that the board was so closely identified with one chief executive, its impartiality and independence were in question. No legal provision, of course, can prevent a politically determined governor, in a state where the climate is right, from soliciting agency resignations to create extra vacancies. In this respect, however, boards of higher education are no more vulnerable to political interference than are other semi-independent boards or commissions. In general, coordinating agencies seem to be adequately protected, at least from crude gubernatorial attempts to pack them, but they are inevitably vulnerable to gubernatorial or legislative influence at budget and appropriations time.

In many states, the law explicitly forbids the members from having any paid or official connection with a higher educational institution. In Texas, for example, no member of the coordinating council may be "employed professionally for remuneration in the field of education"; the wording here would seem to make it possible for trustees of public institutions to sit on the council, but the intent of the provision is apparently to secure public membership. In New Mexico and some other states, however, the agency is considered to be, and in fact is, an all-public board, even though membership by institutional officers or trustees is not explicitly banned by law.

About half of the formal coordinating agencies have further legal requirements for public membership imposed upon them. In some states, all or most of the gubernatorial appointees must be distributed among districts; for example, in Minnesota, the eight public members must be from different congressional districts, and in New Mexico, seven of the eleven members must come from different judicial districts. Oklahoma and a few other states limit the number of alumni of any one institution who may be appointed. Any kind of political bipartisanship requirement is rare. About half of the executive officers of coordinating agencies, however, believe that partisan activity by board members actually damages agency relations with state government, and an even larger number believe that nonpartisanship is of some importance in establishing good relations. Ohio is the only state in which reappointment of members is forbidden, and only South Dakota law is so strict as to prohibit members from residing in any county containing a state educational institution.

Most of the restrictions on the governor's power of appointment are those traditionally used to safeguard public, semi-independent boards. Presumably, the alumni and geographic restrictions are intended to prevent the board from favoring any one institution, a possibility about which colleges and universities are hypersensitive.

But certain problems arise from these restrictions. Formal provision that members come from different districts or informal attempts by the governor to spread appointments over the state may prevent the development of a clique favoring a single institution and may reassure small rural institutions that their interests, as well as those of the more glamorous state universities, are protected. On the other hand, if the members act as ambassadors of localities or representatives of the institutions in their localities, they will be less able to maintain a statewide vision of the public interest. In the early days of the New Mexico Board of Educational Finance, of the seven of the (then) nine members who came from districts where a college or university was located, several were reputed to act aggressively to protect the institutions in their districts; nowadays, some observers complain that choosing members from judicial districts loads the board in favor of the rural areas. If the governor had free choice, the argument runs, then undoubtedly more members would come from metropolitan Albuquerque, which contains a third of the state's population. But this raises the question of whether allotting seats by population rather than by district is any more desirable or appropriate for a higher education board. The basic issue here would seem to be: Does geographic restriction force the governor to pass over a potentially superior board member from district X to select a second-rate person from district Y?

Similar arguments can be used to defend or attack restrictions on alumni membership. Not only may alumni be overprotective of their own colleges, but also board members who are lawyers—as many are—may well have graduated from the state university law school, thus reproducing on the agency the biases that disadvantage smaller undergraduate institutions when they face the legislature, which is also filled with state law school products. But many able candidates may be lost if alumni are excluded; and, in this instance, the bias from such a source may not be very strong.

In any case, when a higher education board makes a difficult decision, political or educational toes will probably be stepped on and the injured party may accuse board members of favoritism. Legal restrictions regarding residence, party affiliation, or educational background may mute these complaints, just as they may restrain an irresponsible governor. But, at the same time, they may create a rigidity which reduces the quality of the agency.

In our investigations, we found the fear of heavy gubernatorial direction to be very real in a number of states, particularly those, like Georgia, in which a history of powerful governors resulted in the creation of a higher education board with constitutional autonomy. In Louisiana, for example, one of the many factors complicating the establishment of a coordinating agency was the reluctance of both state government and higher education leaders to give any governor even restricted authority to appoint all the citizen members. The arguments against giving a governor such power are familiar ones: He may try to pack the board with educationally ignorant cronies and campaign contributors or with strong-minded friends who will base their educational decisions on political considerations of what will be helpful to the governor or his party. Yet a modern governor who aims to be more than a caretaker may well feel that if he is to provide the resources for higher education and accept the higher education board's decisions, he deserves a board to which he can give some direction and with which he can feel some rapport. A possible compromise of sorts has been worked out in Massachusetts, North Dakota, and Rhode Island, where the governor makes the final appointment but only after receiving nominations from a screening body. In Massachusetts, the screening body is the Advisory Council on Education. In North Dakota, a group composed of the State Superintendent of Public Instruction, the Chief Justice of the State Supreme Court, and a representative of the North Dakota Education Association, must unanimously recommend three names. In Rhode Island, an elaborate nominating device was established under 1969 legislation.

Problems of public membership: political relations
The coordinating board plays a political as well as an educational role. Politically naive board members can damage the agency's very real need to gain the confidence of the state government and its ability to present viable higher education policies. (This is discussed further in chapter 8.) One possible way of dealing with this danger is to put public officials on the agency to act as a bridge between it and state government. Although such persons serve on institutional governing boards in quite a few states, rarely are they included on statewide coordinating agencies. Some states, in fact, have laws that prohibit an elected or appointed official from holding more than one position of "honor, trust, or profit." New Mexico had several legislators on its board in the 1950s, prior to a legal ruling enjoining their membership. Ohio law provides that the chairmen of the senate and house education committees sit as nonvoting members on the state coordinating board. Until 1969, the North Carolina board included two legislators; after a series of major disagreements about higher education and the installation of a new administration, the governor and six key legislators joined the board. In Florida and Montana, the governor sits on the state board of education, which has ultimate responsibility for higher education. The new coordinating board established in Washington in 1969 has nonvoting seats for two representatives of the executive office and four legislators.

The comments which we heard about governmental membership are too fragmentary to be reliable, but so far they do indicate that it is a mixed blessing. In New Mexico, the people who remembered the practice had favorable impressions of the way it had worked. But a legislator familiar with the pre-1969 North Carolina board said that on balance he thought it better not to have solons on the board: They were regarded as too pessimistic by their fellow board members but as uncritical boosters of higher education by their fellow legislators. Responses to the Smart questionnaire indicate that the staff of most coordinating agencies do not find the prospect of including government officials on the agencies attractive. In fact, two-thirds of the coordinating board directors judged such memberships to be "clearly damaging," and governing board directors, though less intense in their feeling, were not enthusiastic.

Nevertheless, governmental membership may have some advantages. State officials on the coordinating agency can educate other members to the realities of state politics and finance and can communicate to key legislators the needs and problems of higher education; they can give informed advice to the legislative committees dealing with higher education and appropriations; they can help the agency to formulate proposals and appropriations requests that will be more acceptable to the legislature (though perhaps they cannot, as one cynic suggested, be expected "to kill bills the agency doesn't like"). It is not clear whether these advantages outweigh such difficulties as the legislators' and governor's already heavy workload, the pressures that may be exerted on legislators for decisions favorable to their own constituencies, the potential conflict that might arise in trying to play two policy-making roles, and the possibility that a legislator would either use his elected role to dominate the agency or lose influence with fellow legislators for becoming too sympathetic to higher education. Moreover, the presence of legislators might unduly discourage a board from pressing for the state's educational needs when the legislative climate looked unfavorable.

Problems of public membership: educational expertise

With respect to coordinating agencies composed wholly of public members, one pressing question arises: How does such a board achieve sufficient sensitivity to academic problems to make decisions which are educationally realistic? An obvious answer is that the agency rely on a competent staff composed of persons who have an academic background and who are dedicated to educating the lay members to their jobs. Such a staff would have to undertake careful research work on forthcoming problems, circulate relevant papers well in advance of deadlines, and offer articulate explanations of recommended actions. Good staff work, however, may have a deleterious effect; it may overimpress the agency members and cause them to lean too heavily on staff counsel. Half of the governing boards and two-thirds of the coordinating boards responding to the Smart questionnaire said that they departed but "seldom" from staff recommendations. Even if the staff is correct most of the time, occasions will arise when expert advice from professional educators or tough questioning of the staff's recommendations at the board level might prevent serious error.

Many agency-enabling acts specify that lay members should have some knowledge of and interest in higher education. Moreover, governors have sometimes chosen people—former college presidents or trustees, for example—who bring particular educational expertise and sympathy to their board service. To illustrate, in 1967, the eighteen lay members of the Texas Coordinating Board included three former college presidents, nine former members of boards of trustees, and five persons who were, or had been, connected with colleges and universities outside the state.

But these measures do not meet the objections of those persons who insist that the institutions which will be expected to carry out the agency decisions should have a *direct* voice in the decision-making process. They ask, therefore, that institutions be given minority representation on the agency or that a truly effective advisory system be established: for instance, a council of presidents or technical advisory committees composed of institutional administrators, trustees, and faculty.

Most proponents of strong coordination favor the second course—an advisory system—for they are reluctant to surrender the alleged advantages of an all-public agency: its emphasis on the public interest; its greater acceptability to the state government and, perhaps, to the public; its impartiality toward the institutions; its more effective execution of policies; and its more vigorous exercise of a leadership role in planning.

But this proposed solution runs into at least two difficulties. First, it is much easier to speak of effective presidents' councils and technical advisory committees than it is to keep them operating well (as chapter 8 will indicate). Second, even if this happy result is achieved, those in the institutions cannot be certain that their advice is being delivered undistorted to the all-public board. The agencies which we observed differed markedly in their practices, some welcoming the presence of institutional presidents or other administrative officers and some obviously discouraging it. To illustrate the latter attitude, in some cases, a college president who had to make a formal presentation regarding some item on the agenda was expected to leave as soon as his business was finished. Under these conditions, it is no wonder that some presidents question the effectiveness of advisory procedures.

Yet another factor complicates the problem. It is common knowledge that many agencies—even though the state may have "open-meeting" laws—hold informal "premeetings" or "intermeetings" at which the more controversial items on the agenda are hammered out. Understandably enough, agency members and staff prefer to keep their formal deliberations as serene as possible. If temptations to play to the gallery through newspaper publicity can be avoided, the agency has a better chance of maintaining that minimum internal harmony which any good board must have to be effective, especially in the face of occasional severe disagreements. But the smoothing-over process can be carried too far. Sometimes an agency may retire into executive session far more often than a discussion of the executive's salary could justify. For instance, in one state we visited, a revision and codification of the coordinating council's own policies was discussed at one meeting in public session and continued, during the next month's meeting, in executive session. Although this council was reasonably scrupulous about its relations with the institutions, its retreat into executive session was apparently undertaken to finish consideration of the policies quickly and to avoid interruptions from institutional observers attending the public meeting. Yet the policies were a matter of considerable concern to the institutions, and their effectiveness would depend on institutional acquiescence. In fairness, it should be pointed out that the agency had sent the draft policies to the institutions beforehand and invited prior comment; the institutions had not taken this opportunity but had saved most of their reactions for the open meeting. Nevertheless, the convenience of the executive session could be very tempting for any agency in similar circumstances. In addition, important proposals may be concealed from outsiders under an innocent agenda item labeled "miscellaneous business." Or the executive director or chairman may already have lined up the members on some issue by prior use of the telephone. The minutes of most agencies record a great many unanimous votes and very few rejections of institutional requests. Though institutions are sometimes allowed to withdraw items on which an adverse vote seems indicated (see chapter 7), our observations of the brevity and harmony that characterize the formal sessions of most agencies suggest that a good deal of caucusing of one kind or another occurred. Without institutional membership on the board, the academic world has no certain way of knowing whether its opinions were seriously considered in the crucial stages of decision making.

Problems of institutional membership

Institutional representation on an agency has several advantages besides assuring an input of professional advice. For one thing, a mixed council, once it has made a decision, can claim that just participation was accorded to the academic community; thus, the decision may be more acceptable, both substantively and procedurally, to the institutions, and their confidence in the agency will increase. For another, the institutional members themselves may be educated to the statewide view of higher education problems and the necessity for coordination and planning.

But there are disadvantages as well to including some presidents or trustees as members of coordinating groups. First, the very practice that increases the academic community's confidence in the agency may lessen the faith of the state government. Some legislators feel that the forcefulness and expertise of even a few presidents or trustees may be so overwhelming as to bias the agency's deliberations; in this view, the educational naiveté of the public members will make them captives of the educators. The argument may seem a bit farfetched, given the small proportion of institutional members on most predominantly public councils. Yet our interviews indicated that experience has led some legislators to have a high regard for the persuasive powers of institutional officials, especially presidents.

Second, it is contended that mixed membership may result in delays in deliberations and may make necessary elaborate negotiations in order to produce any results at all, even unsatisfactory ones. Bloc voting by institutional representatives in opposition to public members is not, to our knowledge, a very real danger, given the divisions in the higher education community on many issues. But if such splits were to occur very often, an agency's decisions would be, at the least, tainted. Were the institutional members to engage in successful logrolling, trading off favors among themselves when their interests do not coincide (which seems a more plausible danger), then part of the point of having statutory coordination would indeed be lost.

Another argument for excluding institutional representation is that it may be unreasonable to expect presidents or trustees to play simultaneously the roles of spokesmen for their own institutions and champions of the statewide public interest in higher education. As Paltridge has described this dualism, the institutional members in California

> look after the particular interests of their respective institutions as these . . . become involved in Council deliberations. They also are called upon to take the role of educator-statesmen, as members of a body charged with a major responsibility to the welfare of the state.[8]

In a state having an all-public board, a state government leader told us that presidents should not be asked to play such an awkward double role. Far better for them, he argued, to fight vigorously for their colleges without being expected to be statesmanlike except within the constraints of the general coordinating system itself. In this view, the institutions are liberated by being kept off the coordinating agency.

Finally, devising a pattern of institutional representation on a board presents some practical difficulties. In Illinois, the chairman of each institutional governing board sits on the Board of Higher Education; thus, the Board includes one representative from each of the two major universities, the two boards for state colleges and "emerging universities," and the junior colleges. All major segments of public higher education are represented, and the total number of institutional members, five, is manageable. In Texas, on the other hand, some twenty four-year colleges and universities are governed by eleven different boards, only three of which have responsibility for more than one institution. To design a mixed but predominantly public board of a manageable size in Texas and certain other states, one would either have to use a rotation system for choosing the institutions to be represented (as in North Carolina) or revise the governing structure of the public institutions to reduce the number of boards. In some states—Connecticut, for example—this revision has occurred with the creation of a state board for community colleges and one for the former teachers colleges. But in others, even those with few institutions, restructuring is politically unfeasible. Furthermore, giving representation to junior colleges, in states where the coordinating board has jurisdiction over them, may prove difficult, since often there is no single junior college board, and state controls over community colleges

8. *California's Coordinating Council for Higher Education*, p. 42.

vary. Until recently, the three junior college representatives on the California board were selected from three different sources—a junior college governing board, the state board of education, and a junior college administration—which had "varying opinions on matters related to Council affairs." [9] If representatives of other public segments act cohesively, junior college interests may suffer.

One final question concerning institutional membership on coordinating agencies is whether such members should be presidents or trustees.

Several arguments can be made for choosing trustees over presidents. First, they may be able to speak more freely for their institutions or segments than do presidents, since their livelihood and personal status are not so directly tied to the institutions. Second, the legal basis for compliance with the decisions of the coordinating agency rests with the governing boards rather than with the presidents. Third, trustees may be better able than presidents to combine educational statesmanship with the defense of institutional interests; presidents who must return to the campus to face militant faculty and students may come under severe pressure if they compromise in the context of statewide questions.

However, arguments can also be made for choosing presidents or executive officers of systems as the institutional membership. Professional educators may be more knowledgeable than are trustees about higher education issues, about their institutions, and about how particular decisions will affect their campuses. Moreover, it is the presidents who must carry out the coordinating council's recommendations and deal with the consequences.

We interviewed many government leaders, both in states whose coordinating boards included trustees and in those with all-public boards, who reacted strongly and negatively to the idea of presidents as agency members. In the minds of legislators particularly, presidents can and will press only for the interests of their own institutions. Putting presidents on a council would be, in the words of one, "like asking the thieves to divide up the loot."

The reaction to the notion of including trustees on the agency was more moderate. Their position as laymen seems to make them more acceptable to state government officials, who tended to agree with Arthur Browne that governing board membership should provide "representation without excessive partisanship." [10]

9. Ibid., p. 45.
10. "The Institution and the System: Autonomy and Coordination," *Long-Range Planning in Higher Education*, ed. Owen Knorr (Boulder, Colo.: Western Interstate Commission for Higher Education, 1965), p. 47.

Yet another possibility is to include faculty members on coordinating agencies, as is common in Britain and Canada. The probability that this pattern will be adopted in the United States seems remote (although one of the members of the Pennsylvania coordinating board is a faculty member from a private institution). The argument in favor of the practice asserts that faculty members would be chosen not to represent their institutions but to bring academic values and insights into agency deliberations. It is claimed that they can do this with greater effectiveness than trustees and with greater flexibility than presidents.

Board organization and meetings

Agencies elect their own officers except in Illinois, Pennsylvania, South Carolina, and Texas, where the governor selects the chairman, and in Montana and North Carolina, where the governors act as chairmen. Selection of its own officers helps an agency to establish its independence from the incumbent state administration, although in some cases, a governor—especially one who appoints the whole membership of a new board—may seek commitments from the members to support a chairman agreeable to him. Several governors and agency chairmen told us that there must be some rapport and respect between the two for the sake of the higher education budget and the general political support of the agency.

Most governing and coordinating boards have standing or special committees composed solely of the board membership. Committees manned by both agency members and persons from the institutions are also fairly common.[11] Most of these committees cover such areas as budget and finance, capital construction, and programs and curricula. Service on standing committees can foster the expertise of the public members; it can also ease the workload of both the membership and the staff and provide a counterweight to staff influence. A division of responsibilities may help to "mobilize board energies toward a variety of policy problems," as Browne suggests. But as he also points out, permanent committees have certain disadvantages. They sometimes "delve into various operational areas of the institutions," and he questions their utility as liaison groups with the colleges.[12] Furthermore, committee work may give lay members a false sense of expertise, and the agency,

11. Technical advisory committees composed wholly of institutional personnel are discussed in chapter 8.
12. "The Institution and the System," p. 47.

later acting as the committee of the whole, may come to defer too readily to committee advice. State boards of education that handle both higher and lower education may have special problems here. For instance, committees of the Pennsylvania council on higher education must sell their recommendations first to the council itself and then to the ten other members of the state board.

At least one president we interviewed felt that the agency paid too little attention to his institution's problems and suggested the desirability of having committees to deal with various types of campuses: universities, state colleges, junior colleges. The Texas Coordinating Board has such committees, including a private colleges liaison committee. We were told several times that its junior colleges liaison committee was the price exacted by the junior colleges for agreeing to accept the Board's jurisdiction when the agency was reorganized. The previous council had no responsibilities for two-year colleges and no liaison committees. The chief disadvantage of segmental committees is that they may tempt the board members to try to run the institutions under their particular jurisdiction.

Many coordinating and governing boards hold monthly meetings. Those which may by law meet less often (for example, bimonthly, as in North Carolina, or quarterly, as in New Mexico) are often forced by the pressure of business to hold extra meetings. The better-prepared boards receive agendas and position papers well in advance of meetings, and often the members know informally for some time ahead just what the agenda items are likely to be.

Staffing

The importance of having an outstanding agency director and a highly qualified professional staff has been reiterated in the literature to the point of tedium. Yet our interviews in state after state revealed that acquiring and holding a competent staff is still a key problem for statutory coordinating agencies. Part of the difficulty is a matter of salaries and status; part of it is the scarcity of persons who combine political skill and educational knowledge and are at the same time willing to work in a sensitive area which has no definite career ladder or training ground.

In describing the duties and burdens of coordinating agency personnel, Glenny and Browne, both experienced coordinators, give eloquent testimony to the importance of a high-quality staff. The permanent staff of the agency "has the major responsibility for presenting policy matters to the agency for action."[13] The board's "policy strength," in turn, is built on expert fact-finding and analysis provided primarily by the staff (though sometimes in conjunction with the institutions or with outside consultants).[14] The extent and sophistication of this research and analysis are crucial factors in determining not only the quality of the agency's decisions but also its persuasiveness with the institutions, the state budget office, and the legislature. As Browne puts it, "data do not resolve controversies, but they can shift negotiations to a more sophisticated plane."[15] The increasing emphasis on planning and the more vigorous leadership being exercised by a number of coordinating and governing boards make it even more imperative that the staff be competent and objective.

Furthermore, it seems clear from our own and other persons' observations that the agency's relationships with both state government and higher education institutions will depend chiefly on the staff, especially the executive officer. He is the agency's principal contact with the offices of state government and the legislature. For example, in at least half of the existing coordinating bodies, presentations to the governor and executive department heads are usually made by the director alone rather than by members of the board (although some members of consolidated governing boards play a fairly active role). And the other staff members usually work with lower-echelon state officials on matters such as budgets.

The administrative outlook and style of the executive director and his staff associates are strong determinants of how much and what kind of access the higher education community will have to the board members and to state government officials. Furthermore, staff attitudes and practices will govern the extent to which the institutions participate in data gathering, planning, and policy formulation. Only about half of the coordinating and governing boards responding to the Smart questionnaire reported that they hear formal presentations on major policy decisions from the staff and from institutional representatives on an equal basis. In most agencies, staff studies are prepared with the assistance of institutional representatives, and about half the agency boards "assume" that major differences between staff and other interested parties will have been resolved before the board discusses an issue.

13. Glenny, *Autonomy of Public Colleges* (New York: McGraw-Hill Book Co., 1959), p. 87.
14. Browne, "The Institution and the System," p. 46.
15. Ibid, p. 47.

Quality of staffing

Leaders in both state government and higher education manifest concern about the quality of agency personnel. In many—though by no means all—cases, the state government seems more satisfied with the quality and operations of the staff than does the higher education community. This is partly attributable to the recent trend toward appointing aggressive executive officers to replace older and more easygoing directors, many of whom had long-standing institutional ties and (perhaps) little understanding of the state's expectations about the agency. The new breed of director usually seems to agree with the governor and legislature on the need to exercise the leadership mode of coordination and planning.

The more critical attitude of the higher education community has several explanations. Since administrators of institutions have more frequent contacts with the staff, the possibilities for friction are greater. In addition, they are in a position to question the staff's educational judgment. Finally, they naturally do not share the occasional state government attitude that coordination is meant to "regulate" the institutions and are alarmed to see more staff personnel issuing more regulations and more information (sometimes embarrassing to the institutions) and trying to strengthen the centralized direction of higher education at the cost of the institutions' own scope. As the subjects of the coordination and planning, institutions naturally look askance at the agency staff's power to inhibit their access to the state's political authorities and to a board of laymen who must necessarily rely heavily on staff advice.

In the case of voluntary coordinating systems, staff work is performed by the participating institutions. A few earlier systems (e.g., Colorado, Michigan, Ohio) had a full-time executive director, usually appointed in a last-minute attempt to ward off the threat of statutory coordination. The position of executive director for a voluntary system is something of an anomaly, in that one of the advantages of such a system—in the institutions' view—is that the presidents could deal with each other "without interference from outsiders remote from institutional operation."[16] The executive director is likely to find himself in an impossible position when the institutions which pay him disagree on questions of any magnitude.

The staff members of coordinating boards are usually specialists in budget and finance, academic programs, physical facilities, and, increas-

16. Glenny, *Autonomy of Public Colleges*, p. 247.

ingly, research and Federal programs. They play a crucial role in preparing the agency members for meetings. They also act as the secretariat for presidents' and other advisory committees. Our experience suggests that many agency staffs, often already overworked, tend to neglect these functions (especially for committees), thus causing the board members to rely even more heavily on their unsupported recommendations. In addition, the staff is responsible for informing the presidents and trustees of board actions. Several agencies, such as those in Georgia and North Carolina, publish regular newsletters, but again, this information function is often slighted.

Pliner found that consolidated governing boards, because of their comprehensive responsibilities for the institutions, tended to have larger professional staffs than coordinating boards.[17] Of the nineteen such agencies responding to the Smart questionnaire, three had no more than three professional staff persons, none had over twenty-five and half had between six and ten. Several coordinating boards, however, have increased the number of professional staff positions recently, and this trend will probably continue as needs in research, planning, and Federal program areas become more pressing. Undoubtedly, coordinating agencies have in the past suffered not only from mediocre staffing but also from inadequate numbers. But a larger staff constitutes a danger, even with agencies performing no governing functions, in that it will be more tempted to justify its existence by finding things to do and, perhaps, by dabbling in the operations of the institutions.

In a few states, the creation of an agency—and thus of a staff—solely for higher education has been a delicate issue. Where a state board of education has jurisdiction for all levels, as in Pennsylvania, the higher education staff operates as a division of the state department of education. Some college and university officials, and some state government leaders, feel that in this situation, the small higher education staff tends to be overwhelmed by the influence and perspective of persons with public school backgrounds who are uninformed about or unsympathetic to the special needs of higher education.

Executive officers

The executive officer of a coordinating agency stands at a crucial point in the board's structure. We found state after state grappling with the prob-

17. *Coordination and Planning.*

lem of finding or replacing an executive. In the light of the following summary of the executive officer's duties, it is little wonder that candidates are in short supply.

> In his relationships with the agency he acts as secretary [with some exceptions], as staff director, and as the chief initiator of policy recommendations. . . . He is the official contact for the agency with all persons in and out of the system. . . .
>
> As the initiator of recommendations, he can wield more power and exert more influence on policy than any other person in the system. . . .
>
> . . . He not only enforces agency decisions but also interprets their intent and scope and supplements policy with necessary administrative directives.[18]

Despite the scope and the importance of these responsibilities, agency directors do not necessarily have high prestige. Presidents of universities in the system tend to be paid more, to be better known, and to be more commonly thought of as educational leaders. Furthermore, the agency director has no political base of alumni, voters, or interest groups, whereas most of the officials he deals with are backed by some powerful constituency. Those agency directors who have acquired substantial reputations in their jobs have done so by their vigorous assertion of the agency's powers and by their adeptness in persuasive diplomatic relations with officers of educational institutions and with other arms of state government.

All but three coordinating and governing boards appoint the executive officer. In Pennsylvania, the Superintendent of Public Instruction—an appointee of the governor and a member of his cabinet—chooses another officer to head the higher education staff of the state department of education. In Nevada and Alaska, the president of the state university is the executive head of the single governing board. The executive officer is usually given the title of "executive director," "director," or "executive secretary," though the use of the titles "chancellor" and "commissioner" is increasing, to the consternation of those in higher education circles who recognize that, in giving an executive officer such a designation, the state legislature probably anticipates that he will enlarge his role from executive director of the board to head of the public higher education system.

18. Glenny, *Autonomy of Public Colleges*, pp. 51–52.

The disparate requirements of the executive officer's job, its ambiguous status, and its highly personal nature often make the position extremely difficult to fill. For this reason, a number of new agencies suffer delays in getting under way. This was true of the IIIc-type agencies in Massachusetts and New Jersey. The state boards of education in Michigan and Pennsylvania were also hampered in their early development by periods of vacant superintendencies and by the conflicting demands of the higher education and the public school community, each of which pressed for the appointment of an executive familiar with its own problems and needs.

An additional difficulty is that a board may not know what kind of person to choose. The characteristics of a successful director may even vary through time as the coordinating agency develops. Furthermore, there is no definite experience that will necessarily give a man both the political and the educational knowledgeability relevant to coordination and planning. As a result, the backgrounds of current board directors differ greatly. The chancellors in Ohio and Oklahoma were previously presidents of public institutions in their states, while two commissioners of the Texas council came from private university backgrounds, one from within and one from outside the state. The former directors of the Utah and Illinois coordinating boards were, respectively, an educator who has served as a mayor, and a political scientist who is a major scholar of statewide coordination and planning. Directors in other states have come from within the agency's staff, from public school superintendencies, from the Federal government (although they often have had experience in higher education as well), and even from the White House staff via the ambassadorial service, as in New Jersey.

It seems likely that university and college administrators will continue to be the main source of board officers. State government leaders, as well as college presidents, often demand an educator for the job. They do not, of course, deprecate the importance of political sophistication, but they rarely seem to favor the appointment of someone whose background is heavily political in the conventional sense. Indeed, political skill can be a hindrance. We heard complaints about directors who were too adept in their political role as well as complaints about some who were too naive. If the board director is to earn the cooperation of the higher education community, and if the board is to promote the best interests of higher education as well as of the state, the director's educational credentials and those of his staff associates should inspire confidence.

College presidents and state legislators usually prefer an executive officer who comes from within the state. An outsider, they fear, will be unfamiliar with the state's particular educational and political history and problems. On the other hand, an educator chosen from one of the state's own public institutions may be too dedicated to the status quo, however knowledgeable about the state and acceptable to the institutions he may be. But the history of coordination indicates that previous affiliation with a public institution does not necessarily bias a man. One might convincingly argue that a former poacher would make a good gamekeeper, since he knows all the tricks.

Other staff

Professional staff members under the director usually come to the coordinating agencies from positions in institutions of higher education. Most of the others are likely to be from state government or business, with a smattering of people from research and development organizations, the Federal government, other coordinating agencies, and public school systems. According to summary data on the educational backgrounds of staff in nineteen coordinating agencies, only nine have staffs at least half of whom hold or are working for the doctoral degree, and the figures for governing boards are even smaller. Obviously, staff members without the academic "union card" will be at some disadvantage in dealing with institutional administrators or faculty, particularly if they are working in the areas of academic institution or research.

Obstacles to adequate staffing

Two of the major problems confronting agencies eager to hire and retain qualified directors and staff specialists are salaries and state personnel rules. Unfortunately, the latest salary survey to which we have access dates from 1967, so the absolute dollar figures are not too helpful. But comparative observations are instructive.

Only two executive officers of nine governing boards and twelve coordinating boards were paid more than the highest-paid public or private university president in their states, and only four earned approximately as much; fifteen were paid less. Agency executive officers in ten states received more than the average salary of all public college and university presidents within their states; in twelve states, they earned the same or less. Eight agency directors earned less than the highest-paid state college president, and three were below the level of the highest-paid community college president.

Nearly all executive officers are exempt from state civil service status; thus, the coordinating agency has some flexibility in setting the top salary, if the state budget office and the legislature are agreeable. In at least nine of the coordinating and two of the governing boards, all professional staff positions are exempt, and in a few more, including two state boards of education, some high-level positions below the directorship are exempt or are considered to be academic appointments. In the remainder, the lower professional positions come under state salary schedules, an arrangement which, with other civil service restrictions, probably discourages many qualified persons from serving on agencies.

FIVE

Planning

That planning should constitute the top priority of any coordinating agency is widely recognized today.[1] But this was certainly not the case as recently as 1959 when Lyman Glenny reported that planning was the most neglected function. Planning at all levels—institutional, statewide, regional, and national—has since become so much the vogue that it might be said "we are all planners now." Unfortunately, however, good intentions are not enough, and there is a significant gap between the rhetoric and the reality.

Since the term *planning* can be applied to everything from deciding what will be done tomorrow to attempting to establish a coherent state-wide system of higher education in the face of many complex variables stretching out over the next ten to twenty years, it is important to distinguish here between short-range and long-range planning.

It has been said that "program formulation" is "the single most important task for planners."[2] Moreover, program formulation [should be] viewed as an ongoing activity, continuously practiced, rather than one engaged in only once every five or ten years." This study accepts the first of those statements as consonant with our emphasis on the central importance of program to substantive autonomy, and it accepts the second

---

1. As noted in chapter 3, at the time this study was conducted, at least three other major studies were being carried out. They are: Kent Halstead, *Handbook for State-wide Planning in Higher Education* (Washington: U.S. Office of Education, forthcoming); Lewis B. Mayhew, *Long Range Planning for Higher Education* (Washington: Academy for Educational Development, 1969); and Ernest Palola, Timothy Lehmann, and William R. Blischke, *Higher Education By Design: The Sociology of Planning* (Berkeley: Center for Research and Development in Higher Education, University of California, 1970). We kept in close touch with these studies and conducted our field research so as to minimize duplication of effort. Therefore, this chapter relies more on secondary sources and less on our own investigations than would otherwise have been the case.
2. *Higher Education By Design*, p. 550.

as a realistic description of how most program formulation actually occurs. Chapter 7 analyzes both the form and content of program review, regarded as an ongoing process. In this chapter, we are concerned primarily with long-range planning which, at its best, defines the institutional role and scope missions within which program formulations must occur. Although we are aware that the term *master plan* is already on the way out, because it connotes rigidity, we shall use it (albeit without capital letters) to distinguish it from short-range planning.

Master planning ideally involves the identification of key problems, the accumulation of accurate data about those problems, the analysis of their interrelationships, the extrapolation of future alternatives which might emerge out of present conditions, the assessment of the probable consequences of introducing new variables, the choice of the most desirable (or least undesirable) modified alternatives as the basic goals, a sequential plan for implementing the desired goals, and a built-in feedback system for periodically reevaluating both the goals selected and the means used to achieve them. Naturally, the broader the problems analyzed and the longer the time span covered, the more difficult the planning job.

Judged by the above definition, most of the state surveys undertaken in the first half of this century would not qualify as master planning because of their limited scope and their preoccupation with fact finding. Master planning, the attempt to interrelate the many variables in a statewide system of higher education and to come up with long-range policy recommendations and a scheme of action, is a relatively recent phenomenon.

People are becoming more sophisticated about the process of master planning, viewing it as a package of equally important parts, the parts being the selection of appropriate planning agents; the formulation of the plan itself; provision for implementing and adapting it through time; and provision for its periodic overhaul. For purposes of our analysis, we can examine the package by considering three questions: Who plans? Who implements? Who reevaluates?

Who plans?

The belief that planning is a value-free process of feeding objective data into a computer which then produces "the answers" is fortunately moribund. Our field research tends to confirm Glenny's observation that the values of the planners and the type of planning mechanism chosen have a major bearing on the quality of the planning which results. Concerning the crucial role of the planning staff, he has warned:

> The kind of information which is collected as against that left uncollected, the form in which it is reported, and the attitudes and biases of the persons analyzing it and making recommendations may leave few alternative solutions and little real discretion to those who are to make the final decisions.[3]

The type of planning mechanism used can have both procedural and substantive repercussions. The three major types are: (1) a group of out-of-state consultants, (2) an in-state agency or ad hoc commission, and (3) a commission which employs both in-state and out-of-state personnel. Some states seem to have political climates favorable to outside consultants whereas others are hostile to their use. Thus, the "right" procedure must precede a "right" plan.

With respect to educational results, relying exclusively on either in-state or out-of-state persons has advantages and disadvantages. Out-of-state consultants may be impartial about state issues over which emotions are running high, but their lack of detailed knowledge of a state's problems and their freedom from the responsibility for implementing the plan can sometimes lead them to recommend unrealistic policies.

In our research, we found that use of out-of-state consultants looked especially attractive when in-state planning experience was lacking and when speed was considered important. There is no question but that skilled consultants or commercial firms can get things moving more quickly. On the other hand, we heard criticisms of "instant master plans" and of "slick Eastern planners who lectured everyone under the guise of consulting them."

In-state planning can involve either an existing coordinating agency or a group of citizens and experts assembled ad hoc for the purpose of creating a master plan. The strengths and weaknesses of using an in-state planning mechanism tend to be the opposites of those connected with using outside consultants. A more intimate knowledge of state problems and the necessity for the planners to live with the proposed solutions certainly represent gains, but impartiality and a knowledge of alternatives drawn from other states are sometimes lost. Another possible

3. *Autonomy of Public Colleges* (New York: McGraw-Hill Book Co., 1959), p. 68.

advantage to the in-state method—but one which is realized only if the planning process is very carefully extended to include widespread participation by institutional faculty and administrators—is that it promotes confrontation and dialogue between persons who would not otherwise hear each other's point of view and thus often leads to mutual enlightenment and catharsis. But this happy result does not emerge automatically; it entails considerable effort and risk of delay.[4]

The third, or mixed, approach involves the use of an existing coordinating agency as the basic planning unit, but with in-state laymen and experts serving on working committees and outside consultants engaged for short-term, highly technical problems. This procedure probably takes fullest possible advantage of expertise and participation, but it requires a great deal of planning sophistication, a generous budget, and adequate time.

Now that more and more states have established a central coordinating agency and these agencies are acquiring more planning experience, the third approach will probably become increasingly common. In the past, some states (e.g., North Carolina in 1962, Texas in 1962, Kentucky in 1966) were reluctant to use it, however, since one of the questions to be decided was the future of the coordinating agency itself. If the agency's survival and powers are at issue, then, the state may feel compelled to use outside consultants or an ad hoc commission of citizens.

Who implements?

Glenny has pointed out the crucial importance of explicitly delegating to some appropriate agency the responsibility for seeing to it that the planning is carried out: "It is at this point that many, if not most, plans fail. Plans are not self-enforcing or fulfilling any more than other activities of government. Concerted effort and coordination among the public agencies is essential in order to overcome the myriad of obstacles that confront the plan's objectives."[5] It is conceivable, he notes, that this "concerted effort" would come from a coordinating agency, a state building commission, a scholarship commission, the department of education, the executive and legislative branches of state government, and not least, the several boards governing the colleges and universities.

4. The problems of institutional participation in agency planning are analyzed more thoroughly in chapter 8.
5. "Long-Range Planning for State Educational Needs," *Seven Crucial Issues in Education: Alternatives for State Action* (Denver: Education Commission of the States, 1967), p. 7.

Clearly, an operation of such complexity requires more continuing full-time attention than most legislative or executive agencies can bestow. The experience of several states tends to confirm this: Louisiana, Michigan, and Ohio, for example, all called in distinguished outside consultants to carry out statewide surveys of higher education in the 1950s; but since there was no proper mechanism for implementing the plans, many important policy recommendations were ignored. Since 1900, the Massachusetts legislature has authorized at least thirty-six studies dealing with various aspects of higher education. The latest and largest study, the Willis-Harrington Report, finding that most of the preceding plans had not been properly implemented, recommended that a coordinating board be created and charged with both planning and implementing.[6]

A coordinating agency is in a particularly good position to oversee the implementation of the planning goals because it can use its powers in other areas to reinforce their achievement. For example, a master plan may call for a state university to cut back on lower division enrollments and concentrate on graduate education and research. But the institution will find it difficult to comply if the budget formulas still reward institutions on the basis of student numbers. In this situation, a coordinating agency, through its budget role, can persuade the state to make the formulas harmonize with the planning goals. The agency's functions of program review and capital outlay can also be used to help toward the attainment of planning goals.

The need to integrate Federal programs with state master planning is another argument for assigning to a state coordinating agency the central role in implementation. Real problems arise if Federal grants are made to institutions for which the state master plan has established objectives different from, or contrary to, those which are supported by Federal funds. We talked to some academicians, however, who were distinctly uneasy at the thought of channeling both state and Federal programs through the state coordinating agency; the danger that such monolithic power would be abused, they said, was too great.[7]

A final argument for giving responsibility for implementation to an agency specializing in higher education is that most plans are and should be painted with a very broad brush; therefore they required considerable

6. Cited by Samuel Gove, "The Massachusetts System of Higher Education in Transition" (MS, Department of Political Science, University of Illinois, 1967).
7. This complex question—of whether to channel Federal programs directly to the institutions or through the state government—will be examined in greater detail in chapter 10.

filling in of detail and fine shading of interpretation. In Massachusetts, the Willis-Harrington Report specified

> each institution is expected to enjoy fiscal autonomy and academic autonomy within the limits of its functions, purpose and program as set forth herein *or subsequently altered by decision of the Board of Higher Education.*[8] (Emphasis added.)

Thus, in Massachusetts, as in a number of other states, the authors of the plan for higher education concluded that they could not foresee every eventuality and that a coordinating agency should be empowered to make necessary future adjustments.

Who reevaluates?

A basic maxim of master planning is that periodic updating and reevaluation are necessary to avoid excessive rigidity. Given the extreme complexity of the issues, it is always possible that a recommended policy may have been mistaken or, even if correct in relation to the conditions originally prevailing, may need to be revised or supplemented because of social, economic, educational, or political changes over time. Furthermore, one way to get the "losers" in a particular planning dispute to accept an adverse recommendation and to acknowledge the fairness of the planning procedures is to assure them that they will, in the not-too-distant future, be given another opportunity to raise the issue and to present additional supporting evidence for their point of view. On the other hand, the old admonition against pulling up the carrots every two days to see if they are growing applies here: Too much zeal in reappraisal can easily become self-defeating. Basic policy recommendations must be allowed to take form before being subjected to definitive judgment.

It is important to distinguish between the process of updating a master plan and that of engaging in a fundamental reappraisal of the basic planning goals and the structures of governance and coordination. The New York State Education Law, for example, calls for a new master plan every four years, in addition to annual interim revisions or progress reports. While such frequent updating may be desirable, it seems doubtful that basic reevaluations should occur as often. The natural tendency would be to freeze developments pending the outcome of the reappraisal;

8. Quoted in Gove, "The Massachusetts System of Higher Education in Transition."

and if moratoria on new programs are imposed too frequently in states experiencing rapid growth, severe problems will inevitably develop.

The coordinating agency is the logical body to undertake the updating of a master plan, but some persons have questioned whether an agency charged with implementing existing master-plan goals (which it may have set itself) should also be asked to undertake a fundamental reappraisal of them. Algo D. Henderson, for example, has pointed out that an agency with close ties and responsibilities in higher education can easily "become satisfied with things as they are, can fail to grasp the implications of changes in social conditions and demands. . . . It ordinarily takes a fresh study by a newly constituted body to define the issues, gather objective data, and make recommendations that challenge the status quo."[9]

If the educational status quo is not under heavy attack, and if the coordinating agency's survival is not in question, the existing agency may be perfectly capable of conducting a general reevaluation that will be acceptable to everyone. But if there is serious dissatisfaction with the existing master plan, or if higher education issues have become politically hot, it may be necessary to find other procedures for reevaluation.

Recent history in California illustrates these points well. The California Master Plan, though nationally acclaimed, has been subject to attack from several quarters, chief among them the state college faculty, who, through their statewide academic senate, issued a report claiming that the plan relegated state colleges to second-class citizenship.[10] Militant voices called for a reopening of many questions thought to have been permanently settled and at the same time expressed doubt that the Coordinating Council for Higher Education, with its vested interest in the status quo, was the agency to take the fresh look.

During the same period (1964–66), campus disturbances and a gubernatorial campaign which raised several educational issues (such as the charging of tuition fees for the first time) had inflamed the political situation. A legislative resolution that originally called for an investigation of the university ultimately created a Joint Legislative Committee on Higher Education charged with reevaluating the Master Plan.

The chairman of the Joint Committee then requested the Coordinat-

9. "State Planning and Coordination of Public and Private Higher Education," *Educational Record*, Fall 1966, p. 504.
10. Marc Tool, "The California State Colleges Under the Master Plan" (Report to the Academic Senate of the California State Colleges, Sacramento State College, August 1, 1966).

ing Council to undertake a study of the extent to which the Master Plan recommendations had been implemented. In short, the coordinating agency was used for feedback on the progress and problems of implementation, but the legislature reserved to itself the fundamental reevaluation of goals. Incidentally, one of the matters being reexamined was the pattern of coordination and governance itself, and the committee staff report,[11] as yet not acted upon, recommended that the Coordinating Council be abolished and that the three segments of higher education be merged under one consolidated governing board with regional subboards.

The outside agency for reevaluation does not have to be a legislative committee, of course; it can be any group of persons assembled by the sovereign power of the state and given the proper charge, adequate staff, sufficient funds, and enough time to accomplish its mission.

Coordinating Agencies and Master Planning

The studies by Mayhew[12] and Abrahams[13] give detailed information about each state's planning (or lack thereof) and about the procedures used, the policies recommended, and the problems of implementation. To avoid repeating this material, we will offer instead some general comments (with a few examples) on how the type of coordinating agency is related to its ability to plan, implement, and reevaluate effectively.

As of late 1969, twenty-seven states had formulated either a master plan or comprehensive studies and reports equivalent to it. Of these, seventeen have coordinating boards and ten have consolidated governing boards. An additional six states—three with coordinating boards and three with consolidated governing boards—are in the process of developing master plans. Another five—three coordinating boards and two consolidated governing boards—are planning to develop master plans. Only twelve states have no master plan or its equivalent either completed, in progress, or projected.[14] Table 6 summarizes these data in slightly rearranged form.

Clearly, the tendency is for states to master plan: Three out of four have done so or are doing so. The two states without a formal coordinat-

11. California Staff of the Joint Legislative Committee on Higher Education, *The Challenge of Achievement* (Staff report to the Committee. Sacramento, 1969). It should be noted that the full Committee never approved this report.
12. *Long Range Planning for Higher Education*.
13. Louise Abrahams, *State Planning for Higher Education* (Washington: Academy for Educational Development, 1969).
14. Ibid., Table III, p. 9.

TABLE 6

THE STATUS OF MASTER PLANNING, BY TYPE OF COORDINATING AGENCY

Category of Agency as of October 1969	Master Plan or Equivalent Completed	Plan Being Developed	Plan to Be Developed	No Master Plan
I. No state agency	0	0	0	2
II. Voluntary association	0	0	0	2
III. Coordinating board	17	3	3	4
IV. Consolidated governing board	10	3	2	4
Total	27	6	5	12

SOURCE: Louise Abrahams, *State Planning for Higher Education.* Prepared for the U.S. Department of Health, Education, and Welfare, Office of Education, Bureau of Research, under Contract No. OEC-0-8-980797-4634 (010) (Washington: Academy for Educational Development, 1969), Table III, p. 9.

ing mechanism and the two with voluntary coordinating associations have taken no steps whatsoever in this direction. But slightly more than half of the consolidated governing boards and slightly less than two-thirds of the coordinating boards have completed master plans or their equivalent, and most other states in these two categories are now preparing master plans or have carried out studies in preparation of such plans.

Voluntary coordinating associations

The record of this group is fair to weak on long-range planning and even weaker on implementation. Since the power of the voluntary association depends on continuing unanimous agreement, it can go only as far in planning as all members are willing to go. Even if a plan is authorized, its implementation is contingent on voluntary compliance. To illustrate, at the request of the Ohio College Association (a voluntary group of public and private institutions), John Dale Russell studied Ohio higher education in the 1950s, but his recommendations, considered undesirable to various interests, were quietly shelved.

On the other hand, the California Liaison Committee, the voluntary agency which coordinated the state college and university systems until 1960, had an excellent record in planning. It sponsored the Strayer Report in 1948, the McConnell Restudy in 1955, and the Master Plan itself in 1960. Its record on implementation, however, is much less impressive. Glenny remarks, "Of the 137 recommendations in the Restudy, for example, the Liaison Committee recognized only 104 as of interest to it and endorsed only 89." But, he continues, it is at the board level that the California system reveals its greatest weakness. . . . the university regents were "interested" in 94 [recommendations] but had approved only 37 percent of them, while the state board [for the state colleges] was concerned with 102 and had approved 76.5 percent.[15]

Thus, the Master Plan of 1960 recognized that voluntary planning and implementation were no longer adequate to meet the state's educational problems and therefore recommended the creation of a formal coordinating body to which would be given explicit responsibility for implementing the Master Plan.

The Indiana and pre-1969 Washington voluntary groups both paid modest attention to long-range planning. The Indiana Conference recently moved to cooperate with the state Higher Education Facilities Commission in a major study of the future of higher education in that state. And the Washington Council of Presidents created an elaborate structure of interinstitutional technical committees which acted to lay the groundwork for subsequent planning. But recent studies of voluntary coordination in Colorado[16] and Washington[17] have confirmed earlier pessimism about the ability of voluntary groups to resolve the really controversial issues within a state. If this cannot be done, little should be expected from the voluntary agencies in the way of planning or implementation.

Almost by definition, voluntary groups are the least likely to undertake wide-ranging reevaluation of higher education, for of necessity they operate within the context of the status quo.

Coordinating boards

With the exception of the boards in Arkansas and New Mexico, which were initially confined to coordinating educational finance, all boards in this category seem to have been granted adequate powers to engage in long-range planning. If the power to master plan is not explicitly given, it can usually be deduced from the authority to require data from the institutions and to make studies.

15. *Autonomy of Public Colleges*, p. 259.
16. Harry S. Allen, "Voluntary Coordination of Higher Education in Colorado" (MS, Office of Institutional Research, University of Nebraska, 1967).
17. Frank B. Brouillet, "An Analysis of State of Washington's Method for Coordinating Higher Education" (Ed.D. diss., University of Washington, 1968).

In the realm of implementation, the record is mixed. Boards like those in Illinois and Ohio—which have strong de jure or de facto powers in budget review, program approval, capital outlay review, and perhaps Federal programs—have had few difficulties in riding herd on the implementation of the master plan; but boards like those in California and Pennsylvania whose powers are weak in most of these areas have not been able to push very effectively for the achievement of specified goals. If the institutional governing boards are unenthusiastic, they can simply fail to take action. In California, neither the university nor the state college system moved very fast to implement master plan recommendations calling for the diversion of sizable numbers of lower division students into the junior colleges. But lacking any substantial powers, the coordinating board's only recourse was to recommend to the Department of Finance that state controls over institutional building programs be used to bring about the desired results. In Pennsylvania, the State Board of Education as coordinating agency has not been able to force Pennsylvania State University to comply with the master plan recommendation regarding branch campuses.

The power of the coordinating boards to undertake a fundamental reevaluation of higher education within their states also varies considerably. Those boards that have at least a majority of lay members who are not officially connected with the public institutions are more likely to be asked to undertake reappraisal, whereas those with a majority of institutional representatives are usually judged to be too closely involved with the status quo. Such was the case in California, the only state which to date has attempted fundamental reappraisal of a master plan.

Consolidated governing boards

In theory, the strong governing powers of these boards should permit them to plan effectively and to implement smoothly. As we were told in one state, "planning comes with special force when there are administrative powers to back it up. Unlike some coordinating boards with advisory powers which can only 'urge,' there are many different ways to get something done if our board wants it."

The force of this logic is undeniable, but ease of implementation must still be considered secondary in importance to quality of planning. And here the governing boards' record is not so good. One explanation of this inadequacy is that even though they have ample powers to plan, these boards are so operations-oriented because of their governing responsibilities that they fail to grasp the centrality of long-range planning. A great deal seems to depend on whether the executive officer acts as clerk to the board or as educational leader, the latter type being much more apt to stress the need for master planning. The three governing board states in our study—Florida, Georgia, and Oregon—all had executive officers designated chancellors, and all had carried out some long-range planning, though in Georgia the institutional master plans collectively were said to constitute the state master plan.

The close identification of the consolidated governing boards with the institutions they govern make them suspect when it comes to re-evaluating the original master plan. Mayhew notes, "A single board can develop monopolistic tendencies so that no real look to the future is possible for fear of jeopardizing the status quo."[18] To some extent, this weakness can be overcome by hiring outside consultants to undertake the reappraisal, as the Florida board did in the 1950s.

Summary

In summary, conditions seem generally improved since Glenny noted in 1959 that the various board types seemed to be "about equally inadequate in long-range statewide planning."[19] The coordinating boards would appear to have the best planning records, and the statewide governing boards to be in the strongest position to ensure implementation. The phenomenon of fundamental reappraisal of planning is still too new to permit generalizations, but it seems likely that coordinating boards with public majorities are the most capable of taking a fresh look at higher education.

The Scope of Planning: Jurisdiction

A really strong master plan should probably include, in one way or another, the private sector and, in states where they are governed by a jurisdiction separate from the planning agency, the community colleges.

There are two major ways in which the private institutions can participate in master planning. As in California and Illinois, they can sit on the planning committees and, taking the private sector's enrollment

18. *Long Range Planning for Higher Education*, p. 59.
19. *Autonomy of Public Colleges*, p. 231.

and program projections as given, help to recommend state policy for the public institutions. Or, as in Ohio and Pennsylvania, the master plan can include some substantive recommendations directed to state policy for the private institutions as well. The New York Board of Regents has legal authority over the private institutions in that state, and the Bundy Commission Report (see chapter 9) has recently urged that, in exchange for direct state aid, private sector planning be more closely integrated with that of the public institutions.

Although some state constitutions prohibit direct state aid to private institutions, the trend at the planning level is clearly to include the private sector. This trend is given impetus by Federal programs which distribute funds to both public and private institutions and which increasingly stress cooperative planning.

In some states where planning and coordination is undertaken by a consolidated governing board, persons from private institutions expressed to us some misgivings about closer collaboration. They fear that these boards, with their strong powers and long-standing traditions of administering their institutions, may not be able to back off and exercise pure planning powers vis-à-vis the private institutions. In Georgia and Oregon, this problem was met by the creation of an agency which is confined to planning and which rides lightly over both the consolidated governing board and the State Board of Education. Although the fundamental purpose of these new bodies is to integrate planning across the various public sectors of education, an incidental benefit is that the private institutions may find it easier to collaborate with them.

The problem of integrating junior college development into statewide planning for higher education arises in just a few states where the junior institutions are governed by a body not under the jurisdiction of the coordinating agency. Of the coordinating boards, only North Carolina fails to plan for the junior colleges. Arizona, Florida, Iowa, Kansas, Mississippi, and Oregon among the statewide governing boards lack such jurisdiction. In Florida, separate plans were prepared for the junior and senior institutions in the 1950s and then coordinated informally by the executive officers of the two statewide boards, both of which ultimately report to the State Board of Education. In Oregon, the Education Coordinating Council (mentioned in the preceding paragraph) has been created to act as planning liaison between the State Board of Higher Education and the State Board of Education, which governs the junior colleges. In Iowa, a voluntary coordinating council on post–high school education provides a connecting link between the senior and junior institutions. In Arizona and Mississippi, the Junior-Senior College Conferences achieve the same end.

In our field research, we discovered legislative interest here and there in broadening the coverage of educational planning to include the entire package, from kindergarten through postdoctoral work. But, as of now, not even the states in which all levels are ultimately answerable to the state board of education (Idaho, Michigan, Montana, New York, Pennsylvania, Rhode Island, and, to a much lesser extent, Florida) have attempted to integrate the planning of higher education with that of the public schools. In addition to the new liaison agencies formed to link the consolidated governing boards and the state boards of education in Georgia and Oregon, similar bodies have been created in Massachusetts and New Jersey, states with IIIc-type agencies. In theory, such liaison groups could promote integrated planning from the kindergarten to the postgraduate years, but the problems of attempting to cover such a span are formidable.[20]

The Scope of Planning: Time-Span Covered

Mayhew, in his study of state planning, notes:

> state master plans . . . are rarely projecting beyond 1975 or 1980. Yet it may be crucial to look beyond those dates if the creation of new facilities is to be commensurate with actual need. At present rates of increase of the proportion of college age youth attending college there is a strong possibility of real decline in enrollments after 1980. Yet a number of plans imply that enrollments will continue to increase in absolute numbers even though the lower birth rates of the 1960's are manifest. It would seem logical that states planning higher education should require projections at least to 1987, for the students of that year have already been born.[21]

Lionel J. Livesey, Jr., urges that long-range planning in fact live up to its name: that planners look beyond today or tomorrow to "the day beyond tomorrow and its potential problems which we ought to identify

20. These new planning agencies and the relations between higher education and the public schools are discussed further in chapter 10.
21. *Long Range Planning for Higher Education*, p. 165.

now *before* they reach the crisis stage." [22] Quoting from the Heald Report on higher education in New York, he emphasizes the need to think anew for those who must live part of their lives in the 21st century: "Even the best models of education from the past will not be good enough." But, Livesey warns, the danger is that short-range plans tend to drive out long-range ones and "hard" quantitative data to drive out "soft" qualitative judgments and intuitions. If planners shrink master plans to include only that which can be proved, the plans will probably remain pedestrian extrapolations of existing conditions, and the opportunity for experimentation and innovation will have been missed.

Certainly it is true that most state planning and coordinating agencies are preoccupied with short-range allocative planning. This activity is a necessary one—because planning decisions do have to be made for the short run—but some serious effort and imagination should be directed to the distant future as well. Palola, Lehmann, and Blischke recommend planning for three time periods: short-range (one to four years), intermediate-range (five to twenty-five years), and extended long-range (twenty-six to fifty years). [23]

If an agency does attempt to lengthen the span of its vision, it should do so with full awareness that this may require additional planning staff with somewhat different orientations. (Livesey suggests separate offices for allocative and for long-distance thinking.) Using a staff inexperienced in the special problems of intuitive long-range planning or a staff of utopians lacking the necessary sophistication could result in disaster, and legislators are well known for their impatience about this kind of fiasco.

The Content of Planning

Master planning can be institutional, multicampus-systemwide, [24] statewide, regional, or national. Although certain general problems of quantity, quality, cost, and coordination have to be dealt with in planning

---

22. "Can Higher Education Be Planned?" (MS, State University of New York, Albany, 1968).
23. *Higher Education By Design*, p. 565.
24. By *multicampus system* is meant a corporate entity that governs more than one campus but fewer than all senior public institutions in the state. The term *consolidated governing board* is used for the latter category, and its internal planning would be classified as statewide. For a study of the governance and coordination of multicampus systems, see Eugene C. Lee and Frank Bowen, *The Governance of the Multicampus University* (Berkeley, Institute of Governmental Studies, University of California, 1971).

at each of these levels, the particular topics covered and the emphases given to them differ markedly from level to level and, at the statewide level which is the focus of this study, even from state to state.

Each state undertaking a master plan has to make its own choices about which topics are suitable for central planning and which should be kept at the institutional or multicampus level. Kent Halstead speaks of a continuum, at one end of which are topics so broad as to make them inherently amenable to central planning, and at the other end of which are topics so limited or unique as to require planning at the institutional or multicampus level. He says:

> Between these two positions are many topics which require the attention and viewpoint of both the campus and the central system. . . . It remains the task of the state planning agency, with the concurrence of the various institutional members, to select from among this intermediate group, subjects suitable for statewide study which are also within the legal purview of agency operations.[25]

The following list is not meant to be exhaustive; it merely illustrates the possible range of questions which have to be considered, when deciding whether to plan centrally, locally, or jointly.[26]

1. In undertaking long-range state planning on enrollment capacities and program offerings, should the present and projected activities of the private sector be taken into consideration? If so, how is this to be done?

2. How is the state to provide for the expansion in higher education needed between now and, say, 1985 if (a) the proportion of college-age youth attending college remains about the same; or (b) if it increases dramatically? By expanding existing institutions? If so, which ones and how much? By creating new institutions? If so, what kind and where? Should they be branch campuses or independent institutions? By state-aided support of the private sector (see #11)?

25. *Handbook of Statewide Planning in Higher Education*, chapter 1.
26. Other scholars have discussed this topic in a somewhat different fashion. See: Glenny, "Long-Range Planning for State Educational Needs"; John D. Millett, "State Planning for Higher Education," *Educational Record*, Summer 1965, pp. 223-30; Millett, "State-wide Planning and Coordination of Higher Education," *The Organization of Higher Education* (Proceedings of the Sixteenth Annual Legislative Work Conference, Southern Regional Education Board, White Sulphur Springs, W. Va., August 27-29, 1967; Mayhew, *Long Range Planning for Higher Education*; and Halstead, *Handbook for Statewide Planning in Higher Education*.

3. If the state wishes to effect a significant increase in the proportion of college-age youth who attend college, how should this be done? Through scholarships? Special programs for the disadvantaged? Lower tuition fees? Loans? Urban institutions? Community colleges?

4. What policies should be adopted with respect to student enrollments? In-state admission standards and tuition fees? Out-of-state admissions and tuition fees? State scholarship programs? Loan programs? Transferability of credits? Enrollment mixes, such as suggested percentages of students in lower division, upper division, and graduate work? Enrollment ceilings?

5. Should role and scope (i.e., mission) assignments be made to both new and existing institutions? If so, in how much detail and enforced by whom? How frequently should assignments be reconsidered? By whom?

6. In light of existing and proposed academic programs at all levels, are there unmet needs that should be covered? If so, which institutions should undertake them? Are there duplications in high-cost, low-demand fields that should be eliminated? What provisions, if any, should be made for ongoing planning and approval of new programs? At what level: Ph.D.? professional degree? M.A.? B.A.? new courses? extension programs?

7. Should the institutions' research and public service activities be subjected to an evaluation process similar to that for academic programs listed in #6? What responsibilities do the institutions have with respect to pressing social problems such as pollution, crime, urban congestion, racism, war?

8. How can the quality of higher education be improved? What innovations and experiments should be encouraged? Should new types of institutions be created? Should existing institutions be subject to new arrangements (e.g., cluster colleges)? For the bright students? For the potential dropouts? Can cooperation among institutions be increased? Can the application of modern technology improve library services, the teaching process, administrative operations? Should the faculty/student ratio be altered? Will attempts to meet the problems of quantity affect the level of quality? If so, what is the proper balance?

9. Given the expansion in student numbers, the need for new academic programs and new research and public service activities, the introduction of new techniques, and the search for enrichment in quality, how can the necessary new faculty be recruited and retained? How can faculty quality be improved? How should statewide faculty salary issues

be handled, both with respect to substantive amounts and to procedures for making decisions?

10. Given the estimated future need for faculty, plus all the other variables listed in #9, what are the state's building needs between now and the 1980s? What standards of space utilization should be employed? Should year-round operation of one, some, or all institutions of higher education be considered? How should year-to-year capital outlay priorities be established?

11. Over and above requesting the private institutions to furnish input data on their present operations and future hopes, should the state embark on any programs expressly designed to bolster the role of the private sector? If so, should it be in the form of scholarships? Facilities assistance? Direct aid?

12. If a community college system exists, or is to be created, how should it be governed? What share of the operating and capital outlay expenses should be borne by the state? How can community college functions be coordinated with those in higher education and in the public school system? How is vocational-technical education to be handled?

13. Given all the preceding factors, what are the estimated costs to the state between now and the 1980s? Are estimated tax revenues and the competing demands for other state services likely to allow sufficient funds to comply with all the recommendations? If not, should new sources of revenue be sought or should the master plan be cut back? If some recommendations must be dropped, which ones should go and who should decide?

14. What pattern of governance and coordination will best serve the public interest and higher education? Should one, some, or all institutions be granted constitutional autonomy, or should they all be subject to legislative statute? In either case, which powers belong to the institutions and which to the state? In those many areas where a partnership in decision making is called for, would the quality of decisions be improved by introducing a new coordinating agency or by extending an existing one? If a new agency is to be created, or an existing one altered, should its legal basis be voluntary, statutory, or constitutional? How should its membership be constituted, and how should it be staffed? What powers should it be assigned in the areas of planning, approval of new campuses or institutions, approval of new programs, budget review, capital outlay review, and administration of Federal programs? If no coordinating agency is to be created, or an existing one is to be abolished, who should have respon-

sibility for continuing implementation of the master plan? For periodic updating of it? For occasional basic reevaluations of it?

The Politics of Planning

The preceding list of issues, though not exhaustive, covers more topics than most master plans do. The actual subjects examined in any given master plan will probably depend on two types of decisions: what is educationally desirable and what is politically possible.

With respect to the first decision, educational experts should determine which issues (present or pending) require analysis in the master plan. If adequate time, money, or staff is not available to do the full job recommended, some educational priorities should be established so that less essential topics can be dropped.

But people in the state government may want to make suggestions not only about the topics to be covered but also about the need for practicality in dealing with them, lest the experts fly too high and force the politicians to play the villainous role of "importing reality." John D. Millett, although himself a professional educator, has argued forcefully for realism in master plans:

> No master plan means anything unless it is realizable financially. The easiest task in the world is to dream great dreams and not have to worry about where the money is coming from. But this attitude *is* dreaming. It is not planning.[27]

At the same time, master planners can be overly aware of what is politically feasible and too anxious to forestall anticipated objections. In our field research, we heard complaints that watered-down master plans had missed a crucial opportunity to educate state politicians and the public regarding both the costs and the benefits of supporting high-quality higher education. For instance, some persons criticized political compromises in the Ohio plan treatment of branch campuses and selective admissions. Academic opinion was nearly unanimous that a system of selective admissions was imperative for the orderly development of public higher education in the state; and, in fact, it was admitted that the public universities had long been quietly admitting the better students to the parent campus and the weaker students to the branches. But there is so

27. "State Planning for Higher Education," p. 229.

much popular support for the law which guarantees the right of any graduate of a chartered Ohio high school to admission to a state university that it was evidently felt wiser to say nothing of this practice in the master plan. A later effort by the coordinating board to alter the law was narrowly defeated in the legislature. Conceivably, this might not have occurred if the master plan had softened up public opinion on the issue, though, of course, this can only be a matter for speculation. Whatever the case, many persons feel that master plans should capitalize on the prestige of their sponsoring commissions to "tell it like it is." They contend that if a distinguished team of qualified planners cannot bluntly outline the full extent of the state's needs in higher education—if only to serve as long-range goals to be realized gradually—then their expertise is being wasted.

It is impossible to judge from the outside at just what stage in the planning process the compromise should be made between what is educationally desirable and what is politically possible: whether in the initial charge to the planning authority, in the draft recommendations, in the revisions of the draft recommendations after public hearings have revealed danger spots, in the efforts of the agency empowered to implement the plan, or in the reception accorded to the various recommendations by the organs of state government.

Glenny has described some of the dilemmas facing an agency charged with creating or implementing a master plan:

> Is it better to limit the plan to a few essentials or cover the waterfront? What are the practicable limits of achievable change?
>
> To what extent can a plan become a "package deal"? How do you prevent a sensitively balanced . . . plan from being dissected and mutilated in the political process of approval? Is it realistic to ask a legislature to accept all of a plan or none of it?
>
> How much "reality" should be exposed in a plan? Should the bald financial facts . . . which may frighten the governor and the legislature be given or should they be minimized in order not to jeopardize the plan? How much honesty is required, even though self-defeating? [28]

Most of the state politicians to whom we talked had ambivalent feelings about state planning in higher education. Characteristically, they

28. "Long-Range Planning for State Educational Needs," p. 6.

were disappointed because master planning failed to save the state money. Millett has supplied an answer to this concern:

> The role of the master plan is not to reduce governmental expenditures. On the contrary, the immediate result . . . may be to increase expenditures because of bringing together needs in a clear, comprehensive whole. The purpose of a master plan is to avoid wasteful and duplicating expenditures, to fix some priorities . . . in terms of the relative urgency of various needs, and to help guarantee an effective output . . . of all expenditures. A master plan is not a procedure to improve the efficiency of government.[29]

But other state political figures welcomed long-range planning in higher education, either because they recognized that decisions about such highly complex matters require specialized knowledge and information which they lacked or because they were glad to be relieved of the burden of choice in certain politically sensitive areas.

Strong governors are generally favorable toward master planning, but jurisdictional disputes about who will have the last word may arise as state planning offices grow more powerful.[30] Moreover, by making political commitments concerning educational issues which they expect the planning agencies to endorse, strong governors can create problems for the agencies. Legislatures can create problems too. In North Carolina, the governor tried in 1967 to use his prestige (he alone of the fifty governors lacks the veto power) to plead for a moratorium on major changes in higher education until the coordinating agency could produce a master plan in 1968. East Carolina College, feeling strongly that its cause was just, and openly doubtful that it would receive fair treatment in a master plan prepared by the existing coordinating agency, carried its fight for university status directly to the legislature. After an initial rebuff, it formed an alliance with three colleges in other parts of the state, and together they persuaded the legislature to pass a bill naming them "regional universities."

The reason for citing this incident is not to pass judgment on the substance of the decision but to emphasize that actions of this sort can undermine the whole basis of planning. As a college president in the state remarked to us: "The whole master plan is going to be useless if it is clear

29. "State-wide Planning and Coordination of Higher Education," p. 17.
30. This point is discussed further in chapter 11.

that educational issues are settled in the state legislature by the political process." Credibility must work both ways: If utopian planning lessens legislative enthusiasm, so political shortcuts on educational issues make it difficult for academicians to take master planning seriously.

But master planning cannot be totally divorced from politics. Because it involves recommendations as to who should exercise power and spend public funds, it will inevitably arouse political interest. Because its implementation usually requires both state legislation and appropriations, it must gain political support. Politics cannot be eliminated by avoiding planning, for state power will always exert itself one way or another, if only in a variety of decisions made piecemeal in various state offices. It is far preferable to demand from the state a coherent response to higher education by presenting it with planning that is itself coherent, coordinated, and comprehensive. The way to play down the politics of planning, then, is to formulate plans so persuasive in their facts and in their interpretations that it beomes politically attractive to support what is educationally desirable.

A Critique of Planning

Ideally, master planning should be assessed in terms of both the policies recommended and the procedures used. But even though something of a professional consensus is emerging about the range of questions which planning should explore, there is no agreement on the criteria by which to judge the rightness of the answers for any particular state. Without such criteria, it is impossible, for example, to judge definitively whether the Ohio or the Pennsylvania Master Plan recommended the correct answer to the branch campus vs. community college issue. (One may have private opinions on the subject but none that could be proved to everyone's satisfaction.)

In the absence of generally accepted standards for evaluating the policy recommendations of master plans, this critique focuses on the processes of planning. The following is a discussion of eight weak points often cited by practitioners and scholars in the field.

1. Inexactitude: Planning for the future is an uncertain art at best. Millett, who has participated in planning for higher education at both the national and state levels, illustrates the uncertainty in this field by recounting the variety of concerns voiced between 1949 and 1952 when a national master plan was being developed: fear of declining enrollment,

declining income, inflation, and perhaps even a limited market for college graduates. "None of these fears proved to be realistic. In the light of hindsight [they] seem strange indeed." But he mentions other developments which were correctly anticipated by the planning group and concludes with the mixed verdict: "We look ahead to the best of our ability and with the best available knowledge of the moment . . . and hope that human ingenuity will also serve to augment human thinking."[31]

2. Subjectivity and conventional wisdom: Mayhew agrees that educational planning is an uncertain art and points to two contrasting conditions which contribute to its inexactitude. On the one hand is the subjectivity that prevails in the absence of generally accepted objective standards: "One gets the slight impression that if one knows the background and orientation of a chief consultant, one can predict reasonably well the details of a proposed plan." On the other hand is the conventional wisdom which the profession often falls back on without sufficient scientific examination. Many commonly accepted assumptions may in fact turn out to be essentially correct, but "plans which purport to be rational approaches to a serious problem ought to be at least rational enough as to test assumptions." As one example, Mayhew mentions some of the traditional beliefs about community college systems which tend to be repeated from one master plan to another as articles of faith; he offers some "hard evidence" that suggests quite different conclusions.[32]

3. Preoccupation with short-term quantitative problems: Palola, Lehmann, and Blischke found that the planning which they observed was focused on problems of rapid growth and expansion; preoccupied with the number of campuses, cost of instruction, and classroom size; and essentially routine and means-oriented.

The new challenge of the 1970's will be academic reform, involving reassessment of curricula, programs and methods of instruction and governance. A "qualitative crisis" has resulted from forces such as the growing diversity and needs of students, student and faculty demands for educational reform, and growing interest in utilizing colleges and universities in combating social problems.[33]

31. "State Planning for Higher Education," p. 227.
32. Long Range Planning for Higher Education, p. 162.
33. "Qualitative Planning: Beyond the Numbers Game," Research Reporter, vol. 3, no. 2 (Berkeley: Center for Research and Development in Higher Education, University of California, 1968).

4. Pseudoscience: Livesey warns that, in the quest for objectivity, the uncertain art of planning may try to become the certain "science of planning," with systems analysts inside higher education preparing plans for review by systems analysts outside. Even though, as a planner for the State University of New York (SUNY), he recognizes the need for hard data and the value of using computers to manipulate quantified assumptions in mathematical models of higher education, he objects that "all kinds of present ways of doing things have been programmed into the computer, and they are taken as assumptions for the future without examination of their validity for future use." In other words, tough-minded systems research may have inherent within it some of the same dangers of implicit values as the conventional wisdom approach. Livesey makes an eloquent plea for the continued application of imagination, intuition, and permissiveness in long-range planning that attempts to anticipate problems of the distant future.[34]

5. Inadequate funds and unqualified personnel: A long-standing defect in the planning process—and one which shows no sign of being corrected—is the failure of enabling authorities to provide the time, money, and quantity and quality of staff needed to do a comprehensive job. The debate on whether "some planning is better than none" or "a bad plan is worse than no plan" remains unresolved. While granting that the supply of qualified planners has increased in the past decade, we agree with Mayhew's comment with respect to leaders of state planning and coordinating agencies: "The job specifications and the kinds of people selected appear at times to be quite inconsistent."[35]

6. Sins of omission: Ten years ago Glenny found the private sector of higher education a "problem" because of its open or covert hostility to state planning.[36] Today, however, Mayhew cites a different dilemma: the failure of most master plans to deal adequately with the future of the private institutions.[37] He also faults most plans for their inadequate treatment of the problems of providing higher education in urban areas, in particular for the disadvantaged.

7. Hidden costs of planning: The values of statewide master planning in higher education are now sufficiently recognized that the practice will undoubtedly become more and more common. What is less clear is whether most persons grasp that there are costs involved.

34. "Can Higher Education Be Planned?"
35. *Long Range Planning for Higher Education.*
36. *Autonomy of Public Colleges,* p. 80.
37. State relations with private higher education are discussed further in chapter 9.

First, as mentioned earlier, new programs and new institutions are often frozen while master planning is in progress. For states whose growth rates in higher education have eased back a bit, this may constitute no problem; but states under intense pressure to meet exploding demands can ill afford frequent halts for inventory-taking.

Second, master planning requires accurate and comprehensive data, and this need places heavy burdens on already hard-pressed institutional administrators. Sometimes planning agencies fail to harmonize their data-gathering categories with those of the institutions. In Ohio, one institution claimed that it had to maintain three sets of books: one for the planning agency (The Board of Regents), one for the state auditor, and one for internal management. Planning and coordinating agencies should take care not to abuse their information-gathering powers by collecting data less for its intrinsic worth than for its value in impressing the legislature with the effectiveness of the planning agency.

8. Inadequate institutional participation in master planning. A final sensitive area is the degree and manner of institutional participation in master planning. Ten years ago, Glenny criticized the planning agencies for their failure to involve presidents and faculty members in their efforts.[38] Today, the situation has improved somewhat. Planning typically involves the use of several statewide technical committees on which may sit administrators, faculty, and trustees; the circulation of draft proposals to a presidents' advisory council; and perhaps even public hearings at which institutional reactions can be voiced. Yet, for all this, criticism still abounds, most of it centering on the difference between consultation in form and consultation in substance. For example, we heard of a technical committee which never saw its draft report in final form before it was published. Several presidents complained that their advisory council meetings seemed pro forma and that the public hearings were essentially public relations sessions. And from faculty ranks came sharp comments that the faculty participants in statewide planning always seemed to be chosen from above. (Only Illinois has a master plan advisory committee composed of faculty selected by their own academic senates.)

Of course, not every criticism can be accepted at face value. Sometimes attacks on the planning process or the planning staff reflect a personal or institutional disenchantment with the substance of the plan rather than a bona fide assessment of the opportunities for institutional participation.

38. *Autonomy of Public Colleges,* p. 82.

Nevertheless, the basic charge of inadequate consultative practices seems to us basically correct and, in chapter 8, on general relations between the institutions and the coordinating agency, we will offer a detailed discussion of ways in which consultation can be turned into a meaningful device in the planning process.

SIX

Budget review

Whereas statewide planning for higher education has moved steadily from the periphery to the center of the coordinating process, the function of budget review has had a more erratic history. At first, most people in state government seemed to regard coordination of higher education as essentially a process of fiscal rationalization, and accordingly coordinating agencies were given heavy responsibility for budget review. But with the passage of time, this assumption came to be questioned here and there, and while some agencies have continued to stress the primacy of budget review, many others have given more attention to planning and program review and a few have even deemphasized their budget functions. Thus, at present, the budget review role varies so markedly from one type of agency to another—and, within the category of coordinating boards, from one state to another—that one must analyze the variations in some detail to understand the nuances of problems in fiscal coordination.

Following a brief overview of budget relations between higher education and state government, this chapter will examine the various roles of coordinating agencies as middlemen in such relations and then analyze certain aspects of the newer budgeting techniques: formulas and cost analyses, and program budgeting.

James L. Miller, who has done the major study of state budgeting in higher education, reports that the greatest friction occurs over the matter of fiscal controls (preaudit, transfer of line items, central purchasing, central personnel) but that "coordinating boards, in general, have not been involved in these areas."[1] Thus, consistent with our goal of stressing substantive rather than procedural autonomy, we will examine those aspects

1. *State Budgeting for Higher Education: The Use of Formulas and Cost Analysis,* Michigan Governmental Studies no. 45, University of Michigan (Ann Arbor: Institute of Public Administration, 1964), p. 30.

of the budget process which precede decisions about appropriations (who gets how much to spend on what programs), omitting consideration of state controls on how the institutions subsequently spend their money.

The Appropriations Process: An Overview

The appropriations process involves an abrupt confrontation between long-cherished plans requiring public monies and political realities. On one side are the many hopeful aspirants seeking support for their real or imagined needs; on the other are the legislative brokers who must decide first how much money to require of the taxpayer by force of law and then how to spend it in the public interest.

In our interviews with persons in state government, we found, not surprisingly, a disinclination to vote higher taxes and a fairly strong conviction that the public interest requires them to insist on strict accountability for allocated funds, wherever these may go. This means that when the various demands for state support exceed the estimated resources, requests are more often rejected than resources increased. It also means that state budget authorities usually want to decide just where the cuts should be made. Moreover, since the power to spend public funds is the mother's milk of politics, some politicians frankly admit that they are reluctant to surrender any of this power. Persons in higher education, on the other hand, naturally hope for as much money and as few controls as possible. They recognize that determining the gross amount of available state funds is a political decision in the broadest sense and that higher education can expect no exemption from critical scrutiny; its needs must be evaluated alongside those of other claimants. What they do ask is that decisions on relative needs and on whether to specify flat reductions or selective cuts reflect a sensitivity to those aspects of higher education which make it very different from other state-supported activities. As they point out, the normal standards of utility and productivity simply do not apply to the "output" of universities and colleges. More important, the problems raised by the issues of academic freedom and institutional autonomy are unique to higher education and set it apart from all other state activities.

State criticisms of institutional budgeting

A few states have recognized the special status of higher education by granting their universities constitutional autonomy or by appropriating funds in a lump sum.[2] But the tendency of most state government officials whom we interviewed was to be cautious about giving special privileges to higher education. A few said candidly that a tight appropriations process is one way (and sometimes the only way) to teach humility to those students and faculty members whose behavior is shocking the taxpayers. Others justified their restrictiveness on purely budgetary grounds, citing examples of ways in which they had been misled by university and college presidents and trustees. We heard tales of the excess from underestimated fee income being used to build a barbecue in a president's backyard, of funds ostensibly voted for higher faculty salaries being used to establish new departments, of class credit hours being claimed in the "rich" graduate category for specially numbered elementary foreign language courses designed for graduate students. These and other similar examples, though involving relatively modest amounts of money, are like red flags waved in front of politicians and budget staff members conditioned to "save the taxpayers' money." A key North Carolina legislator told us: "Higher education people are just as bad as anyone else, . . . but we know these people and we are pretty well able to separate the wheat from the chaff." In Florida, we heard allegations that the institutions sometimes furnish "perverted statistics." In New Mexico, a powerful solon said bluntly: "I will listen carefully to those people who give a straight answer and whose answers check out, but if somebody delays or gives false information, I will strike him off my list."

Legislators also complained to us of excessive institutional lobbying for funds. The right to press for adequate appropriations is, of course, a basic prerogative in a democratic society and will inevitably be expressed in one form or another. But some institutions carry their campaigns to extreme lengths. One president confessed to us that he would "drink with the tipplers and pray with the pious" if that would promote the interests of his institution. In the hopes of improving the institution's financial prospects, everything from free football tickets to reduced prices at university hospitals are offered to legislators. To be sure, many colleges and universities enjoy excellent relations with the state government and with the public merely by virtue of their excellent programs and their service activities (extension, research, and the presentation of artistic

2. The fiscal freedom which lump sum appropriations bestow is real but not necessarily total. They make it easier to transfer funds from one category to another, but we heard of definite implicit conditions being attached to so-called lump sum appropriations in at least two states.

and lecture events). Nevertheless, there is some truth in the comment of one state budget officer, who noted sadly, "If the universities would take the energy they invest in seeking tax funds and apply it to the improvement of their programs, they would be much better institutions." Unfortunately, a single institution cannot easily afford to make a noble gesture. If several colleges or universities who wage aggressive campaigns for state funds "win," the others are under intense pressure to match their efforts.

Institutional criticisms of state budgeting

Legislative complaints about lobbying and about the unwillingness of some institutional administrators to give the straight facts are met by the countercharge from higher education that budgetary practices in many states bring out the worst in everyone. For example, according to Moos and Rourke, the experience of some universities and colleges had been that "information supplied in good faith has come home to roost in the form of control . . . [and] that disclosure brings control over areas of educational policy that have previously been immune from interference." [3]

We ourselves met college presidents and business officers who were almost pathetically eager to open their books to legislators and to explain the full extent of their needs. But, they complained, legislators were usually too busy to sit down for extended sessions and *really* listen, especially in states where the legislative session in the off-year is constitutionally limited to sixty days.

Furthermore, the special complexities attached to assessing performance in higher education make judgment difficult for even those legislators with time and goodwill. We were told by a member of the Louisiana Senate Appropriations Committee that he had once studied the state budget intensively for two weeks and found many things to question—but not in education. It was a subject he was simply unable to handle without more staff assistance. Not all legislators are so modest. The chairman of an appropriations committee told us that a sensitive and experienced politician could determine true needs in higher education, as in other areas, by cutting to the point where the inevitable protests became genuine: "Everyone complains when you cut their budgets, but you can tell by the quality of the screams when it is time to stop."

3. Malcolm Moos and Frank Rourke, *The Campus and the State* (Baltimore: Johns Hopkins Press, 1959), p. 88.

Another institutional grievance concerns the uncertainties of some state budget procedures. In Texas, for example, before cost estimate and formula budgeting was introduced for higher education, the conference committee of the two houses of the legislature could completely rewrite the appropriations bill, and each house then had to accept or reject the conference bill in its entirety. Thus, an institution's budgetary fate depended primarily on having friends on that powerful committee.

Nor is the situation much better in the executive and legislative budget agencies where professional staffs are maintained. In our field visits, we more often than not found such offices chronically undermanned and overworked. Our impressions were at least partially confirmed by responses to the Smart questionnaire indicating (*a*) that while twenty-seven out of thirty-two states replying had some kind of executive office responsible for budget review, only fourteen were rated as very effective; and (*b*) that of the twenty-four states reporting that they had a legislative fiscal office, only six were rated as very effective. In only two of the thirty-two states responding were *both* state budget offices rated very effective.

Moreover, when a state is able to obtain a first-class budget officer, it runs the risk of seeing him hired away by the state university, which can justify paying higher salaries than does the state civil service on the grounds that it must remain competitive in the national market. In other states, the chief budget officer is usually forced by press of work to delegate review of the higher education budget to others, and here the staff quality may drop off markedly. We met several bright and earnest, but very young, budget analysts who had had this heavy responsibility thrust upon them.

The situation is even worse with respect to staffing the legislative budget review operations. A few states provide no committee staffing beyond a legislative reference service available to all members. In other states, appropriations committee chairmen complain that it is impossible to undertake a sophisticated budget analysis with the limited staff provided.

The coordinating agency as middleman

Miller suggests that while better staffing in the executive and legislative budget offices and longer legislative sessions could improve budget review processes, the basic problem in budgeting for higher education is that the appropriations cycle is not really effective unless it is linked with careful long-range state planning. It is, he says, a "myth that major decisions about the state appropriation are made by the legislature during the legislative session." In reality, cuts may be made here or there, but the great bulk of the budget is already committed to established programs whose intrinsic worth to the state cannot be meaningfully evaluated by the legislature during its normal business.[4]

Miller proposes that, to attack this problem, an important role be given to a planning and coordinating agency which could share with the government a statewide point of view transcending the interests of any given college or university and yet share with the institutions a specialized knowledge of, and concern for, higher education. Such an agency could, at the least, perform two functions vital to effective state budgeting for higher education: It could require information from institutions and then organize these data in common categories, thus making it easier for state budget offices to judge comparative needs and costs; and it could, with the help of the institutions, undertake comprehensive planning, subject to approval by the organs of state government, which would then conduct their review of the higher education budget in such a way as to implement the agreed-upon planning goals.

But a much larger role for the coordinating agency is claimed by some enthusiasts, who maintain that, since it must have highly detailed budget knowledge to help develop and implement its planning, it might as well go all the way and become, in effect, the principal agent for reviewing the higher education budget. According to this argument, if the coordinating agency does its job well, the state government will develop enough confidence in it to appropriate a higher percentage of the funds requested and to allow the agency, in law or in fact, to decide where cuts should be made. These results, in turn, would reassure the institutions that their budgetary fates were in educational rather than political hands, and they could relax their lobbying efforts and in-fighting, and get on with the business of education.

Looking at the actual practices of various state coordinating agencies, however, one finds that each type of agency has some characteristics that suit it for a greater budgetary role and some that suggest a lesser one. We will examine each of the three types—consolidated governing board, vol-

4. James L. Miller, "Budgeting Processes," *Financing Higher Education* (Proceedings of the Fifteenth Annual Legislative Work Conference, Southern Regional Education Board, Asheville, N.C., July 27–30, 1966), p. 29.

untary coordinating association, and coordinating board—to see how its general role and its legal powers affect its capacity to become a major participant in higher education budget review. In particular, we will present in detail several case studies involving coordinating boards, the largest and most heterogeneous category.

The Consolidated Governing Board: Role and Powers

Both the role and the budgetary powers of this type of agency are sharply defined. Because it directly governs the institutions under its jurisdiction, the consolidated governing board is clearly identified with higher education rather than with the state government[5] and has strong internal fiscal powers.

This close identification with higher education usually makes the state government unwilling to defer major budget review to a consolidated governing board. In our field work, we found that most legislators and budget officers in states with governing boards clearly felt that the lay trustees, though appointed to govern the system in the public interest, were too apt to be influenced by institutional loyalties or too open to the persuasion of college and university administrators.

But if the governing board's lack of disinterestedness makes it unfit to recommend the gross amount of needed public funds or to seek exemption from normal state review of its consolidated system budget, its strong internal administrative powers and intimate knowledge of the institutions make it the logical agency to determine where the budget should be cut. If it were given this power, bickering among institutions over budget cuts could be kept within the system rather than carried out at the state capital, and the decisions could be made on educational rather than political grounds.

By and large, our observations in Florida, Georgia, and Oregon confirmed these generalizations, though Florida was atypical on one side and Georgia on the other. Under the peculiar political structure in Florida, the top elected statewide officers serve collectively as the Budget Commission (*and* the Board of Education, as well as some other roles!), exercising tight controls and thus depriving the governing board of considerable fis-

---

5. On the Smart questionnaire, ten out of fourteen governing boards responded, and of these the following numbers checked these self-characterizations of the agency: primarily a part of higher education, 10; the primary spokesman for higher education, 9; primarily an agency of state government, 2; an extension of the state budget office, 0.

cal discretion over the higher education budget. In 1965, a Chancellor was appointed and, more recently, the position of Vice-Chancellor for Business Affairs was created, and this reorganization of the governing board may ultimately counteract what we found to be a reputation for looseness in internal budgeting.

By contrast, the governing boards in Oregon and Georgia both receive lump sum appropriations, although there are signs that this permissiveness may be somewhat modified in the future. In Oregon, for example, a legislative fiscal office recently served notice that it would be seeking much more information about the budget for higher education.[6]

In Georgia, two factors have combined to give the statewide governing board unusually broad fiscal powers. For one thing, because of excessive political intrusions into higher education, the Regents were given constitutional autonomy in 1943; for another, until recently there was no executive budget staff to speak of, and the legislative appropriations committee could conduct no more than a superficial review of the budget for higher education. The Regents were allowed to present their budget in terms of statewide categories (e.g., faculty salaries, equipment), thus eliminating any danger of legislative logrolling for individual institutional budgets. In 1967, the Regents asked for and received, even over the governor's objection, a sizable additional sum for "enrichment of quality." Nevertheless, we saw indications that, in Georgia as elsewhere, both the executive and legislative branches of state government were moving to strengthen their budget review procedures. Reapportionment may have a greater impact on the legislative process in Georgia than in most other states; and that, coupled with talk we heard about Georgia's adopting an annual appropriations system, makes it difficult to know how the higher education budget will be treated there in the future.

The Voluntary Coordinating Association: Role and Powers

The voluntary groups have without exception been identified with higher education, but their powers in budgetary matters have varied from state to state, with some agencies undertaking no budget work at all and others submitting joint budget requests after extensive preliminary analyses. Because these groups have been composed predominantly of institutional presidents and their administrative aides, state officials have generally

6. Samuel Gove, "The Oregon State System of Higher Education" (MS, Department of Political Science, University of Illinois, 1967).

been even less receptive to their total budget requests than to those of consolidated governing boards. The feeling is that the presidents have too great a stake in the results to subordinate their institutional interests to statewide concerns. Thus, the question of delegating final state budget review to such voluntary groups has never even arisen.

Since voluntary associations by definition can go only as far as all members are willing to go, most have limited themselves in budgetary matters to working out common definitions and categories for reporting to the state on operations, income, and expenditures.[7] In Indiana and Ohio, however, in the 1950s, the presidents of the public universities hammered out an internal agreement on submitting joint budget requests, with the understanding that each institution would accept the same share of any reduced appropriations as was proposed for it in the initial budget request. The Ohio system has since been superseded by the creation in 1963 of a formal coordinating board, but the Indiana pattern continues to the present, albeit staggering a little, as will be indicated later in this section.

Three major gains are claimed for this kind of budgetary cooperation among the public institutions. First, Miller[8] and Glenny[9] quote persons, in Indiana and Ohio respectively, who maintain that more state support was forthcoming than would have been the case without the joint budget requests. Second, open competition among institutions for funds was reduced. And finally, the institutions, not the state government, decided where to make selective cuts in the higher education budget.

This third claim needs to be examined more closely. The bald fact that power was transferred to the institutions is, of course, true. But was this transfer in the best interests of higher education and of the state? There has been criticism both of the procedures used to determine what share of the initial appropriations request should go to each institution and of the agreement of each to accept, if necessary, the same flat percentage reduction as all the others. The latter has come under fire because, according to critics, it is a default in educational leadership to pretend that all programs eliminated by flat cutbacks are of equal value to higher education or to the state. By this reasoning, educational criteria operate only

---

7. See, for example, Brouillet's account of this in "An Analysis of State of Washington's Method for Coordinating Higher Education" (Ed. D. diss., University of Washington, 1968), p. 82.
8. "Budgeting Processes," p. 66.
9. *Autonomy of Public Colleges* (New York: McGraw-Hill Book Co., 1959), p. 145.

when selective cuts are made within institutions; flat reductions accepted among institutions remain essentially political in nature.

Criticism leveled against the procedures used to determine initial shares are exemplified in the case of Ohio in the 1950s. There, the Inter-University Council used crude estimates of student costs and previous fall-term enrollments as points of departure for negotiations among institutions about their respective needs. But the divisions were based on the existing pecking order, with Ohio State University usually getting 52–54 percent of the requests and the other institutions sharing the remainder in a relatively fixed ratio. Once, Glenny notes, "an extra million dollars was added to the total request of all institutions in order to overcome some inequities because of one institution's asking for relatively more than another."[10] John D. Millett, himself a participant for many years in the Ohio voluntary group, has recently described its former budget deliberations as paralleling "almost exactly" those of the Defense Department in the pre-McNamara days when the service chiefs split up the defense appropriations on the basis of relatively fixed percentages of the total, and each branch went its own way. Governor Rhodes and the Ohio legislature evidently felt that the voluntary system's defects outweighed its virtues, because in 1963 they created one of the strongest coordinating boards in the country and gave it a powerful role in formulating the budget for higher education.

The Indiana system demonstrates considerably more sophistication in its cost analyses, breaking down all institutional costs (for research and public service as well as for instruction) by student for each level of instruction. The per-student figures, different for each institution because of differing programs, are then multiplied by estimated future enrollments to obtain the base support to be requested. Additional amounts are asked for (a) improvements in salary levels, (b) new programs, and (c) large specialized programs found in only one institution, such as medical school and agricultural extension services. These additional amounts are arrived at by rough negotiation among the institutions, although some of the specialized needs can be quantified.

The Indiana system of budgetary coordination, which has functioned since 1951 and has steadily improved its analytical techniques, occasioned strong praise from M. M. Chambers.[11] Nevertheless, both Glenny[12] and

10. Ibid., p. 124.
11. *Voluntary Statewide Coordination in Public Higher Education* (Ann Arbor: University of Michigan, 1961), p. 23.
12. *Autonomy of Public Colleges*, p. 147.

Miller[13] found major flaws in the procedures used. Glenny noted, for example, that "the practice of projecting current costs to future enrollments continues and even increases the inequities of the past. If an institution applies reserve funds to support a given program in a particular year, the increased cost per student . . . is automatically used in projecting the next budget." Usually up to 80 percent of the budget request has been divided up between Indiana University and Purdue University, the larger and wealthier institutions, both of which have high-cost graduate and technical programs. Ball State and Indiana State Universities have received around 10 percent each; but since both have moved from teachers college to university status and have recently acquired new presidents, who—in their drive to improve their institutions—may feel unconstrained by past agreements to which they themselves were not a party, it seems likely that these two institutions will press for a larger share of the appropriations. The 1967–69 biennial joint request did, in fact, include an additional $10 million for their "program improvement," but it also included for the first time some $28 million for expansion of the regional campuses of Purdue University and Indiana University. The overall ratios thus stayed about the same.

The governor, apparently dissatisfied with the system, engaged a management firm to survey the cost analysis procedures used, and the firm recommended a change to program budgeting. Perhaps as a result of this new budget format or of gubernatorial intercession or of internal splits in higher education, the 1967 legislature, departing from a sixteen-year-old pattern, voted differential appropriations to the four institutions: Indiana University and Purdue each received about 84.5 percent of their initial requests, Ball State 88 percent, and Indiana State University 94.5 percent. Furthermore, a legislative rider used since 1949 to require that the four institutions collaborate on their budget presentations was dropped. The universities have arranged to consult with each other if the state decides to retain program budgeting, but they did not promise to agree among themselves for the next budget presentation. Although, as reported earlier, various bills to create a statewide coordinating agency with powers of detailed budget review were defeated, the executive budget office gave every sign of being ready to play a more aggressive role.

<hr/>

13. *State Budgeting for Higher Education: The Use of Formulas and Cost Analysis*, p. 97.

The Coordinating Board: Role and Powers

Boards of this type range all the way from completely lay bodies, which exercise strong budget powers and are regarded as arms of the state, to councils predominantly institutional in membership, which engage in no detailed budget review and are identified as part of higher education. Most coordinating boards, however, do not fall neatly into either category. Responses to the Smart questionnaire make apparent this role confusion. Asked whether they would characterize themselves as primarily an agency of state government or primarily a part of higher education, eight boards chose the first label, five the second label, and six checked both! In short, the role and budget powers of this type of agency are subject to considerable debate.

The institutions feel strongly that an agency which specializes in higher education should be constantly ready to press the state for badly needed funds. But more often than not, the governors and legislators who originally established these coordinating boards over existing institutional governing bodies did so to achieve fiscal economies and prevent program duplication. Given these diametrically opposed views, it was inevitable that the early role of these agencies would be controversial. Glenny noted ten years ago: "It is possible that the agency, because it stands between these two groups, may expend its energies on budgets without satisfying either group." [14]

Boards caught in cross fire: Virginia, North Carolina, and Texas

The history of budget review procedures in three states will illustrate the ways in which coordinating boards sometimes get caught in the cross fire. In Virginia, the State Council for Higher Education, created in 1956, was given a statutory mandate to review institutional budgets but very little staff to carry out the charge. Therefore, the budget director and some legislators were displeased when in 1958 the board recommended basic support of the requests as submitted by the universities and colleges. After the accession of a new and more aggressive director, the Council in 1960 took a tougher line and did, in fact, recommend specific cuts in some institutional budget requests. The angry institutions then used their power in the state legislature to have a rider attached to the appropriations act stripping the Council of its powers of budget review. The budget director

14. *Autonomy of Public Colleges*, p. 115.

joined forces with the institutions in reducing the board's budget role because its executive officer allegedly favored having all state appropriations to higher education granted to the Council in a lump sum for distribution. The restrictive rider to the appropriations act was repeated each biennium until two factors finally combined to get it dropped: A new council director, more acceptable to the institutions and less threatening to the state budget officer, was appointed; and a nationally known outside consultant, after a survey of Virginia higher education, recommended strongly that the rider be eliminated. Now the Council exercises certain powers of budget review, but since it renders advice confidentially to the governor and the state budget officer, its impact is difficult to assess.

At about the same time, in the neighboring state of North Carolina, the institutions were directing similar criticisms against the coordinating board for its exercise of budget review. The University of North Carolina had originally supported the creation of the Board of Higher Education in the hope that some of the detailed fiscal controls exercised by the state Advisory Budget Commission would then be removed. But the enabling legislation, as it finally emerged, withheld from the Board any significant discretion regarding fiscal controls (the final tally failed by one vote to accord even the power to authorize transfer of funds within an institution) but nevertheless made it responsible for reviewing institutional budgets. One of our interviewees noted the results:

Probably the most tedious and time-consuming function that the small staff performed was in an area where it appeared unlikely that they could exert any real influence—in the review of the biennial budget requests of nine institutions and the submission of their recommendations. This they laboriously did. They recommended more or less what the institutions requested and sought to justify any changes. In most of this they simply joined the chorus of the presidents of the institutions and their boards of trustees.

But when the new Board felt obliged to overrule the University of North Carolina in two matters relating to salaries and one relating to housing for married students, the university marshaled its considerable support within state government to reduce some of the Board's powers. The state had just created a new layer of review, the Department of Administration, over its own budget office, and the university found it intolerable that the Board should begin to exercise its budget powers more vigorously at the same time that another review agency was coming into existence. Authorized to negotiate with the Board and the state government, the Executive Committee of the University of North Carolina trustees presented its case against this multilayer system of review which required the university to submit every feature of its work, including its biennial budget requests, to more and more points of reference, clearance, and negotiation.

Whatever the relative merits of the opposing positions, the two sides waging the battle were unevenly matched. The university had a century-and-a-half tradition and a hundred-man Board of Trustees, with the governor serving ex officio as chairman. The Board of Higher Education had been in existence for only four years and had no political constituency to turn to for support. The resulting legislation, passed in 1959, stressed that in budget matters, the Board would merely determine that the institutions' requests were "consistent with their primary purposes," concentrating "on broad fiscal policy" and avoiding "a line-by-line detailed review of budget requests." As this procedure has worked out, the Board does not inquire into the institutional "A" budget requests, which cover ongoing programs, but it does notify the Advisory Budget Commission and the institutions if any of the latter's "B" budget requests, which are for new programs, are not approved by the Board.

A variation on this theme occurred in Texas in 1965 when, in response to a report of a Governor's Committee on Education Beyond the High School, the old Texas Commission on Higher Education (TCHE) was abolished and in its place was established a new coordinating board with much stronger powers of planning and program review but weaker powers over budget matters. Because this story revolves primarily around dissatisfaction with the TCHE's permissiveness in authorizing new programs and new institutions, it will be treated at greater length in the next chapter. Suffice it to say here, the TCHE was required by its enabling legislation to create an advisory committee of at least one person (usually the president) from each institution; that this Presidents' Advisory Committee soon got a reputation for wielding too much influence with the all-lay board; and that the TCHE aroused some legislative resentment by recommending greatly increased state support for higher education although its review of institutional budgets was confined to verifying that their formula data were based on accurate statistics.

The new coordinating board in Texas can make financial recommendations outside the approximately 70 percent of the budget covered by formulas only if requested to do so by the governor or the legislature. Thus, like the North Carolina board, it has been told to concentrate on planning and program review and leave the budget details to the fiscally dominant legislature. Where there were three higher education budgets before—those of the TCHE, the executive, and the Legislative Budget Commission—there are now only two, with the understaffed executive budget office relying on the coordinating board for technical data and analysis.

The variety of coordinating board budget roles

Of course, not all coordinating boards are caught in such a cross fire of criticism. Some are "all the way in" the budget review process, and others are "all the way out." One atypical example is the Oklahoma Board of Regents, founded in 1941 as a reaction against excessive political intrusions into higher education and given both constitutional autonomy and lump sum appropriations. No other coordinating board has been granted either of these powers, but several have been awarded de jure, or achieved de facto, a major role in reviewing higher education budgets. The titles of New Mexico's Board of Educational Finance and Arkansas's Commission on Coordination of Higher Education Finance indicate the primary fiscal mission of these boards. The Illinois and Ohio boards are well-known for their strong budget roles even though, legally, both bodies can only make recommendations to their state governments. But their solid statutory powers in planning and program review, plus statehouse confidence in the aggressive leadership roles assumed by their executive officers, have combined to make their so-called advisory budget roles regulatory for all practical purposes. In addition, the boards in Colorado, Connecticut, and Wisconsin appear to be developing stronger budget review powers.

In contrast, the coordinating boards in California, Maryland, Minnesota, and (since 1959) North Carolina, plus the three state boards of education acting as coordinating bodies for higher education in Michigan, New York, and Pennsylvania, all play very modest roles in the budget review process.

It is still too early to judge the probable budget review patterns that the newer boards in Alabama, Massachusetts, New Jersey, South Carolina, Tennessee, Washington, and Wyoming will develop.

We were told during our field research that a board should go into budget review either deeply or not at all. But which of these two alternatives is the proper choice for a given coordinating board would seem to depend on a variety of factors: the intensity and effectiveness of budget review procedures in the state executive and legislative branches; the ways in which people in state government view higher education, and vice versa; and the particular role into which the coordinating board has been cast by virtue of its membership, staffing, powers, and experience.

California: a case study of light budget involvement

Some of the dilemmas of boards with weak budget powers are revealed by the California experience.[15] There, the Coordinating Council for Higher Education searched long and hard for a way to contribute to the budget review process in higher education without duplicating the very thorough work of the executive and legislative branches. The weak budget role accorded to this board at its inception in 1960 was not accidental. Neither the state government nor the institutions wanted another layer added to the already four-layered review process: by the local campus, by the headquarters of the university or state college multicampus system, by the Department of Finance (governor's budget), and by the Legislative Analyst (for the legislative appropriations committees).

According to Paltridge, state fiscal officers were willing to let the Council share in the "mechanical" (fact-gathering) aspects of budget review, but they insisted that overriding considerations of public policy required them to retain the "judgmental" prerogatives.[16] In 1963, a state Director of Finance mentioned the possibility that the Council would become a "successor to the Department of Finance in making certain higher education judgments," but when later asked for a clarification, he in effect withdrew the statement.

The university and state college systems were willing to accept the existing budget review process for several reasons:

1. The University was fearful that any substantial reorganization of

---

15. This section is based on the following three sources: John Marshall Smart, "Political Aspects of State Coordination of Higher Education: The Process of Influence" (Ph.D. diss., University of Southern California, 1968); James G. Paltridge, *California's Coordinating Council for Higher Education: A Study of Organizational Growth and Change* (Berkeley: Center for Research and Development in Higher Education, University of California, 1966); and California Coordinating Council for Higher Education, *The Budget Review Role of the Coordinating Council for Higher Education,* CCHE, no. 10, May 23, 1967.

16. *California's Coordinating Council for Higher Education,* pp. 68–79.

the governance and coordination of higher education would interfere with its precious constitutional autonomy.

2. The state college system—which, formerly under Board of Education jurisdiction, had been tightly controlled by the Department of Finance—was led by the Master Plan to hope that its newly created Board of Trustees would receive constitutional status and therefore fiscal freedom similar to the University's. (The legislature, however, did not grant this status, and therefore the state college system has subsequently been in favor of an expanded budget role for the Coordinating Council. The Council, in turn, has pushed, not very successfully, for wider fiscal freedom for the state colleges.)

3. The University had strong representation in the state capital and so evidently preferred to take its chances in the existing political milieu. Perhaps it wanted to deal directly with the men making the central decisions about overall allocation of state resources; or perhaps it expected that "uninitiated" state fiscal officers would ask less awkward questions than would an agency specializing in higher education.

With such marked lack of enthusiasm on both sides, it is not surprising, then, that, at its inception, the Coordinating Council was given only advisory budget powers. To be sure, its fiscal charge was broad: "review of the annual budget and capital outlay requests . . . and presentation of comments on the general level of support sought." But since nine out of its fifteen members represented the public institutions (and three more, the private ones), the early Council and its staff implemented this charge with the utmost sensitivity toward university and college feelings. The general principles of the Council's budget review role from 1962 to 1964 were later summarized as follows:

1. An emphasis on the broader and larger problems facing higher education rather than a line-item analysis of the budget which would duplicate the review of other agencies of state government.

2. Collection of only that information which is necessary in arriving at decisions.

3. The orderly collection of data accommodated to reporting systems already in effect.

4. The initiation of uniform procedures for reporting budgetary information.

5. Provision for intensive studies in selected areas.

6. A hands-off policy in the area of intercampus relationships

and a recognition that matters of equity and balanced development are appropriate responsibilities of the governing boards.[17]

When the Council issued its annual budget reports, it generally endorsed the funds requested by the segments, on the grounds that they
were to be used for purposes consistent with the Master Plan, and included an interstate comparison section which showed that California
was "neither particularly low nor high in overall tax burden and public
higher education tax effort among the most appropriate comparison
states."

In view of the Council's deference toward institutional prerogatives,
its reluctance to recommend budget cuts, and its implicit suggestion that
taxes might well be raised in order to finance higher education more adequately, it is small wonder that the Legislative Analyst officially went on
record in 1965 with the judgment that it

> has contributed very little through its annual review of the uni-
> versity and state college budget requests, largely because of a
> failure to adopt a viewpoint which is significantly broader than
> that of any one of the individual segments.[18]

Although some of its intensive studies did affect the state's budget decisions (e.g., on faculty salaries, student fees, year-round operations), the
lack of sufficient staff and the very awkward timing of the budget cycle
prevented the Council from having a serious fiscal impact on either the
institutions or the state government. Smart reports that Council staff
were not present even as observers at the executive and legislative budget
sessions on higher education. Nor did the Council help to determine the
budget formulas (different for each segment) which reportedly cover 85
percent of the state funds for higher education.[19]

Recognizing its own shortcomings, the Council in 1965 and 1966
adopted a new budget role. First, it revised budget categories so that new
programs could be handled with much more sophistication.[20] Second,
it altered its emphasis from a broad and largely descriptive overview

17. *The Budget Review Role of the Coordinating Council for Higher Education*, p. 5.
18. Quoted in Paltridge, *California's Coordinating Council for Higher Education*, p. 72.
19. "Political Aspects of State Coordination of Higher Education," p. 155.
20. The following budget categories were established: maintenance of continuing programs, new programs, improved programs, program development, discontinuance and
reduction of programs, changes in funding. (*The Budget Review Role of the Coordinating Council for Higher Education*, pp. 11–15.)

to in-depth analyses and evaluations of significant new programs. Finally, it changed its timetable so that its views might be presented to both the institutional and the state authorities before all the crucial decisions had been made.

However, a subsequent Council appraisal indicated that this second phase was also a failure. Cited as the immediate cause of this failure were the Council's inabilty to examine the overall level of support sought, to develop satisfactory cost-benefit analyses of new and improved program requests, and to develop a satisfactory model for measuring relative benefits of competing requests in a context of scarce resources. But the underlying causes were described as general lack of power in fiscal matters, ignorance about the statewide financial constraints within which decisions about allocations of scarce resources had to be made, and a failure to convince state officials that its budget recommendations were realistic. This last shortcoming was attributed to the fact that "in comparison with coordinating agencies in some other states, the Council has appeared to identify more with higher education (and its resource and autonomy needs) than with state government (and its annual resource limitations)." [21]

In 1967, the Legislative Analyst again turned his critical attentions to the Council's budget role:

> The Council itself is unsuited to the task of making a detailed and comprehensive review of the college and university budgets. In our opinion it would be of greater service to the state if it looked instead at the whole span of planning, programming, budgeting and performance and chose those areas in which it can complement the activities of other agencies. . . . the Council staff could take the initiative in important areas such as organized research, health education, student and library resources to provide a more comprehensive and carefully developed statement of program requirements in each area. At the same time, it could review new programs broadly in terms of the functions of each segment, the availability of resources, the adequacy of planning, possible alternatives and priorities in relation to other new and continuing programs. [22]

21. Ibid., pp. 29-30.
22. As quoted in ibid., Appendix E.

The Council evidently agreed with the Legislative Analyst for, in a later report on its budget review role, it recommended two long-range roles, both involving aspects of the Programming and Budgeting System (PABS) which the governor in 1966 had directed be installed in all regular state departments by 1967–68. These long-range goals were (a) to improve the program accountability of higher education and (b) to use this knowledge to engage in multiyear budget planning that would be closely integrated with master planning in higher education. It was hoped that, if program accountability were improved, some of the traditional fiscal controls over institutions, particularly the state colleges, could be eliminated. And if effective multiyear budget planning could be tied to master planning, the annual budget review of program changes and improvements could become something other than a case-by-case project based on ad hoc criteria.

The Council reported in early 1968 that the University was making substantial progress toward complying with the state PABS, but that the state college system felt it could not submit a multiyear program budget before 1970–71.[23] The University had had a running start in this area, for several years earlier Charles Hitch had been brought to Berkeley as administrative vice-president for the express purpose of seeing if the Planning-programming-budgeting system techniques used by the Defense Department could be adapted to the multicampus university system.

At that time, Hitch wisely warned that it might take five years before the feasibility of the effort could be judged accurately. Presumably, it will take at least that long before the more complex task of extending the PAB system to *all* public higher education can be evaluated.[24] In the meantime, the Coordinating Council will probably be moving toward the assumption of its two long-range budget review roles, seeking through them the means of becoming a central participant in higher education decision making without encroaching unduly on either institutional autonomy or state government prerogatives.

Illinois: a case study in deep budget involvement

On the basis of his experience in Illinois, Glenny has presented the larger case for giving to coordinating boards a major budget role. Such a role, he

23. California Coordinating Council for Higher Education, *Budget Report to the Legislature, 1968,* (Staff report, CCHE no. 3, February 20, 1968).
24. Some of the problems of applying the PAB system to higher education in California are examined in: California Coordinating Council for Higher Education, *November Report on the Level of Support for Public Higher Education, 1968–69,* Staff report, CCHE no. 16, December 6, 1967.

believes, will operate to the ultimate good of both state government and higher education. His line of argument is as follows: [25]

1. The state government makes judgments about the fiscal needs of higher education in one way or another. In the absence of advice from a specialized agency, these judgments will normally tend to be based on either or both of two elements: the relative political influence of the various universities and colleges and the efforts of the usually understaffed executive and/or legislative budget offices to apply crude cost analyses to higher education.

2. Such a situation is good neither for the state nor for the institutions. There must be better grounds than political ones on which to judge budget proposals. But efforts by regular state officers to make such judgments often turn out badly. The misguided conscientiousness of many state budget offices may seem to save the taxpayers thousands of dollars but may lose them millions. Either the budget office fails to realize where the real savings are (Glenny indicates that his board's space utilization survey showed that $32 million could be saved in two years by increasing utilization rates by 16 percent), or it chops away at expensive instructional and research programs that in the long run may be vital to high-quality education and to the state's future growth. (Many legislators, Glenny states, tend to look at costs primarily in terms of numbers of students enrolled, ignoring the justification for research, public service, and some high-cost programs.)

3. A coordinating board which is granted adequate powers in planning, budget review, and program review and enough funds to recruit well-qualified staff can, judging from the Illinois experience, bring about the following results:

    a) Using an intimate knowledge derived from detailed budget review and special planning studies, the board, in cooperation with the institutions, can formulate long-range plans which are then presented to the state government for approval or modification.

    b) Once planning guidelines are accepted, the coordinating board can recommend institutional budget cuts according to the degree to which the proposed expenditures conform to the established

25. Glenny's views are reconstructed from a variety of sources but primarily from the testimony which he gave to the state of Washington Interim Committee on Education, January 21–22, 1966. In addition, some material has been used from studies of coordination in Illinois: Robert O. Marsh, "Coordination of State Higher Education in Illinois: A Case Study" (Ed.D. diss., Illinois State University, 1967); James Heck, "Coordination of Higher Education in Illinois" (MS, School of Education, University of Delaware, 1968).

goals and in keeping with statewide priorities. (Glenny reports that the cuts recommended by the Illinois coordinating board varied from 2–3 percent for some institutions to 12–14 percent for others.)

c) The executive and legislative organs of government, having helped to set planning goals and being reassured of the seriousness, thoroughness, and accuracy of the board budget review, will tend to accept the board recommendations. (James Heck's study of Illinois coordination includes a table showing that the proportion of the state budget going to higher education mounted steadily from a 1957–1963 preboard average of 6.8 percent to 10.3 percent for the 1967–69 biennium. And the board has consistently received over 94 percent of its biennial requests.)[26]

4. According to Glenny, all parties benefit from this process:

a) The institutions have the satisfaction of seeing educational criteria substituted for political or fiscal criteria when budget cuts are made. Moreover, they are freed from having to squabble with other institutions for funds. Finally, they have the cheerful prospect of receiving higher appropriations than would have resulted from traditional budget processes.

b) The state, though it cannot look forward to "economies" (savings may occur here and there, but overall expenditures will probably increase), will know that its limited resources are being utilized in the most effective way to achieve desirable quantitative and qualitative goals in higher education.

c) The coordinating board will find that its planning, program, and budget review activities mesh more easily and that its powers in other areas will be enhanced as a result of its advice being taken more seriously in light of its playing a substantial role in budget review.

Although Heck's study shows that most interested persons in Illinois state government and higher education probably agree with the basic thrust of these arguments, there are pockets of dissent here and there. For example, Robert O. Marsh quotes one critic who says that the coordinating board should confine itself to asking, "Is the proposed program needed, and if so, are the requested funds sufficient but not excessive?"

26. "Coordination of Higher Education in Illinois," Table 1.

Then, the job of deciding whether there is enough state money for all the "needed" programs should be left to the governor and the legislators.[27]

Some institutional voices have suggested that the board's excellent record in obtaining most of its budget requests may be at least partly attributable to its taking cues from the governor's office about what amounts are politic to request. And some members of the legislature, a bit overwhelmed by the flood of data presented to them by the board, have acted to make themselves less dependent on board recommendations by passing a bill that establishes a legislative commission on higher education. The governor vetoed the bill, however, on the grounds that the board should remain the chief adviser on higher education.

Outside of Illinois, we came across much skepticism in both political and educational circles about giving so large a budget role to a coordinating board. Politicians had several grounds for misgivings. Some powerful appropriations leaders were reluctant to forego control over the details of expenditure. Others were genuinely worried that the legislature would be defaulting on its responsibility for overseeing public policy if it deferred so heavily to a coordinating board. Upon hearing Glenny's explanation of the partnership whereby the state government helped to set policy through the master plan and then ceded authority to the coordinating board for its budgetary implementation, one Washington state legislator remarked: "My trouble is that the answer sounds all right, but when I get home I still won't believe it."

Many of the negative reactions centered on the susceptibility of the board and its staff to the persuasive abilities and expensive ambitions of higher education. The chairman of the senate appropriations committee in one state and the chief budget officer in another each told us that the board in his state was a "spending agency" and that it was better to have someone outside give the tough scrutiny necessary in the budget review process. The same sentiment was reflected in our interview notes from another state:

> R.O.B. then asked how [Mr. A] would feel if the state budget analyst for higher education were to work for the coordinating board and lend them his wisdom. [Mr. A] replied that he preferred the analyst to stay where he was. If he were with the board he would be exposed to educators and their viewpoint and would stop looking at budgeting from the standpoint of the overall

27. "Coordination of State Higher Education in Illinois: A Case Study," pp. 180–81.

availability of funds. Higher education was not the only area which needed funds. The analyst, however good, would inevitably reflect the opinions of the men for whom he was working.

Opposition from university and college personnel was based on several grounds. First, as in California, some powerful universities with well-established representation in the state capitals were not anxious to have anything come between them and the persons making the crucial decisions about allocation of state resources. They obviously felt that they could do better financially on their own. Some also recognized the de facto power which detailed budget review would give to a coordinating board, even if, from a legal standpoint, its recommendations were only advisory. As one president put it, "The budgetary process is highly political, and such powers would bring the coordinating board into real decision-making matters which are not its functions." Finally, others were extremely reluctant to see another step added to the process of budget review unless one were dropped or the total appropriation to higher education promised to be significantly higher. Otherwise the additional review would represent just another slice off the top of their budget.

The debate over the Illinois setup versus the California setup probably cannot be settled absolutely, since each board is responding to the particular situation within its own state. However, three observations seem pertinent: (1) the California experience may indicate that no board can hope to do an effective job of coordinating and planning if it does not play a substantial role in the budget process; (2) the Illinois pattern will probably become less and less appropriate to other states as they move to strengthen their executive and legislative budget offices; and (3) the whole current trend in budgeting for higher education—from simple subjective judgments, through formulas and cost analysis, to some form of program budgeting—may offer a middle way that will allow coordinating agencies to participate meaningfully in the budget process without duplicating the efforts of other state offices.

Formulas and Cost Analysis

Miller, who has written the authoritative study on the use of formulas and cost analysis in state budgeting for higher education, reports that these techniques emerged in the 1950s out of a need for objectivity and quantification stemming from the vast increase in state expenditures on higher education. Briefly, *cost analyses* are attempts to *measure past actual costs* per unit (e.g., teaching introductory chemistry to a freshman student) by dividing total institutional expenditures into various cost categories; whereas *formulas* are attempts to *estimate future fiscal needs* on the basis of certain assumptions about enrollments, faculty/student ratios, average teaching salary, ratios of instructional expenses to other institutional outlays, etc.[28]

Frank Rourke and Glen Brooks point out that although cost analyses (if well done) are extremely helpful for internal management, they are used much less frequently than are formulas for external budgeting because of the danger of legislative and public misunderstanding about high-cost programs. They found that, of 259 state universities and colleges surveyed, 53.3 percent used both formulas and cost analysis; 25.3 percent used formulas without cost analysis; 5.9 percent used cost analysis without formulas; and 15.5 percent used neither.[29]

These proportions are similar for coordinating agencies. Emogene Pliner's study indicated that some seventeen agencies were using formulas as a basis for institutional requests;[30] and we know of at least three states in which cost analyses are of primary importance. The better formulas, incidentally, now make considerable use of cost study data.

These quantifying techniques have been adopted by one or more boards in each of the three categories of agencies—voluntary, coordinating, and consolidated governing—and in most cases the agency's budget role has become less controversial as a result. The use of formulas and cost analyses, whatever their limitations, seems to meet certain needs in both higher education and state government.

Benefits to institutions

For higher education, the major benefits claimed are fiscal flexibility, more adequate support by the state, and equitable treatment of institutions. It may seem strange to attribute fiscal flexibility to a system that calls for maximum objectivity of data, but the explanation lies in the fact

28. Further technical information concerning both cost analysis and formulas may be obtained from Miller's *State Budgeting for Higher Education: The Use of Formulas and Cost Analysis*. For more immediate reference, Appendix A of this report has two examples of formula budgeting applied to higher education.
29. *Managerial Revolution in Higher Education* (Baltimore: Johns Hopkins Press, 1966), p. 81.
30. *Coordination and Planning* (Baton Rouge: Public Affairs Research Council of Louisiana, 1966).

that formulas and cost analyses are presently used to formulate *asking* budgets, not *spending* budgets. Thus, depending on the particular mode of appropriations within a state, an institution may be allotted so many dollars on the basis of formulas and other justifications and then left fairly free to spend the funds where they are most needed. An official at one large state university told us that his institution "lost money" on the fine arts and regained it on the law school, but as long as the funds granted did not have to be spent in the exact spot where they were earned, the institution would probably find the formula system a net gain.

It is less easy to show that these techniques result in more adequate support. Miller cites opinion from four states that more state money to higher education was forthcoming because of the introduction of the newer budget procedures, but at the same time, he warns: "Such judgments . . . are subjective and may not make proper allowance for other factors which should be considered." [31] Certainly the institutional officers to whom we spoke expressed doubts that state support levels had in fact been substantially raised by the use of formula budgets. In New Mexico, Oklahoma, and Texas, for example, we heard complaints that formulas were not resulting in the appropriations necessary to finance higher education's growth in size and quality. This is not too surprising in that no state government is likely to surrender, through a predetermined formula mechanism, its right to set the gross amount of state support for higher education. For instance, the Texas legislature in 1965 approved 100 percent of the library and faculty salary formulas, 66 percent of those for organized research, 97 percent of those for building maintenance, and 84 percent for custodial services. This kind of juggling plays havoc with the notion that the use of formulas will lead to adequate support.

In New Mexico, it was said that the Board of Educational Finance, pressed to submit politically realistic budget requests, was working backwards: Taking cues from the state as to the maximum amount that could be expected, the board then devised various assumptions about faculty-student ratios and average teaching salaries so as to end up with the "right" answer. Quantification in this sense may further equity among institutions but bears little relation to achieving adequate support.

Even so, the value of achieving rough equity among institutions—if that, indeed, is all that formulas do—should not be underestimated. Rourke and Brooks tend to confirm this observation:

31. *State Budgeting for Higher Education: The Use of Formulas and Cost Analysis*, p. 153.

Many legislators assert that the determination of an over-all level
of support for higher education within a state . . . can be made
rather quickly in any legislative session. The real conflict arises
over the distribution of funds among state institutions of higher
education. It is here that an allocation formula enters the picture
as a politically acceptable means of slicing the academic pie.[32]

Glenny notes, "Where the president, using information collected by the
central agency, can compute the major part of the budget for any institutions in the system by employing formulas which he had approved and
clearly understood, there is at least some assurance of fairness."[33] This
general assurance is important for several reasons: The fear is lessened
that a coordinating agency will make arbitrary budget decisions intended
to punish some institutions for having criticized the agency or its policies;
institutions will be able to spend more time on forward planning and less
on competing with other colleges and universities; and the image of
higher education will improve if its public clamor for funds is muted.

Of course, institutional equity does not derive automatically from
just any set of formulas or cost data. Some of the early crude models erred
drastically by calling unlike things like. But with the passing of time,
refinements have occurred, and now some systems (e.g., Ohio's) make
as many as seven different distinctions between types and levels of programs. Thus, extremely expensive doctoral students are no longer counted
in the same category as undergraduates, and high-cost science and technology programs are no longer lumped together with general studies. If
institutional equity is to be achieved, the next step is to recognize the
higher costs per unit of getting new institutions started and the atypical
cost patterns in urban institutions which are trying to deal with the disadvantaged.

Benefits to state governments

Our field research largely confirmed the findings of Miller, Glenny, and
Rourke and Brooks that state political figures and budget officers are
basically in sympathy with the use of formulas and cost analyses, although
we did come across patches of cynicism here and there: for example, in
Texas, "formulas are a subterfuge to get funds without argument and

32. *Managerial Revolution in Higher Education*, p. 79.
33. *Autonomy of Public Colleges*, p. 145.

bear little necessary relation to actual costs and needs"; in Georgia, "formulas are a public relations device, used when it is politically expedient." But unquestionably, busy legislators need and welcome these quantitative techniques as a guide in understanding the huge increases in appropriations to higher education. Furthermore, just as the use of formulas has probably lessened interinstitutional competition for funds, so it has probably lessened (though by no means eliminated) some of the legislative conflict about specific allocation of funds for higher education.[34]

Benefits to coordinating agencies

Given this fairly high degree of support for formulas and cost analysis from both the state government and higher education, coordinating agencies seem to have found a more comfortable role in the budgetary process. In gathering the data needed, they gain that intimate knowledge of the institutions which will aid their work in other areas—the creation and implementation of a master plan, program review, and capital outlay review—in a way that does not threaten to substitute the coordinating agency's judgment for that of either the state officials (concerning the overall level of support) or of the institutional authorities (concerning their internal priorities).

A critique of formula cost analysis budgeting

All is not rosy with the use of formulas and cost analysis, however, and several problems are worth examining.

1. Absence of quality considerations: Otto Feinstein has leveled a frontal assault on these techniques for what he regards as their preoccupation with numbers and disregard of considerations of quality and personalism: that is, of the best ways to educate the mind and to develop the whole person. He argues that, even within similar categories of studies, to treat each student credit hour and each square foot of classroom space like any other is to ignore that some of these units of measure contribute to supreme achievements in education and others to practically nothing.[35]

Millett would argue that state support *should* be based on quantitative equity of similar types of activities and that institutions should seek

34. Rourke and Brooks, *Managerial Revolution in Higher Education*, p. 80.
35. Otto Feinstein et al., "Economics of Higher Education: Quality and Personalism" (MS, Wayne State University, 1967).

qualitative distinctions by means of their nonstate income. In Texas, we heard that it was only the existence of "available funds" (in effect, private endowments created by the state) which permitted the University of Texas and Texas A&M to maintain excellence in the face of formula budgeting. But in Oklahoma and New Mexico, the institutions "lose" their nonstate income by virtue of its being taken into consideration when the level of state support for higher education is set. This not only pushes equalization deeper into the process but also removes most of the incentive for institutions to seek outside research grants.[36]

2. Pseudo-objectivity: Some experts maintain that the so-called objectivity of formulas and cost analysis can be exaggerated, that often they contain implicit values, and that they are no substitutes for the policy judgments that have to be made at some time in the process. As Glenny puts it, formulas

> contain hidden subjectivity and arbitrariness. Value judgments such as the "right" class size, the "right" teaching load, and the "right" per-unit cost are implicit in all formulas. . . . How . . . can the need for a bevatron unit or a psychiatric hospital be measured against the needs of conventional programs, such as lower-division liberal arts. . . . How can a board compare the benefits to be derived from expenditures on medical education, hospitals of various types, advanced research, scientific centers and institutes, and agricultural and extension services?[37]

Defenders of formula budgeting comment on this dilemma in several ways. First, there is the obvious and logical point that if everything does not lend itself to being measured, you quantify that which does and take it from there: in other words, that some comparability is better than none. Thus, costs in departments with similar functions have been compared within an institution, and items such as lower-division liberal arts costs have been compared between institutions, often with fairly interesting results. But since even this modest type of comparison does not eliminate the problem of relative quality, the budget analyst must simply be aware of this danger and take it into consideration.

Second, there is an admitted need for periodic and frequent revision

36. There does, however, seem to be some justification for a state to require, as North Carolina does, that its public universities and colleges inform state fiscal officers if they are seeking nonstate funds which may subsequently involve expenditure of state funds (e.g., maintenance of new buildings, continuation of faculty salaries).
37. *Autonomy of Public Colleges*, p. 144.

of the formula and cost analysis formats. If this is done with sensitivity and open-mindedness, valuable feedback about possible mistaken facts or value assumptions should result.

Third, institutional participation in the setting and revising of formula and cost analysis formats, quite apart from its intrinsic merits, will also help to lessen the danger of the coordinating agency's feeding arbitrary values into the process.[38]

3. Dangers of control: Another problem arises in that formulas and cost analysis could be used as either actual or latent control mechanisms. Since these procedures have, at least until now, been applied only to asking, and not to spending, budgets, the dangers of control may seem slight. But institutional decision-makers—knowing that certain new developments "earn" more credits and that new high-cost programs are, in their cost-analysis nakedness, more difficult to justify to the legislature—may shy away from the latter and veer toward the former. For instance, the relatively "rich" Ohio formula figures for lower-division students at branch campuses would seem to be one device employed by the coordinating board to persuade the universities to divert more students to these branches and away from the parent campuses. Feinstein, in his polemic against formula budgeting, stresses that external standards have a way of becoming internalized when administrators learn that this is the way to beat the game.

Related to the issue of control are the complaints we heard in Ohio and Oklahoma that coordinating agencies employ formula budgets but insist also on conducting a detailed review of the entire institutional budget. Presumably one of the advantages of formula budgeting is that when the central agency is assured of the accuracy of the relevant information, the institution is left largely free of other kinds of budget controls. Institutional officers, while admitting that an occasional thorough budget inquiry can help the coordinating agency to evaluate the propriety of the formulas being used and can serve as a form of audit of the institutions' data, question whether this detailed scrutiny should have to occur each year and find in some of the questions asked an unwelcome influence over policy.

38. As pointed out in earlier chapters, such institutional participation never comes without a certain cost in agency staff time and nervous energy. The difficulty in getting agreement on the relative weights of differential formulas among educators representing widely different types of institutions is obvious. The temptation, then, is for the staff to avoid frequent revisions and the dangers inherent in reopening old wounds. Yet only by revisions can the formulas and cost analyses be kept viable, and only by institutional participation will they remain acceptable to the universities and colleges.

Finally, Rourke and Brooks have called attention to the danger that quantitative mechanisms set up to speed the flow of funds during periods of expansion and affluence could be turned around during periods of scarcity and become devices of control. Asking budgets could become spending budgets; high-cost programs could be flatly forbidden rather than merely discouraged; the trend toward objectivity could sweep all before it.

Some educators, therefore, reject the whole movement toward objective budgeting. They say that

> subjectivity, not objectivity, has brought some of the greatest gains to higher education. . . . "free money," unencumbered by state regulation or central control and most easily made available under more subjective budget formulations, has been responsible in no small degree for the outstanding buildings, libraries, laboratories and the superior instructional programs and experimentation of many institutions.[39]

Miller, while highly sensitive to the need to encourage creativity and innovation in higher education, nevertheless implies that it is Canute-like to curse the incoming tide of objective budgets; he quotes Logan Wilson as saying that "our fundamental consideration in the matter of evaluating costs . . . is not whether we shall employ admittedly imperfect methods, but merely which kinds we are going to use." Miller thus urges that instead of yearning nostalgically for the "good old days," we apply imaginative thought to the problem of building creativity and innovation into formula budgeting. This might be done, he suggests, by incorporating some "formal recognition of the obvious and continuing costs of change. . . . (only a limited amount of which can be expected to be entirely 'successful')."[40]

In a recent interview, Miller expressed strong disappointment with the failure of practitioners of formula budgeting to make the kinds of improvements which might have met some of the problems just discussed. Although the use of formulas as rather crude rules of thumb continues to spread among the states, he now expects that some form of program budgeting adapted to higher education will supersede the formula system.

---

39. Quoted in Glenny, *Autonomy of Public Colleges*, p. 147.
40. *State Budgeting for Higher Education: The Use of Formulas and Cost Analysis*, p. 168.

Program Budgeting

Though one could say a great deal about what program budgeting in higher education may become, very little can be said about what it means now, for no state has had sufficient experience to justify confident assertions.

Planning-programming-budgeting systems (PPBS) are built on a series of steps. In higher education, these can be described roughly as follows:

1. The program units must be defined at various levels of generality, and their "boundaries" determined for purposes of assessing costs and benefits. Programs can vary from the minutiae of individual courses through huge blocks of institutional activities like teaching, research, and public service.

2. One must be able to estimate costs for any given program on a multiyear basis, five years being the period most frequently mentioned.

3. The anticipated benefits of the programs must be made explicit and criteria established by which to measure their achievement.

4. Information systems, which will provide a steady flow of data on both costs and benefits, must be established.

5. Program alternatives, with accompanying cost-benefit analyses, must be presented to decision makers in both the planning and budgeting operations of higher education.

Obviously, it constitutes a huge challenge to introduce so complex a system into so delicate a field as higher education.[41] Some institutional administrators have wondered whether the results would justify the effort since: (a) it would impose a substantial burden on already overworked institutional business officers: (b) universities and colleges are not faring too badly under existing budgetary techniques; and (c) in any case, it might prove impossible to devise adequate measurements of "benefits" in higher education.

It is possible to measure far more precisely the number of miles of highways constructed, the number of patients cared for in a mental hospital, the number of planted fish caught from the lake, the reduction in the maternal death rate, the response of the crime rate to police measures, or the effect on traffic accident

41. See, in this regard, Anthony G. Oettinger's incisive article—"The Myths of Educational Technology," *Saturday Review*, May 18, 1968, pp. 76–77, 97—which warns against excessive hopes for applying PPBS to education and notes the enormous amount of preparation which was needed to use it within the Defense Department.

rates of law enforcement procedures. But the benefits of education are beyond such precise measurement and evaluation; they
are often slow to develop, and then difficult to interpret or identify except in general terms. They are most often reflected in
social, political, economic gains made over periods of decades,
coming far too slowly and imperceptibly to be assayed critically
by legislators working on year-to-year appropriations.[42]

An implicit answer to these concerns was recently voiced by a state
government proponent of PPBS whose general theme was that the spread
of program budgeting among the states is rapid; that it will inevitably be
applied to higher education; and that, notwithstanding earlier successes
under other budgetary procedures, it is vital now that higher education
cooperate with the new system rather than fight it:

> The degree to which education can respond with sophisticated
> PPB-type tools to aid decision making may well have a direct
> bearing on its future effective participation in the resource-
> distribution process. . . .
>   Questions which I have repeatedly heard raised in the legis-
> lative halls relating to the values of research, the returns from a
> counselling program, the cost-benefit rationale of Operation
> Headstart, the workload level of the teaching faculty, or the eco-
> nomic and social benefit of a college education itself are not out-
> side the realm of measurement, evaluation *and* redirection, if
> redirection is indicated.[43] (Order transposed.)

PPBS and the setting of educational priorities

Although it is still too early to offer any substantial analysis of the
workings of PPBS, one issue seems certain to cause some friction between
higher education and state government and may ultimately draw the
coordinating agency into a central budget role.

This issue concerns the level of generality at which institutional programs are to be defined for purposes of state budget review. There are
both administrative and political reasons why persons in state government
may prefer to keep the program packages small. One legislative analyst

42. Quoted in Moos and Rourke, *The Campus and the State*, p. 320.
43. Wayne F. McGown, "How Can States Develop a Good Program-Planning-Budgeting System (PPBS) for Education?" *Seven Crucial Issues in Education: Alternatives
for State Action* (Denver: Education Commission of the States, 1967), p. 6.

insisted that he could operate under PPBS only if reasonably precise techniques of measurement and evaluation had been developed, and he assumed that this would require, at least initially, that programs be broken down into fairly small components. And several legislators to whom we talked confirmed Aaron Wildavsky's thesis[44] that politicians feel more comfortable dealing incrementally with traditional budgets and dislike having to choose between major policy alternatives. If they are made to go the PPBS route, they will undoubtedly prefer to keep the programs as small as possible.

On the other hand, college and university spokesmen point out that since, to permit later evaluation, program budgets must necessarily be spending budgets, the institutions' administrative flexibility will be considerably narrowed if the program packages are too small.

As one possible solution to this dilemma, ways for measuring costs and benefits of larger programs might be devised and then legislators persuaded to accept the revised pattern. But if they were to embrace such a role too enthusiastically, a different dilemma might arise: They would then be in a position to substitute *their* judgments about major educational priorities for those recommended by the authorities in higher education.

Democratic theory has, of course, always required that duly elected representatives of the people make basic public policy; but in many states there has emerged a tacit modus operandi whereby legislators usually confine their role to making incremental budget changes and defer to the institutions' setting of internal priorities.[45] This has not prevented occasional complaints from higher education (e.g., the report of the Committee on Government and Higher Education, *The Efficiency of Freedom*) that this kind of budget review sometimes leads to a situation in which fiscal officers make educational decisions. But even though state cuts here and there in a budget based on the objects of expenditure (salaries, desks, lightbulbs, etc.) can obviously affect an institution's overall level of quality, they do not necessarily alter its priorities with respect to educational policy.

But a PPB system based on broad program definitions may raise ques-

44. Aaron Wildavsky, *The Politics of the Budgetary Process* (Boston: Little, Brown, and Co., 1964).
45. "In most states, the changes which the legislature makes during the session are principally along the lines of modifying a few sections of the act to increase or decrease the amounts for a few departments or programs." (Miller, "Budgeting Processes," p. 29.)

tions about exactly this point. If, instead of salaries and lightbulbs, legislators are asked to fund certain major programs, and if the estimated costs and benefits of these programs and their alternatives are laid out for all to see, politicians may yield to the temptation to rearrange the priorities recommended by the educational authorities. This change from formal to substantive budget decisions is described in Wayne F. McGown's account of higher education budget review in Wisconsin:

> In the past, the budget submitted by the state's educational institutions permitted decision making in form—consideration of the numbers of books purchased, teacher-pupil ratios, the proposed purchase of laboratory equipment and classroom supplies and the number of cleaning staff and yardkeepers. Examination that did take place did so without reference to a framework of output objectives. In contrast, today's requests are set in broad program terms—teaching the underclassman, financial assistance to students, continuing education for adults, research for industrial application—substantive matters for the decision makers. In this framework, costs of administration, physical plant, libraries, and registration offices become identified as ingredients to program ends—not ends in themselves.[46]

If such a change does occur, then the tacit modus operandi will have broken down. Some legislators may reply to this, "The sooner we reclaim our rights over public policy, the better." But most educators will answer that universities and colleges have normally done their best when persons in state government, either by choice or by default, have refrained from exercising their full powers.

We raise the problem here not to solve it (for the arguments can be neither subtantiated nor refuted) but to outline its possible dimensions and to indicate the ways in which coordinating agencies may become involved. With costs in higher education soaring and with tensions between the campuses and the state capitals intensifying, the politicians' self-restraint in PPBS will become increasingly more difficult to maintain. In this situation, the coordinating agency may have a vital role to play. First, through its ability to emphasize the importance of long-range planning, it can ensure that the state and the institutions will have reached essential agreement on educational priorities, thus reducing some of the danger

46. "How Can States Develop a good PPBS for Education?" p. 9.

of clashes in program preferences. But there will always be other areas where interim revisions are needed. Here the coordinating agency can use its budgetary powers to recommend program priorities that will command the support of both state government and higher education. Politicians and university and college authorities may not like to have their own preferences second-guessed by the coordinating agency, but it is difficult to see how the agency can avoid assuming a central budget role under PPBS when planning is so closely linked with fiscal review. (We return to the issue of PPBS and the related development of management information systems in chapter 11.)

SEVEN

Program review

The term *program review* is used here to refer to all decisions relating to the substantive development of higher education. As explained in chapter 1, it is conceivable that a state could respect scrupulously the boundaries of academic freedom, impose the minimum number of procedural controls, and still do great damage to its system of higher education either by intervening too heavily in, and imposing the wrong criteria on, substantive decisions or, paradoxically, by intervening too little and allowing a sweet anarchy to weaken the system from within.

Centrality to the Coordinating Process

It becomes a matter of considerable delicacy, then, to strike a balance in this area between the various interests of the state and those of the institutions. Louisiana, the one state in our survey which had neither a voluntary nor a formal coordinating agency at the time, attempted to solve this problem by a kind of unofficial division of labor: The state assumed the dominant role in deciding on new institutions, and the governing boards of the two systems (university and state college) were allowed to determine internal procedures for approving new courses and degree programs. This arrangement worked well for neither the state nor the institutions. (Louisiana's establishment of a statewide coordinating board in 1969 would seem to validate this judgment.)

Our field research in Louisiana confirmed Emogene Pliner's observation that state action resulted in the proliferation of new institutions (seven were authorized between 1964 and 1967) which were inadequately planned for, with respect to both their location and their type.[1] Previ-

1. *Coordination and Planning* (Baton Rouge: Public Affairs Research Council of Louisiana, 1966), p. 54.

135

ously, the pattern had been to establish two-year branches of Louisiana State University (LSU), allow them to develop into four-year institutions, and then transfer them to the jurisdiction of the State Board of Education, which ran the state college system. But more recently, the LSU system acquired a four-year campus in New Orleans and another in Shreveport, while the State Board of Education acquired at least one two-year institution. We were told by persons both in state government and in higher education that these arrangements had been the result of political tradeoffs rather than careful planning. Certainly all reports indicate that the branch campus in Eunice was thrust upon the LSU system without being formally requested and that the New Orleans branch of Southern University (a black institution) was authorized so hastily that even the president of the university and the mayor of the city were not informed in advance. It is perhaps no coincidence that it was in this state—where political criteria were applied freely in deciding on new institutions—that we heard stories of heavy contributions from building contractors to the party in power.

Nor do the institutions themselves have a very impressive record with respect to avoiding duplication of courses and degree programs.[2] An examination of Pliner's list showing the numbers of students enrolled in various classes and in various degree programs reveals considerable unnecessary proliferation. A state must, of course, provide some instruction in fields for which the demand is limited, but Louisiana institutions seem to have been too relaxed in their self-regulation on this matter.

Most scholars have concluded, on the basis of similar situations in other states, that neither the organs of state government nor the institutions of higher education are capable of conducting the finely balanced assessments involved in program review, the former because the issues are too complex for nonprofessionals to handle and the latter because their own self-interest often inhibits their objectivity. Thus, coordinating agencies —because they combine a statewide perspective with a specialized knowledge of higher education—have increasingly been called upon to play a central role in these decisions. Such a role, however, requires that both the state government and the universities and colleges yield some of their traditional powers, and this they have not always been willing to do. State governments find it difficult to give up even de facto powers, especially

2. Here we rely entirely on Pliner, since our own investigation in Louisiana did not cover the technical details of course proliferation. Incidentally, Pliner's study has been criticized by some institutional officers as too severe.

a power as politically and economically loaded as that of creating new institutions. On their side, colleges and universities find role and scope assignments and degree and course approval so intimately linked with substantive autonomy that they become very nervous over the prospect of the coordinating agency's having increased authority over these areas.

In view of such sensitivities, it was hoped at first that program control could be achieved through the coordinating agency's exercise of its budget review powers alone; more recently, program review has been regarded by some persons as an almost automatic process of approving or disapproving proposed programs on the basis of their compatability with master-plan guidelines. But close examination shows that neither process—budget review or master planning—obviates the need for a thorough process of program review in its own right.

Relation to budget review

New Mexico's Board of Educational Finance was founded on the philosophy that the best way to coordinate higher education without violating institutional autonomy is to concentrate on fiscal relations. Thus, the original statute (in 1951) gave the Board no direct authority in the area of program review. Yet Lyman A. Glenny, in his 1959 study, pointed out that the Board was able to use its considerable budgetary powers as a "means of influencing and controlling programs and their allocations."[3] Among the techniques it used to influence programs, the Board requested—and sometimes published—data on class size, teaching loads, costs per student-credit hour, and number of degree graduates per year in each program; in addition, it asked that all new programs and services be listed in budget documents as separate items and fully justified. Using this information, the Board of Educational Finance then pushed steadily to cut back on redundant courses and degree programs by pegging faculty salary increases to increases in class size, by refusing to budget new faculty positions when data indicated that a department lacked self-restraint, and in one case—in spite of the executive officer's reminder that it lacked power to disapprove new programs—by sending a letter to an institutional president warning that it did not look with favor on the development of more graduate programs. Of the New Mexico experience, Glenny concludes: "The eventual legislative grant of authority to the agency to control grad-

3. *Autonomy of Public Colleges* (New York: McGraw-Hill Book Co., 1959), p. 96.

uate programs shows that, however powerful and successful the indirect methods are, the surest method of control requires full legal authority."[4]

With the exception of the Arkansas Commission on Coordination of Higher Education Finance, created in 1961, all other coordinating agencies have been given explicit responsibility—even if only advisory—for program review. Because of recent developments in program budgeting (described in the previous chapter), program review, budget review, and master planning are coming to be integrated more tightly. The long-range goal of PPBS is to have multiyear estimates of both the costs and the benefits of every proposed program and its major alternatives; if this ideal is realized, then the master plan can make much more knowledgeable recommendations about program choices.

Relation to master planning

Master planning might seem to be a better device than budget review for accomplishing the purposes of program review, since it involves guidelines which have been agreed upon by both state government and higher education and which are used in making what might otherwise be controversial ad hoc decisions. A master plan that sets forth the criteria for establishing new institutions or for assigning basic role and scope missions should help to lessen tension when the coordinating agency is later called upon to make decisions in these areas. But since only twenty-three states had completed serious master plans by 1969, and since many of these did not cover all the major topics relevant to program review, it is obvious that, at its present stage, planning is only a partial answer.

Even if a greater number of states produce more comprehensive master plans, the evidence suggests that controversies over subsequent program decisions will continue. In Illinois, for example, certain private institutions which had participated fully in the deliberations leading to Phase II of the Master Plan opposed its recommendation for three new public institutions and carried their fight to the legislature. In California, the state college system is now pressing for certain changes (university designation, faculty salaries equal to the university scale, lighter teaching loads, more state support for research) which were thought to have been precluded by its acceptance of the role and scope mission assigned in the Master Plan of 1960. Finally, in North Carolina, East Carolina College justified its recent bid for independent university status by saying that conditions had

4. Ibid., p. 97.

changed substantially since its president signed a 1962 governor's commission report endorsing a monopoly on university status by the consolidated state university.

Given all these considerations—the lack of master planning in many states; the failure of some state plans to include guidelines on major program issues; and the need to make interim adjustments in, and periodic reevaluations of, such guidelines as do exist—one can see that master planning may contribute to, but cannot replace, the program review function of the state coordinating agencies.

Content and pattern

Program review concerns itself with such decisions as the following: whether to establish new institutions, branch campuses, or professional schools, and, if so, where; what role and scope missions, if any, to assign to new or existing institutions; which new degree programs or courses to establish; which to reallocate or eliminate; which research and public service activities to institute; and what degree of control to exercise over programs funded from nonstate sources. It should be pointed out that the pattern of program review varies markedly from state to state: Some of the decisions are made by institutions, some by coordinating agencies, some by state governments, and some by combinations of these parties.[5] The remainder of this chapter is devoted to a consideration of the coordinating agency's role in each of the above-mentioned areas.

The Establishment of New Institutions

The decisions to be made in this area are numerous and complex. Is it preferable to expand existing institutions or to establish new ones? If the latter, what kind should they be: two-, four-, or six-year colleges? limited or comprehensive universities? or separate professional schools, perhaps? Should they be established as independent institutions, equal branches of a multicampus system, or satellite campuses partially controlled by a parent institution? Where should such new institutions be located: in high-cost urban areas, where they will be accessible to commuting students, or in low-cost rural areas, where more residences will have to be

5. The Utah Coordinating Council of Higher Education (before it was superseded by a consolidated governing board in 1969) made a study of program review in other states. This survey was reported in *The Importance of Coordination in Higher Education* (Salt Lake City: Coordinating Council of Higher Education, 1968).

provided? How will their establishment affect existing public institutions and, more particularly, existing private ones, with their higher tuition rates?

With so many complex educational criteria to take into consideration, one might suppose that decisions in this area would be left completely to the coordinating agencies. But they have tended to be very cautious because of two factors: the strong urge of some persons in state government to introduce political criteria; and the highly controversial nature of such decisions among educators.

To take the first point, it is obvious that legislators sometimes win votes by promising new institutions to their local constituents. As Glenny notes: "The successful politician [proves] his merit by bringing home an insane asylum, a prison or a college. Frequently it [makes] little difference which."[6] On a statewide basis, a governor or a state official may want to locate a new institution on the basis of its potential contribution as a "smokeless industry" to the economic development of a particular region. Nor is it improper—in cases where the educational arguments are fairly evenly balanced—for a politician to urge that the needier of two alternative regions get the new institution. It is improper, however, to allow political or economic considerations to supersede important educational ones. And the practice of handing out huge construction contracts in return for contributions to party coffers hardly merits comment.

In the face of these political pressures, a coordinating agency which tries to have a greater say in recommendations regarding new institutions needs unified institutional backing for its proposals. But this support is hard to get. University and college administrators exhibit many anxieties over new institutions (which may, after all, be controlled by others): economically, that these institutions may divert already inadequate state funds; academically, that they may compete aggressively for the best staff and students; politically, that either as separate new bodies or as parts of some other multicampus system, they may alter the existing balance of power. Given the fairly large number of public institutions in most states and the natural tendency of administrators to protect the interests of their own campuses, it is not surprising that so little consensus results.

The inability of educators to agree on this issue is best evidenced in the reluctance of most voluntary coordinating agencies to deal with the problem of new institutions. For example, Frank B. Brouillet reports that

6. *Autonomy of Public Colleges*, p. 13.

in Washington, the Council of Presidents declined to recommend the location of a new four-year institution; at its suggestion, the legislature created an ad hoc Temporary Advisory Council on Public Higher Education, which subsequently hired a consulting firm to undertake the necessary studies.[7]

As long as Purdue and Indiana University dominated, the Indiana voluntary group had a fairly good record in handling new branch campuses and professional schools; but now Indiana State (ISU) and Ball State (recently given university status) have begun to take an interest in branch campus expansion, and unanimity has become more difficult. The four institutions were unable to agree on the location and affiliation of a new state medical school; moreover, the Evansville branch of ISU was evidently launched amidst internal dissension. The Regional Campus Coordinating Committee which has been set up will have its hands full dealing with such issues as the admission of the Fort Wayne and Indianapolis branch campuses to independent university status.

The voluntary coordinating group which operated in California until 1960 had one of the better records in planning new institutions; but ultimately, even that issue became the subject of discord between the university and the state college systems. A study made in 1957 had outlined six basic criteria for deciding on new institutions and then offered a priority list of desirable locations for each type of institution. All but one of the new campuses authorized by the 1957 legislature were on the priority list, but that one exception proved too tempting to many communities and therefore to many legislators. John Marshall Smart reports that the next legislative session was besieged with twenty-three bills, three resolutions, and two constitutional amendments relating to proposed new institutions or changes in the structure of higher education.[8] This sudden flurry of political interest broke through the united front of the university and state college systems in supporting the 1957 plan, and subsequently the governing board of each system made its own approach to the legislature regarding desired new campuses. This problem, along with increasing disagreement over other issues, led to the Master Plan study of 1960 and the implementation of its recommendation to create a formal statutory coordinating council.

7. "An Analysis of State of Washington's Method for Coordinating Higher Education" (Ed.D. diss., University of Washington, 1968), p. 101.
8. "Political Aspects of State Coordination of Higher Education: The Process of Influence" (Ph.D. diss., University of Southern California, 1968).

Statutory coordinating agencies do not operate on a principle of unanimity, as most voluntary systems do, and can therefore make recommendations without the agreement of all parties. Ten of the thirteen consolidated governing boards responding to the Pliner questionnaire indicated that one of their functions was to approve the establishment of new institutions or campuses; only ten of the nineteen responding coordinating boards had this function.[9] But statutory agencies, like voluntary ones, run into problems with both state governments and institutions.

For example, the Georgia Board of Regents—one of the most powerful, with its constitutional autonomy and lump sum appropriations—has, we were told, found it prudent in the past to pay careful heed to gubernatorial preferences about the placement of new institutions. Since the governor in question had been a good friend fiscally to higher education, refusal to cooperate would presumably have been awkward.

Nor did California's problems end with the creation of a statutory coordinating board. Even though the board's legal powers in recommending new institutions were advisory only, the legislature, in a policy statement attached to the enabling act, declared that it would not authorize or acquire sites for new institutions unless they were recommended by the Coordinating Council.[10] This worthy intention was soon put severely to the test. In 1963, legislators who favored the early acquisition of certain sites for future state colleges tried to persuade the agency to advance the date of its scheduled 1965 study of the need for new institutions. Failing that, they reacted by passing a bill that called for a state college to be established in a particular county; only a gubernatorial pocket veto saved the Council's face. For the next two years, the Council in general and its director in particular came under heavy critical fire from some disappointed legislators. When the 1965 study was finally published, it still did not give top priority to a college in the county in question, and political hostilities reached their climax. A compromise of sorts was reached whereby supporters of the Council agreed to accept legislative action in acquiring recommended sites well ahead of target dates, with the understanding that construction would not begin until the Council said so. Thus modified, the Coordinating Council's de facto powers stand, and it

9. *Coordination and Planning*, p. 39.
10. James G. Paltridge, *California's Coordinating Council for Higher Education: A Study of Organizational Growth and Change*. (Berkeley: Center for Research and Development in Higher Education, University of California, 1966), p. 55.

continues to make careful studies of the need for, and appropriate location of, new institutions.

In Illinois, by way of contrast, opposition came not from state government but from parts of higher education itself. As mentioned earlier, some private institutions opposed the coordinating board's proposals for creating two new public four-year colleges, on the grounds that the capacities of existing private institutions were not being fully utilized. The state legislature supported the coordinating board, authorizing both recommended campuses; at the same time, however, it approved the appointment of a commission to study the problems of private higher education in Illinois.

Not all states undergo epic political struggles over the establishment of new institutions. For example, Florida in the mid-1950s accepted the Brumbaugh Plan recommendations for new senior institutions and the Wattenbarger Plan recommendations for the development of a comprehensive junior college system; it has kept fairly closely to those guidelines. The difficulty there is imprecise role definition, and this will be discussed in the next section.

A problem of another kind arose in Pennsylvania. There, the State Board of Education (which acts as the statewide coordinating board) recommended in its master plan that a system of community colleges be created and that the extensive network of Pennsylvania State University two-year branch campuses gradually be transferred to that system. Not only did Penn State react adversely to this recommendation, but also it insisted on its independent right to seek legislative approval for additional branch campuses, even if they competed with community colleges scheduled for the same general area.

One such clash occurred in Delaware County, where the State Board planned a community college. It discovered then that it had neither the statutory authorization nor the broad political support necessary to oppose Penn State. The legislature had never delegated the powers it had asked for in the master plan. The competitive situation was an interesting one: Penn State branch campuses are supported partly from fees and partly from funds allocated by the state; therefore, they do not, as do community colleges, constitute an additional burden on local tax roles. Quite apart from the respective merits of branch campuses and community colleges in their quality, prestige, responsiveness to local needs, and so forth, one can understand why many local taxpayers would prefer branch campuses. The State Board was reduced to the gesture of recommending that the legislature cut Penn State appropriations by an amount equivalent to the cost of founding the Delaware County branch campus.

Finally, the creation of new medical schools is a phenomenon unto itself. In addition to the Indiana problem already mentioned, we came across spirited controversies over the location of new medical schools in Ohio and Texas and incipient disagreements in Virginia and Georgia as well. The stakes in the game are high, and everyone plays to win. One institutional president in Virginia remarked that the coordinating board would be foolish indeed to get caught in the cross fire over a decision which had such politically loaded implications.

The Texas Coordinating Board, apparently finding good reasons for violating its own declared moratorium on new institutions, recommended that new medical and dental schools be established in Houston and Dallas. It thus managed to enrage both certain private institutions in those cities and certain West Texas legislators who wanted the professional schools for their own area. In Ohio, whatever the educational justification for locating a new medical school in Toledo, the decision (as was pointed out to us) was hardly displeasing to the editor of a major newspaper in that city who had been a strong supporter of the governor.

One can see why, ten years ago, Glenny found coordinating agencies so timid about recommending new institutions: "The central agencies often are passive, do not take a stand, and do not lend advice on the matter without specific requests from the legislature."[11] No doubt the wrong types of institutions have often been put in the wrong places over the last several decades, but these errors of judgment have usually been buried under the avalanche of new institutions and of new programs required by the rapidly growing demand for higher education. But projections into the 1980s indicate that there will be a slowdown in the creation of new institutions. If the decisions made in this area are to be wise ones, then excessive political interventions and unbridled institutional ambitions must be curbed. Happily, as pointed out in chapter 5, planning techniques are steadily improving, and coordinating agencies are gradually acquiring more competent staff.

Role and Scope Assignments

Decisions in this area involve the determination of an institution's basic type (e.g., two-year, four-year, or graduate institution) and of its curricu-

11. *Autonomy of Public Colleges*, p. 208.

lar emphasis (e.g., liberal arts, teacher training, vocational-technical, professional). (The process of approving specific degree programs within these general boundaries is discussed in the next section.)

From the point of view of the institutions—at least the most powerful ones—each campus would ideally be allowed complete freedom to determine its own basic type and its own long-range program goals, toward which it would move as fast as it could persuade the state to support them. Campus administrators would have to decide whether it is more effective to present a complete campus master plan and hope that the attractiveness of the package will outweigh the shock of the total costs involved, or, alternatively, to advance plans piece by piece for ad hoc state reactions and risk that important parts will be rejected. The latter path seems the more heavily traveled, not only because fears about legislative sensitivity to huge price tags are justified but also—and perhaps even more frequently—because many institutions simply have not done a thorough job of long-range planning.[12] They tend to present one major goal at a time because they have not thought ahead any farther. But even campuses with master plans may be reluctant to reveal them in toto since publicizing their dreams of grandeur could awaken similar longings in other institutional bosoms, and the sum total of these aspirations would probably alarm legislators even more.

For this very reason, ad hoc responses to institutional requests for changed role and scope missions are, from the state point of view, unsatisfactory. Such requests can be judged rationally only after all institutional plans are put alongside each other and some attempt is made to assess their combined relevance to long-term state needs and resources. If, as is usual, such an inventory reveals an aggregate of desired program developments and fiscal demands which exceeds either state needs or state resources or both, then clearly some cutting back must be done, Fiscally, this can be accomplished by applying a flat percentage reduction to each institution's request for state support and allowing it to juggle its own internal program priorities; but such a response fails to recognize that some institutions are more effective than others and that some proposed programs are more badly needed than others.

What is needed, then, is a process whereby the state, in cooperation

12. See, for example, Frank Rourke and Glen Brooks, *Managerial Revolution in Higher Education* (Baltimore: Johns Hopkins Press, 1966); and Lewis B. Mayhew, *Long Range Planning for Higher Education* (Washington: Academy for Educational Development, 1969).

with the institutions, makes role and scope decisions designed to achieve both educational diversity and fiscal economy. Negatively, such a process will discourage most institutions from aspiring to become high-cost, research-oriented, comprehensive state universities and will curb unnecessary duplication of educational programs. Positively, it will encourage the creation of diverse types of institutions and will stimulate the addition of new programs to meet unfilled needs. Moreover, such approved new programs will receive more adequate support since state funds will not be spread too thin through undue proliferation.

The two main questions relating to role allocation are: How diverse should the pattern of institutions be to meet the state's needs? And how much flexibility should be built into the system to satisfy the desires of campuses which want to change roles?

Tier patterns

Most states have a three-tiered system: two-year colleges, four- to six-year institutions (the older of which are usually former teachers colleges with broadened liberal arts curricula), and the state university or universities. In some states in our survey (e.g., California, Maryland, Massachusetts, North Carolina), the land-grant college had been combined with the state university and developed into a multicampus university system. In others (e.g., Georgia, New Mexico, Oklahoma, Oregon, Texas, Washington), the land-grant institution developed separately and, until recently at least, tended to emphasize agriculture and engineering, in contrast to the state university, which emphasized the traditional liberal arts and the professions.

A variation of the three-tiered system is the existence in some states of two-year branch campuses of senior institutions rather than community or junior colleges. Kentucky, Louisiana, and Pennsylvania have such a pattern; the essential structure of their middle-level state college system remains intact, although these colleges are sometimes given university titles. In Ohio and Indiana, on the other hand, the former state colleges have assumed some of the functions, as well as the titles, of universities, and the pattern has thus become two-tiered: universities and their branch campuses. Though Ohio and Pennsylvania have established some community colleges, the relation of these to the existing two-year branch campuses of senior institutions has not yet been finally determined.

Yet another variation occurs in Florida and is being considered in

Illinois, New York, and Pennsylvania: the establishment of "senior colleges" which offer only upper division and master's work. The theory is that this kind of institution, drawing its enrollment from nearby junior or community colleges, reduces to a minimum the overlap with existing public institutions and private colleges. But the pressures at such institutions to extend the programs both up and down are enormous. Already Florida Atlantic University at Boca Raton is pressing to award the doctorate, claiming that only then can high-quality faculty be attracted and retained. And cynics have long noted that freshmen and sophomore classes are essential not only to winning football games but also to employing impecunious graduate students as teaching assistants in introductory courses.

In Illinois, Phase II of the state Master Plan calls for the creation of such three-year senior colleges; in the meantime, a fourth tier has been added to the existing three: "a liberal arts university" inserted between the traditional comprehensive university and the state colleges. This new tier—composed of the two largest state colleges already granting the doctorate in several fields, and of a new campus in Springfield—has been given its own separate board of regents and an explicit role assignment:

> to concentrate its efforts to establish institutional programs of graduate education leading to the doctorate in a significant number of fields but whose breadth of offering is restricted to the liberal arts and sciences and other related undergraduate programs, with only a limited number of associated graduate professional schools, usually education or business administration. . . . The dominant challenge both quantitatively and qualitatively, for these institutions during the immediate years ahead is to fill the vast and growing need for college and university teachers.[13]

The pattern of tiers and the number of institutions in each are matters which every state must determine for itself. Usually, of course, the choice is limited by the existing pattern but may be opened up when new institutions are created or old ones want to change their mission. In theory, a very small state could offer all the desired programs to all qualified students at the university level alone; this would require admitting students whose abilities varied widely and offering programs as diverse as two-year vocational-technical training, four-year liberal arts curricula, and gradu-

13. Illinois Board of Higher Education, A *Master Plan for Higher Education in Illinois: Phase II* (Springfield: Board of Higher Education, 1966), p. 58.

ate and professional work. In practice, all states have two or more tiers. The feeling is that a heterogeneous pool of students is best served by a diversity of institutions, perhaps with different admissions standards. Thus, it is felt that, quite apart from fiscal considerations, it is not desirable for every public institution in a state to strive for full university status.

Firmness or flexibility?

The next question is whether institutions should be discouraged from changing from one tier to another, and if so, how? That this is no small issue is indicated by the following summary of changes that occurred during the 1953-54 to 1963-64 period:[14]

Type of Change	Public	Private-Nonsectarian	Church-Related
Junior colleges becoming senior colleges	11	23	38
Four-year colleges initiating master's programs	85	44	49
Senior colleges initiating doctoral programs	40	12	17
Totals:	136	79	104

Though most of this movement took place in the private sector, enough public institutions changed their missions (and, in particular, in the expensive graduate area) to raise the question of whether such flux is in the public interest. M. M. Chambers, cited in chapter 3, insists that the public interest is best served in higher education by a pluralistic free market limited only by constraints accepted through voluntary coordination. He argues that rigid role definitions—"fixed and imposed from above, and enforced by an 'abominable "no" man' "—are particularly abhorrent, for they box in an institution and attack its morale, the indispensable element in its pursuit of excellence.[15]

But high morale and the absence of restraints may not be sufficient to attain excellence in "vertical extension of programs" (i.e., changing an institution's basic role). Money and planning, both in large doses, are also needed. But, as Raymond Schultz and Hugh Stickler point out, they are seldom available.

14. Derived from Raymond Schultz and Hugh Stickler, "Vertical Extension of Academic Programs in Institutions of Higher Education," *Educational Record*, Summer 1965, p. 234.
15. *Freedom and Repression in Higher Education* (Bloomington, Ind.: Bloomcraft Press, 1965), pp. 15–17.

Only in occasional cases are careful study and planning undertaken in advance of vertical extension. . . .

Governing boards generally do not have . . . essential facts about need for additional facilities, staff, library resources, and finances if vertical transition is to be accomplished successfully. . . .

Institutions that undertake vertical extension without reasonable assurance of substantially increased financial support are in danger of propagating a travesty if not an outright fraud on higher education.[16]

This does not mean that vertical extensions are never proper; as mentioned earlier, in times of rapid expansion like the present, what is required is not a hatchet man but a traffic director who will make sure that needed programs are undertaken at the right place and properly financed. The "right place" may be a new institution, an existing institution with similar programs, or an existing institution which is changing its role.

Role changes in some states depend more on political influence than on deliberate educational planning. But critics of excessively tidy planning point out that, had central planning and control been too heavy-handed in the past, many normal schools might never have become the fine state colleges and universities that they are today. And others cite, as examples of the desirability of fluidity, the successful efforts of Michigan State and Southern Illinois to achieve university status and national recognition.

One must recognize, however, that raw political influences have also produced travesties in institutional role changes, some of which have been fortuitously obscured by the continuing demand for rapid growth in higher education. And—as was mentioned in connection with the establishment of new institutions—such factors as the projected deceleration of the expansion rate, the wider operation of coordinating agencies, and the development of more sophisticated planning techniques should result in more careful educational screening with respect to future changes in role and scope.

In making statewide role and scope assignments, two alternative approaches are used: *across-the-board* and *selective*. The first involves the

16. "Vertical Extension of Academic Programs in Institutions of Higher Education," pp. 240-41.

stipulation (in a master plan or a set of statutes or through coordinating agency action) of explicit role assignments for each institution, or for each type of institution, and the requirement that all subsequent program changes be made within the boundaries of these assigned roles. In California, for example, the Master Plan of 1960 recommended, and the state legislature subsequently enacted, the following roles for the various institutions:

the University of California is the primary state-supported agency for research.

The university may provide instruction in the liberal arts and sciences and in the professions, including the teaching profession. The university has exclusive jurisdiction over instruction in the profession of law, and over graduate instruction in the professions of medicine, dentistry, veterinary medicine and architecture.

The university has the sole authority in public higher education to award the doctoral degree in all fields of learning, except that it may agree with the state colleges to award joint doctoral degrees in selected fields. . . .

The primary function of the state colleges is the provision of instruction for undergraduate and graduate students, through the master's degree, in the liberal arts and sciences, in applied fields and in the professions. . . . Faculty research is authorized to the extent that it is consistent with the primary function of the state colleges and the facilities provided for that function. . . .

Public junior colleges shall offer instruction through but not beyond the fourteenth grade level, which instruction may include, but shall not be limited to, programs in one or more of the following categories: (1) standard collegiate courses for transfer to higher institutions; (2) vocational and technical fields leading to employment; and (3) general or liberal arts courses.[17]

The Illinois pattern represents the selective technique: "Orderly expansion of public higher education in Illinois can be best achieved under the guidance of the State Board of Higher Education . . . rather than

17. California Master Plan Survey Team, *A Survey Plan for Higher Education in California, 1960–75* (Prepared for the Liaison Committee of the State Department of Education and the Regents of the University of California. Sacramento: State Department of Education, 1960), Education Code, Division 16.5.

by detailed fixed powers and limitations written into state laws."[18] The California pattern was explicitly rejected because of its "tendency toward inflexibility and rigidity and a resulting waste of educational resources." The Illinois Master Plan continues:

> Our educational system has grown to its present dimensions and quality by allowing each institution to develop freely the programs in which it has outstanding faculty resources and competence.
>
>   . . . experience has shown that excellence often arises out of fortuitous combination of faculty members and resources with little or no planning. When this happens, rigid limits placed on program level or research function may stifle a potentially outstanding contribution to the educational world. Faculty resources can easily be wasted at the very time when they must be maximized merely to maintain current levels of quality.[19]

To achieve flexibility and yet maintain diversity within order, the Illinois coordinating board proposed the previously mentioned four-tiered "system of systems." Diversity and order are achieved through the efforts of each system, under the direction of its central governing board, to realize its own particular purposes rather than merely trying to emulate the University of Illinois; flexibility is achieved insofar as the possibility of basic change is not dismissed out of hand:

> The system of systems concept is not intended to type institutions indelibly or to predetermine their ultimate destiny. They can be expected to respond to social, economic, and demographic conditions in order to render maximum service to their respective clientele. If through such accommodations the functions of an institution change radically, it may then become necessary to transfer that institution to another more appropriate governing system. It is anticipated, however, that such transfers will not be frequent.[20]

Relation to type of coordinating agency

Among the states in our survey, type of coordinating agency seemed uncorrelated with the approach used in making role and scope assignments.

18. A Master Plan for Higher Education in Illinois: Phase I (1964), p. 42.
19. Ibid.
20. Ibid.: Phase II (1966), p. 57.

Prior to 1969, when it was in the voluntary association category, Washington had firm across-the-board guidelines written into its constitution; another state in the voluntary category, Indiana, permitted its two former teachers colleges to become universities and to expand their graduate work accordingly. In the governing board category, both Georgia and Oregon have restricted advanced graduate work to the state universities, although state institutions in Atlanta and in Portland are pressing hard to join the club. Florida, on the other hand, has indicated that its newer campuses at Tampa, Boca Raton, and Pensacola—each of which has been granted the title of university—may include selective doctoral programs.

Among states in the coordinating board category, the patterns are extremely varied. Like Illinois, Ohio and Wisconsin have chosen the selective method (although in the case of Wisconsin, it is prospective rather than actual: A 1967 plan mentioned that some state colleges might, in the future, be authorized to grant doctorates, depending upon the special needs of the regions). In addition to California, Kentucky and North Carolina use the across-the-board method, making explicit in state law the differentiation of functions. The boards in Massachusetts, Oklahoma, and Texas have used their strong role and scope powers to confine doctoral programs to certain institutions. The boards in Maryland, New Mexico, Pennsylvania, and Virginia all lack the authority to allocate role and scope (though Virginia's board can limit curricula offerings "with the approval of the governor"), but all have either recently completed or will soon complete state master plans which say something about role and scope missions.

Special problems in role changes

What particular considerations enter into changing an institution's role and scope? What kinds of changes occur? Which approach is preferable: across-the-board or selective? These and similar questions can best be answered by focusing on one tier at a time.

Changes in Two-Year Colleges: The major variable in this sector is not the method of role allocation but the kind of two-year institution involved. Most states with highly developed community college systems have acted to prevent these institutions from becoming four-year (or beyond) institutions. This is as true for Illinois (a coordinating board state) and Florida (a governing board state), both of which use the selective approach, as it is for California (coordinating board) and Oregon (governing board), which use the across-the-board approach. The feeling is that the community colleges serve an important public function by providing two-year vocational-technical curricula along with college-parallel curricula and general education courses. But this very fact makes transition to a four-year college difficult.

The same is not true, however, for two-year branch campuses of universities or senior colleges or of junior colleges with exclusively college-parallel curricula. Thus, Ohio (a coordinating board state) and Indiana (a voluntary association state)—both using the selective method—either have authorized or will soon authorize one or more of the branch campuses in the state to become independent senior institutions. North Carolina (coordinating board) and Georgia (governing board)—which make across-the-board assignments—have permitted some junior colleges to become four-year institutions. More recently, North Carolina has developed its other junior colleges into a community college system and, barring outright political interventions, no further transfers are anticipated.

When an excellent community college is prevented from changing its status, frustration may result. A concerted political effort was mounted in Pensacola, Florida, to turn the local community college into the new senior institution projected for that region by the Florida Board of Regents. But the Board agreed with the community college governing structure in the Department of Education that such a change was undesirable. Instead, as a compromise, the new institution was planned as a "senior" college (upper division and master's work).

The California community colleges, in their drive for "excellence at their own level," have encountered a dilemma. Because of their locations and salary scales, many are able to recruit a highly qualified faculty, a large proportion of whom hold the doctorate. Such faculty members, often university-oriented, lead efforts to introduce changes (e.g., pressing for professorial ranks, establishing academic senates, emphasizing college-parallel programs) that may lead to neglect of the two-year terminal programs.[21]

Four-year Colleges Initiating Master's Degree Programs: That the most common change in role mission involves the addition of master's programs by four-year colleges (see figures on p. 148) is explained partly by the growing market demand for persons educated beyond the B.A. and partly by the relative ease and economy with which this kind of change

21. T. R. McConnell, "State Systems of Higher Education," *Universal Higher Education,* ed. Earl J. McGrath (New York: McGraw-Hill Book Co., 1966), p. 26.

can be effected. The faculty, library resources, and laboratory facilities required for master's programs usually differ in extent rather than kind from those required for baccalaureate programs. Thus, both across-the-board and selective states have seen fit to allow most of their four-year institutions to add a fifth and sixth year. The only question is whether to confine master's programs to certain institutions, and the usual answer is to do so in the case of high-cost, low-demand fields.

Senior Institutions Initiating Doctoral Programs: Such factors as costs, degree standards, state and national needs, and academic prestige combine to make the issue of changing a senior institution into a doctorate-awarding institution one of the hottest in the area of role allocation. Advocates of the across-the-board approach argue that state and national needs for more doctorates should be met by expanding existing universities rather than by trying to upgrade state colleges. Citing Allen M. Cartter on the difficulties of achieving an outstanding reputation for graduate programs,[22] they urge that the state concentrate such work in one or two "centers of excellence" rather than distributing it more widely and ending up with a larger number of mediocre universities. To allow state colleges to enter the doctoral field, they say, is to court trouble in at least four ways: (1) such a move siphons off limited state funds from existing programs and thereby jeopardizes their quality; (2) it increases costs because of unnecessary duplication of expensive library and laboratory facilities; (3) it traumatizes the institutions that must struggle to adapt themselves to a new and demanding role; and (4) it diverts from their essential purposes those state colleges that are left behind. The last two points require further elaboration.

The traumatic effects arise from the difficulty of upgrading faculty in the face of tenure considerations and from the shortage of outstanding scholars to supervise advanced graduate work. Sometimes, ill feeling is generated by the need to eliminate those degree programs and departments considered inappropriate to the newly acquired university role. Naturally enough, the faculty and students involved, as well as the outside groups served by the threatened units, resist such changes resolutely. All in all, it may take a decade or longer to complete the transition. In the 1950s, after suffering the labor pains of bringing a state college into the university sector, a University of California administrator was said to

22. *An Assessment of Quality in Graduate Education* (Washington: American Council on Education, 1966).

have muttered: "Never again!" Later, when student enrollment projections pointed to the inescapable need to expand doctoral work beyond the capacity of existing university campuses, it was decided to create new institutions rather than take over any more state colleges. In other states, the response has been to absorb existing private universities into the state system, either as state universities (e.g., Buffalo, Houston, Louisville, Omaha) or as state-assisted universities (e.g., Akron, Cincinnati, Pittsburgh, Temple, Toledo).[23]

No doubt some of the problems of upgrading an institution could be avoided if it were merely a question of allocating an isolated doctoral program here and there on the basis of a special regional need. But to achieve real excellence, doctoral programs should operate in at least clusters of allied subjects. Thus, the situation should realistically be seen for what it is: a very large camel's nose under the tent. Almost inevitably, other clusters of departments will soon be demanding equal treatment. Their ambitions can be checked, but only at considerable psychological cost.

Nor should one overlook the possibility that, once it is decided, special circumstances justify the introduction of doctoral work at one or several state colleges, the others will quickly become obsessed with the desire to be next in line. This obsession may distract them from concentrating on their own special purposes in a differentiated system and thereby distort their activities. The states adopting the across-the-board technique of role allocation evidently hope that an explicit and relatively fixed definition of the state college role will serve to make the persons associated with those institutions more inclined to accept the assigned status and to channel their restless and potentially creative energies into improving the colleges within their defined limits. Experience has shown, however, that such hopes have not been realized. So long as greater prestige is attached to the university label and its concomitants—higher salaries, lighter teaching loads, more research opportunities, better libraries and laboratories, tighter admissions standards—just so long will the ambitious state college faculty members, often supported by administrators, trustees, students, alumni, local legislators, and the chamber of commerce, campaign vigorously for changed status.

Thus, across-the-board role allocations have not prevented state colleges from seeking university status in California, Kentucky, or Wash-

23. More is said about state relations with private higher education in chapter 9.

ington, provisions in state law notwithstanding; or in North Carolina, Oklahoma, Pennsylvania, or Texas, coordinating board plans notwithstanding. Four state colleges in North Carolina and five in Kentucky won the approval of the legislatures involved to change their names to universities, even though this was acknowledged to be primarily an aid to faculty recruitment rather than approval to initiate doctoral programs. Similarly, Pennsylvania's Indiana State College, through astute political leadership, received legislative permission to become Indiana University (but not to offer the doctorate); the remaining state colleges, however, were then prohibited from making any further changes. The Oklahoma legislature also consented to let Central State College change its title to university, but the governor blocked this move through a veto.

In other cases, state colleges have sought university status in more than name and have generated considerable political turmoil in so doing. When the Texas coordinating board, whose program review powers were greatly strengthened in 1965, ruled that doctoral programs at institutions other than approved universities would have to be terminated by September 1968, East Texas State College went over the board's head and got legislative approval to retain its doctoral programs; only a gubernatorial veto upheld the board's action.

The faculty of the California state colleges felt strongly that the 1960 Master Plan had, under the guise of giving their institutions "separate but equal" status and functions, relegated them to second-class citizenship within the state system. Therefore, through their statewide academic senate, they commissioned the Tool Report,[24] which made a detailed plea for altered status. Later, the legislature, generally dissatisfied with other aspects of coordination and irritated over student unrest, created a Joint Legislative Committee on Higher Education. Its staff report recommended, among other things, that rigid role allocation be abandoned in favor of greater flexibility.[25] Clearly, the across-the-board approach has not brought peace and quiet to the area of role and scope allocation.

Proponents of the selective approach would observe that peace and quiet are unrealistic and undesirable goals in higher education. Tension is inevitable in so sensitive an organism as a campus; the only real question is whether it is manifested in a vital striving for excellence or in rage and

24. Marc Tool, "The California State Colleges Under the Master Plan," (Report to the Academic Senate of the California State Colleges, Sacramento State College, August 1, 1966).
25. California Staff of the Joint Legislative Committee on Higher Education, *The Challenge of Achievement* (Staff report to the Committee, Sacramento, 1969).

impotence. The selective philosophy assumes that the carrot of hope is preferable to the stick of rigid role assignments. Thus, institutions granting the master's degree are usually led to believe that if they become good enough, they can expand into doctoral work as fast as state conditions permit. Advocates argue further that, in assessing state needs, the selective approach takes into account three factors often overlooked by the across-the-board school of thought. First, concentrating doctoral work in a few centers runs counter to the priority of attracting more students into advanced graduate work; the connection between wider geographic availability of education and higher proportionate student enrollments is well known. Second, some of the difficulties of developing doctoral programs in single departments or small clusters can be overcome by promoting much closer interuniversity cooperation in matters of faculty exchange, libraries, closed circuit TV, and the like. Third, as the Ohio Master Plan points out:

> Some competition in graduate study and research seems desirable. Monopoly in higher education may be as harmful to progress and freedom as monopoly in other social institutions: economic, social, and religious. When only one institution undertakes graduate study and research, there may not be any basis for comparing its accomplishments and failures with those of other institutions. Competition, moreover, is a spur to effort.[26]

Thus, Illinois and Ohio have authorized most of their existing senior institutions—and, up to 1969, Indiana and Florida all of them—to grant doctoral degrees in at least some subjects. This policy has gone a long way toward reducing major tensions, though it leaves one smaller issue unresolved: Unless all institutions are granted doctoral programs, the ones excluded will probably come to resent their status.

In Illinois, as already mentioned, the two state colleges offering the most graduate work were placed under a new Board of Regents system to become "limited universities," and the two remaining state colleges, joined by a new campus in Chicago, retained that status. In Ohio, the master plan called for Cleveland State University, the State University at Dayton, and Central State College to confine their offerings to the master's level, the first two also to concentrate on serving a commuter population. It has not yet been determined what role and scope will be assigned to

26. Ohio Board of Regents, *Master Plan for State Policy in Higher Education* (Columbus, 1966), p. 88.

the new public campuses emerging in Fort Wayne and Indianapolis, Indiana, or to the institutions planned for Miami and Jacksonville, Florida. If prohibited from offering doctoral work, they will probably begin to clamor for a change in status before long. Now that reapportionment has given more political strength to the cities and suburbs, institutions with large metropolitan power bases behind them will be in a position to push hard for a change in their restrictive state-assigned missions and to seek national prestige as full universities. (Georgia State College at Atlanta and Portland State College in Oregon already show signs of such yearnings.)

The main difficulty with the selective approach, however, is that by permitting all or most senior institutions to award the doctorate in at least some fields, it throws an enormous burden on the coordinating agency and taxes severely its procedures for approving new degree programs. No longer will requests for new doctoral programs come only from universities long experienced in advanced graduate work and capable of conducting their own rigorous screening. If the agency is to keep the doors from being flung wide open, it must have strong determination. It must also have procedures for degree approval which not only *are*, but also are *seen to be*, both fair and firm.

Approval of New Degree Programs

There are three main issues in this area, each one with its own complexities: (1) which degree programs to review; (2) what kinds of judgments to make about them; and (3) what type of review machinery to use.

Selection of programs to review

The question of which degree programs to review is easily answered for states with consolidated governing boards, since these boards have full legal power to approve all curricular changes in the institutions under their jurisdiction. But in states with coordinating boards or voluntary associations, the universities and colleges may balk at the agency's being given extensive control over degree programs, preferring to police themselves, particularly if the proposed degrees fall within the defined boundaries of their role and scope assignments.

But because of considerations of costs, particularly in expensive graduate programs, eleven coordinating boards have been granted the authority to approve new programs, and thirteen coordinating boards, plus the voluntary association in Indiana, have the authority to recommend approval. Only the Arkansas coordinating board has no say at all in the matter.

Still, one must not judge a board's powers alone on the external evidence. For instance, a board with strong legal powers that turns down very few proposed new programs may seem at first glance to be failing to use those powers fully enough; but in fact the situation may be attributable to an effective communications network which operates to spare institutions the embarrassment of a formal rejection. An institution may sound out the agency and staff beforehand and, through informal premeetings or intermeetings, learn whether its proposals are likely to be rejected. If they are, then the institution will simply not submit the proposal; indeed, some boards permit an institution to withdraw its formal request even after a negative vote. Thus, a board's effectiveness as a watchdog over new degree programs cannot always be assessed from its rejection record. Furthermore, even mere advisory powers may be effective in that having to make a formal presentation before an agency, in full view of other institutions, may sometimes deter a university or college from proposing some program which, were it left on its own, it would have quietly adopted.

Most coordinating board statutes mention review of "new programs" or "new degree or certificate programs" without specifying the exact coverage intended. In New Mexico, the board's formal jurisdiction extends only to new graduate programs. In Illinois, the term used is "new unit of instruction," and this is defined to include establishment of any college, school, division, institute, department, or other unit not heretofore mentioned. It does not, however, include "reasonable and moderate extensions of existing curricula," although the board has the power to determine just what constitutes such reasonable and moderate extensions. In California, the coordinating board "advised" on only seventeen instructional programs between 1962 and 1967, its inactivity being attributable to a very permissive definition of "new programs." The board examined overall academic plans for the university and the state colleges each year; degree programs were reviewed only if they had been developed subsequent to the overall plan and had no "functional counterpart" within the segment or constituted a major departure from existing programs.

Criteria of judgment

The California experience is relevant here too. The state's Coordinating Council is charged with seeing that new programs are "appropriate to the orderly growth of public higher education." More specifically, a proposed instructional program must fall within the segment's function as defined by the Master Plan and must represent a response to present and projected needs for graduates. In addition, its estimated costs must be reasonably related to the number of students to be educated.

A Coordinating Council document in 1967 described and explained the results:

> all programs presented . . . so far have been approved. Both the University and State Colleges have able sophisticated planning staffs and have developed internal review procedures. Both segments have followed Council criteria in good faith.[27]

Yet within a year of this statement, a study of engineering curricula called into question some previously approved programs. The Council made this observation:

> Existing Council procedures for review of new programs and the blanket approval of programs once they appear in an academic plan received and reviewed by the Council have not resulted in significant coordination activities on the part of the Council.[28]

Consequently, as a preliminary to giving much more careful attention to program review, the Coordinating Council decided to survey annually the educational offerings of the university and the state colleges, but this move did not save it from a biting indictment in the staff report to the Joint Legislative Committee on Higher Education, which charged that it was a "protective association" for the segments and had allowed "orderly growth" to proceed on three fronts rather than one.[29]

Whether this general condemnation is justified or not, it is clear that at least up to 1968, the California board had done an inadequate

27. California Coordinating Council for Higher Education, Committee on Educational Programs, "Council Review of Proposed New Academic Programs," September 25, 1967, p. 1.
28. California Coordinating Council for Higher Education, Committee on Educational Programs, "Preliminary Plan for Annual Survey of Educational Offerings, California State Colleges and University of California," May 20, 1968, p. 4.
29. *The Challenge of Achievement*, p. 47.

job with respect to new degree programs. One of the basic causes of this deficiency, as was pointed out in Chapter 4, is the composition of the board: i.e., an institutional majority all too ready to defer to the wishes of the colleges and universities. Other factors contributing to its apparent sluggishness are the purely advisory nature of its program review powers, its overly narrow definition of "new programs," and the vagueness of its criteria for suitability.

The three major criteria for passing judgment on proposed new degree programs—institutional readiness, state need, and state ability to finance—require further comment.

Institutional Readiness: This criterion covers a whole range of matters involving the adequacy of institutional faculty, facilities, funds, library resources, and so forth; they add up to the institution's ability to create and maintain a new program at a high-quality level. The main problem in applying this criterion on a statewide scale is that institutions vary considerably in their ability to judge their own readiness. Some have excellent internal screening procedures, and some do not. Obviously, to function effectively, the system must cover its weakest link; but obviously, too, regulations must be applied equitably to all institutions. Thus, an institution with long experience in creating high-quality graduate programs and in having them judged by outside experts must submit to the same screening process as does a college that is just expanding into master's or doctoral work. If the experienced institutions can suppress their distaste at having to fill out another set of papers (or perhaps can use the same reporting forms as the coordinating board), they will probably soon learn that board reactions will tend to be pro forma and thus fairly easy to live with.

State Needs: On the criterion of state needs, however, there should be no pro forma judgments; proposals for new degree programs from *all* institutions must be evaluated in the light of carefully estimated state needs. The universities and colleges, though they may try to ascertain such state needs, are obviously in a much poorer position than the coordinating agency to make judgments about unnecessary duplication of facilities. Moreover, if expansion seems indicated, the agency is better able to determine where it should occur.

The coordinating agency, in carrying out its important role as assessor of state needs, should be mindful of several facts. First, a distinction may have to be made between student *demands* for a program and state *needs* for it. A Florida university administrator pointed out that he had more requests for a doctorate in education than for one in mathematics; yet he was sure that the state had a greater need for more highly trained mathematicians.

Second, in judging need, regional and even national, as well as state, factors should be considered. At the graduate level, particularly, the market tends to transcend state boundaries, and a state that "imports" doctors or teachers (for instance) should be aware of its responsibility to educate its fair share of professionals for other states. (The various regional associations of higher education are helpful in working on this problem.)

Third, it is crucial to underscore the word *unnecessary* when talking about duplication, for in these days of rapid expansion, a considerable amount of legitimate overlap will occur. All institutions should probably provide a core of general education; and many should probably offer liberal arts baccalaureates and perhaps even master's degrees, teacher education, and business administration. But in the more esoteric subjects, where demand is small, and in the more advanced and professional degree programs, where costs are high, even a small degree of duplication may be unnecessary.

John D. Millett has described how the Ohio board views this problem.

> Replication is not necessarily duplication. . . . The real test of duplication which needs to be applied in every statewide system or structure of higher education is that of desirable enrollment size needed in any instructional program in order to make that program viable, in order to achieve a satisfactory utilization of capital plant, and in order to maintain overhead costs at a reasonable level per student. . . . Scholarship, like atomic reaction, depends today upon a critical mass. It is a fine part of the academic art to determine at what point this critical mass of facilities and scholarly talent is realized.[30] (Order transposed.)

In setting a minimum critical mass, however, an emerging institution must be given enough time to develop its new departments. One must remember, too, that frequently a wider geographic spread of various programs elicits larger enrollments than would have occurred had the programs remained concentrated.

30. "The Role of Coordination in Public Higher Education" (Address to the Select Committee on Post-High School Education, University of Southern Florida, Tampa, September 18, 1968).

State Ability to Finance: The final reason for giving the coordinating agency a powerful voice in the approval of new degree programs is that, even granting that an institution is ready to offer a high-quality program which the state stands in need of and which is not being unnecessarily duplicated in some other institution, it does not always follow that expenditure of state funds for the program represents the best investment of scarce resources. We will not go into the matter of the competition between higher education and other state services; such conflicting demands must be resolved chiefly in the political domain. The point here is that an effective coordinating agency will attempt to make difficult judgments about relative priorities for new programs in higher education, and, in doing so, should either use guidelines previously established by the planning process or create a working group—including institutional representatives—to evolve new guidelines. In this way, purely ad hoc responses to projects put forward in piecemeal fashion may be avoided.

Review machinery

Review procedures for judging institutional readiness, state needs, and state ability to finance new programs are important under any circumstances; they become crucial when agencies using the selective approach to role and scope allocations must pass judgment on a flood of new doctoral programs proposed by institutions just entering the field.

The administrative procedures employed in program review differ widely and seem to have no particular correlation with type of agency. Quite a few agencies in our sample rely chiefly on staff analysis (Georgia, New Mexico, Oklahoma, Texas); at least one uses a standing committee of lay board members (Oregon); several employ statewide committees composed of persons from the institutions (Indiana, Ohio, Washington); some lean heavily on outside consultants (North Carolina, Virginia); a few favor a mixed pattern, using interinstitutional committees for most judgments and outside consultants for a few others (Florida, Maryland); and one state has a standing advisory committee whose members are drawn from both inside and outside the state (Illinois).

Bearing in mind that the review procedures not only must be fair and firm, but also must be *perceived* as such, one can examine the problems inherent in each technique.

Heavy reliance on staff review makes for firm control over new degree programs, but even when that control is also in fact fair, institutions whose programs are rejected may not regard it to be so. Lay members, faced with long and highly complex agendas, are necessarily influenced by staff recommendations. Thus, if too many new programs are rejected, institutional hostility may come to be focused on the staff.

Although the use of a standing committee of public members may counterbalance excessive staff influence, it also raises the specter of a few powerful laymen dominating in highly delicate academic matters. Furthermore, the danger of explicit or implicit tradeoffs among lay members with different geographic or institutional sympathies is present.

Early in their existence, the North Carolina and Ohio boards attempted to draw on expertise outside the agency staff and membership: They asked highly respected professors at the state university to make confidential judgments on new degree programs proposed by emerging colleges. Inevitably, some judgments were negative and, when their source was somehow leaked, disappointed institutions protested volubly that the state university was thwarting them in order to protect its primacy and prevent state funds for graduate work from going to other institutions. In short, however expert the judgments in fact were, their source made them suspect.

North Carolina then made use of consultants from outside the state. While this solved the problems of objectivity and secrecy, it raised another issue brought to our attention by a college president in that state. He noted that experts from high-powered, out-of-state institutions tended to have unrealistically high expectations and to judge modest local needs by Berkeley or Harvard standards. Presumably this problem could be met by selecting consultants more carefully or by giving them a charge more consistent with realities in the state.

For its part, the Ohio board then turned to a statewide advisory committee composed of institutional representatives (mostly graduate deans) to review at least the new graduate programs. The dangers of this approach are all too clear.[31] Unless it has strong and careful staff leadership, the committee can turn into a giant logrolling operation, accepting most programs whether they are in the public interest or not. Alternatively, if those members whose institutions have long experience in advanced graduate work take a firm line with respect to standards of quality in new programs, the committee may find itself divided into the "have-nots"

31. The topic of institutional participation in agency activities is examined in greater detail in chapter 8.

and the "haves" and the former (usually more numerous) may gang up on the latter.

This danger seemed imminent in Florida, even though its Board of Regents had established careful procedures for reporting and justifying new programs to the academic advisory committee. One sensed that the newer institutions, which outnumbered the two older ones, might unite in their common aspiration to initiate new graduate programs. If they did so, the agency staff—which on other grounds might have backed the older institutions—would then have to take note of the political realities. Because of legislative reapportionment, the power of the newer institutions, whose ambitions were supported by the major population centers, has increased, whereas that of the rural-based older universities has declined.

Such problems as committee logrolling and the overwhelming of the few by the many can often be handled by strong staff leadership. Particularly in the early days of the advisory committee structure, when the institutional members are being educated to the problems of higher education, staff work must be of high quality and continuous for a year or two (rather than sporadic). Well done, this investment of staff time may pay handsome dividends. First, by making institutional advice more to be desired than feared, it will allow the agency to tap the invaluable experience, wisdom, and judgment of institutional personnel. Second, it can help to establish the reputation that procedures are both firm and fair; at that point, responsibility can be delegated, thus lightening considerably the agency's heavy workload. Finally, to the extent that key institutional personnel learn to work together on program review and to see problems from a statewide perspective, the basic coordinating and planning process must profit.

Illinois has evolved an intermediate type of procedure which embodies some of the virtues of both the in-state and the out-of-state approach. Its Commission of Scholars was created with the following conditions. It was to be composed of nine persons nationally known for their teaching and research, the majority of them from outside the state. Members were to be selected by the Board of Higher Education from lists submitted by "each state-supported university which offers advanced graduate programs and from nominees suggested by such other collegiate institutions as the Board may solicit." Their duties were as follows:

    i) Study areas of critical need for doctoral programs to determine at which institutions they should be offered and how their initiation and sound development may be expedited.

ii) Review applications by any state university to offer a degree program requiring six or more years of education or training. In appropriate cases the Board may act without referral of an application to the Commission.

iii) Evaluate the intrinsic merit of the particular proposal.

iv) Determine the need for each program.

v) Investigate the qualifications of the faculty and physical resources of the institution proposing the program.

vi) Conduct such studies and employ, with the approval of the Board, such consultants as are necessary to inform the Commission.

vii) Make a recommendation to the Board.[32]

James Heck reports that the members chosen from inside the state act not as representatives of their institutions but as scholars with broad and varied educational interests.[33] The Commission, with the agency staff assisting it, meets privately but may grant hearings to persons from the institutions which are proposing programs. During the first two years of its existence (1965–67), it rejected four-and-a-half programs, and in each case the decision was unanimous. No division between in-state and out-of-state members has emerged, and the agency staff has so far supported all Commission recommendations. Though understandably not over-joyed, the institutions whose programs were rejected seemed to accept the decision as legitimate. Some programs resubmitted after being revised in accordance with the Commission's suggestions have been subsequently approved.

Illinois, then, seems to be fairly successful in handling control of new degree programs. Each state must come to grips with this problem, whether it be through the efforts of the staff, outside consultants, inter-institutional committees, or some combination of these.

Course Approval

As was the case with review of new degree programs, approval of new courses raises no problems in states with consolidated governing boards

32. *A Master Plan for Higher Education in Illinois: Phase I* (1964), pp. 36–37.
33. "Coordination of Higher Education in Illinois" (MS, School of Education, University of Delaware, 1968).

since their plenary powers include this authority, if they choose to use it. Often, however, as a matter of administrative practice and academic tradition, the power is delegated to local campus officers or faculty senates.

In states with coordinating boards or voluntary associations, the agency almost never has the power to review new courses. Yet some observers feel that control over new degree programs is by itself an inadequate protection of the public interest. T. R. McConnell, for example, argues that if a coordinating agency lacks the power to eliminate existing programs, it should have a say about course offerings:

> A coordinating board should also have the authority to discontinue educational programs. Such power may save the board from being confronted, as is now often the case, with what amounts to a *fait accompli*, that is, with a request to give approval to a *program* or *curriculum* on the ground that the institution already offers all or nearly all the necessary *courses*. If the authority to discontinue programs does not control this sort of academic one-upmanship, some continuing review of course offerings may become essential.[34]

In Texas, just such maneuvers as these resulted in the coordinating board's being give the following authority in 1965:

> Each governing board shall submit to the Board immediately following the effective date of this Act, and thereafter once each year on dates designated by the Board, a comprehensive list by department, division and school of all courses, together with a description of content, scope and prerequisites of all such courses, that will be offered by each institution under the supervision of said governing board during the following academic year. The Board may order the deletion or consolidation of any courses so submitted after giving due notice with reasons therefor and after providing a hearing if one is requested by the governing board involved.[35]

A recent count indicated that over thirty-six thousand courses had

34. "The Coordination of State Systems," *Emerging Patterns in American Higher Education*, ed. Logan Wilson (Washington: American Council on Education, 1965), p. 139.
35. See Robert L. Williams, *Legal Bases for Coordinating Boards in Thirty-Eight States*. (Chicago: Council of State Governments, 1967), pp. 106–07.

been registered with the board. A knowledgeable observer commented to us:

> The Board has stated that the power would be used with discretion and only to control unauthorized expansion of academic offerings; nevertheless, the power is present without the provision of any basis or criteria for its exercise. The requirement of public hearing provides some protection, but such protection might be scant for courses in politically unpopular subject areas or in areas likely to be unappreciated by a lay Board. The basic area of higher education which has always been recognized as the exclusive province of the faculty is now subject to the control of a statewide lay Board. The fact that this power has not been misused by the Board and probably will not be so misused by *this* Board does not remove the inherent danger to higher education in Texas.

A few boards might claim the power to scrutinize individual courses by very broadly interpreting their authority over new programs or units of instruction. The Wisconsin board, for example, reported as follows:

> Although the Council's legislative charge gives it jurisdiction over the development of any new higher education program in the State of Wisconsin, it has, up to this point, only reviewed new majors or new schools. The Council now is beginning to recognize that such self-imposed limitations may, in some cases, interfere with a coordinated planning function and it is now contemplating some method whereby it could, without excessive demands upon staff time, review new courses of study, new associate degree programs, or new programs at the minor level, which may have an impact upon the total State picture.[36]

But most will restrain themselves, realizing that state action in this sphere may well ruffle academic sensitivities. The legislation creating the New Jersey coordinating board was explicit about the limits of the board's power:

> "Programs" as used in this subparagraph means areas or fields in which degrees or non-degree certificates might be granted and shall not include individual courses nor course content nor shall

36. As reported in Utah Coordinating Council on Higher Education, *The Importance of Coordination in Higher Education*, p. 90.

it include the course composition of areas or fields already in existence.[37]

Program Reallocation

Paradoxically, universities and colleges can be very eager to take on new functions and very reluctant to drop old ones. The first tendency becomes dangerous when institutions slide into new programs which they are unprepared to handle and for which they have not received approval. The second tendency causes trouble when institutions cling to outworn and useless programs; the Illinois Master Plan comments on this problem:

> The constant changes in career requirements for occupational and professional fields and the economics of education make it imperative to discontinue obsolete or clearly unproductive programs. Chief administrators sometimes allow continuance of acknowledged obsolete curriculums because of certain faculty forces working with sympathetic interest groups outside the college. With diminishing demands for some programs the state may find it advantageous to center in one or two places the resources now scattered in several institutions.[38]

Again, the statewide governing boards have substantial powers in this area. During the depression of the early 1930s, the newly created governing boards in Georgia and Oregon used these powers to redistribute functions and programs more rationally among the institutions. The Georgia board even closed down ten two-year and four-year colleges.

The coordinating boards have given less emphasis to the reallocation and elimination of existing programs. Indeed, in one recent study, this was cited as the major shortcoming of the planning systems observed.[39] Only in Massachusetts, New Jersey, Oklahoma, and Texas have the boards been given regulatory powers in this matter, while in Colorado, Illinois, Ohio, and Utah they have merely advisory powers. The boards in North Carolina, Virginia, and Wisconsin may recommend that programs be reallocated, but some form of state government approval is

---

37. Williams, *Legal Bases for Coordinating Boards in Thirty-Eight States,* p. 61.
38. *A Master Plan for Higher Education in Illinois: Phase I* (1964), p. 43.
39. Ernest Palola, Timothy Lehmann, and William R. Blischke, *Higher Education By Design: The Sociology of Planning* (Berkeley: Center for Research and Development in Higher Education, University of California, 1970), p. 536.

required before their recommendations take force. No voluntary association has undertaken reallocation as a major responsibility, although Indiana has attempted some functional adjustments on branch campuses.

The power to reallocate and eliminate programs is seldom exercised because past experience has shown that such moves have unfortunate political repercussions, stirring up controversy and even leading to the agency's decision being overturned. Such was the case in Texas, when the board moved to eliminate some doctoral programs at East Texas State College; and in Oklahoma, when the board tried to reallocate certain programs and mentioned that the military academy might be closed down. Powers to reallocate programs are little used during periods of rapid expansion, but should a severe recession or depression occur, this function of coordination might well become central.

Review of New Research and Public Service Programs

Problems arise in this area not at the level of the individual research project or the isolated concert series but at the level of new research institutes and broad public service activities such as adult education and agricultural extension service programs. At this higher level, the same criteria as are used in judging new degree programs should be applied: institutional readiness, state needs, and state ability to finance.

While all consolidated governing boards have the power to approve new programs in research and public services, only in Illinois, Oklahoma, and Texas do coordinating boards have similar explicit authority. The boards in Colorado, Massachusetts, and Virginia have been given regulatory power in the specific areas of adult education and extension programs. Advisory powers over research and public service activities are exercised by the boards in California, Maryland, New Jersey, and Ohio.

Two main problems arise in this area. First, overly ambitious institutions often wage aggressive campaigns to expand their extension programs into ever-larger areas of the state, with consequent overlapping of jurisdictions and conflict between the institutions involved. To prevent such a situation from developing, the Texas board was given power to designate the "limitations of extension programs for credit to specific geographic areas." In Oklahoma, a statewide institutional committee has been established to advise on extension policies and disputes.

The second problem is finding proper criteria for making judgments about proposed research institutes. The California Coordinating Council found that the two it tried to apply—contribution to knowledge and cost considerations—were completely unsatisfactory:

> There is no basis for judgment by the Council staff, the Council, or even a panel of experts in the appropriate field as to the degree to which a particular research center might contribute to knowledge—at least not for a long period of time after such a center has been established.
>
> Costs for research obviously vary with the type of activity, and under present systems of accounting and reporting, the costs and benefits of research are nearly impossible to assess.[40]

In view of these comments, it is not surprising that between 1962 and 1967, all twenty of the university's proposals for new research institutes or centers were approved. Obviously, the answer is not to consider separately each proposal for a new research institute but rather to judge relative priorities among proposals in light of available resources. Review machinery that draws on collective academic advice (such as some of the procedures discussed in the section on degree program approval) might be helpful here.

Approval of Nonstate-Funded Programs

Initiating new teaching or research programs funded from nonstate sources (e.g., endowments, gifts, Federal grants) presents budget and program problems which deserve attention, though we gathered only a little data on them.

With respect to finance, some states that use a budget formula insist on reducing "earned" state funds by an amount equal to the outside income. While this procedure would seem to save the state money, it obviously dampens institutional ardor about seeking outside funds. It would seem preferable to leave a substantial part of the extra income to the institutions to aid them in their quest for quality above the threshold of normal state support.

With respect to program, the question is whether an institution using outside funds for a new program must have the approval of the coordinating agency. A North Carolina law requires that all such programs receive board clearance on the grounds that they may involve indirect costs to

40. California Coordinating Council for Higher Education, Committee on Educational Programs, "Council Review of Proposed New Academic Programs," p. 6.

the state or that the state may ultimately be expected to take over the program. The more devoted proponents of program control claim that only in this way can institutions be held to their allotted role and scope. A more moderate view would exempt programs financed *entirely* (including cost overheads and indirect costs) from outside sources; the argument here is that some leeway must be left for institutional initiative and risk taking, particularly when no state funds are endangered.

Summary

Looking over the ways in which various coordinating agencies have tried to meet the problems of establishing new institutions, allocating role and scope missions, approving new courses, reallocating programs, and surveying research and public service activities, one can readily see that the consolidated governing boards have far and away the most impressive powers. If rigorous control is the criterion, they score highest, followed by coordinating boards, with voluntary associations trailing in the rear. But when one recalls that an institution's programs are intimately linked with its substantive autonomy, then the criterion of rigorous control seems less appropriate; more desirable is the kind of partnership between state government and higher education that is discussed in chapter 1.

Under this criterion, the coordinating boards do not come off so poorly. Certainly their performance in program review has, in general, improved enormously since it was condemned by Glenny in 1959 as inadequate.[41] It seems likely that boards will become more regulatory and less advisory in the program review area.

41. *Autonomy of Public Colleges*, p. 231.

EIGHT

The agency as intermediary

Although occasionally a state government may send an unsolicited policy directive to its coordinating agency for transmission to the state university and colleges, the normal and healthy flow of business is in the reverse direction. The agency first assembles a mass of planning, budget, and program data from the various institutions; then reviews such data from the standpoint of the public interest in higher education; and finally passes its recommendations to the state government, hoping for full approval and fiscal support. Once state policies in higher education are funded, the agency usually has the responsibility of overseeing their implementation.

The quality of the agency's policy recommendations to the state, and certainly its ability to win the institutions' cooperation later in carrying out state-approved policies, are greatly influenced by the nature of its procedural relations with those institutions. Similarly, the degree to which agency recommendations receive state approval and funding will be greatly influenced by the nature of its relations with the organs of state government. This chapter will examine both these relationships—with higher education and with state government—to discover what problems each of them entails and how these problems affect one another.

Relations with the Universities and Colleges

The extent and manner of consultation and communication between the agency and the institutions of higher education is a matter of prime importance in coordination. In states which have voluntary coordinating systems or coordinating boards that include institutional representatives, this presents no serious problem, because some or all of the universities and colleges are, through their presidents or trustees, directly involved in

173

the final stages of policy making. Similarly, in states with consolidated governing boards having only a few institutions under their jurisdiction, the lay board members will probably be able to plan and coordinate the system, administer the separate institutions, and still find time to get to know the various presidents and administrative officers, and perhaps even some faculty members and students. But in states whose governing boards must oversee many institutions (Georgia, for example, which has some twenty-five institutions under its jurisdiction), and in states which have coordinating boards composed entirely of public members, difficulties may arise in channeling academic opinions from the institutions to the boards. However familiar with educational issues public members may become through continuing board service, their distance from the institutions deprives them of important professional advice.

In addition to having institutional membership on the coordinating agency (discussed in chapter 4), academic advice is made available to the lay members in three major ways:

1. Institutional personnel—from presidents and administrators through faculty and students—may attend agency meetings to express their opinions in general or on specific issues;

2. Institutional personnel and agency staff can make contact with one another informally and frequently, and the staff can then incorporate academic opinion in papers and verbal reports to the agency; and

3. Through specially created formal structures, institutional personnel can be drawn together periodically to advise and react on given subjects.

These three methods are by no means mutually exclusive; some states employ all three. Certain aspects of each method, however, require further comment.

Attendance at agency meetings

Agencies differ considerably in the extent to which they encourage institutional personnel to attend their meetings and comment on the issues. We observed several meetings of both governing and coordinating boards at which presidents and other institutional administrators waited outside the meeting chamber, to be called in singly when an item relevant to their own institution came up for discussion. In marked contrast is the practice of the Florida governing board (made possible by its having only six or seven senior institutions to govern, since community colleges are handled separately) : it invites all the presidents to attend its meetings and seats them opposite the Regents. Each president makes a formal presentation on developments and problems concerning his institution and later comments informally on matters touching on his knowledge or interest. One of these presidents told us that before this practice was introduced, he would have had to rent a hotel room in the city where the Regents were meeting, wait around for his five-minute appearance, and leave none the wiser about the problems of other state institutions or the overall process of coordination.

Institutional attendance at meetings does not always depend on the agency's attitudes and policies. At one point, it was discovered that the university and college presidents in New Mexico had tacitly agreed among themselves not to sit in on coordinating board meetings while each other's business was being discussed. Neither the governor nor the board leadership regarded this self-imposed absenteeism as healthy, so now presidents or administrative officers or both attend meetings on a regular basis, stay for most of the items, and speak at will on the issues.

Though presidential attendance at agency meetings may seem desirable as a general principle, in operation it runs into a number of difficulties. First, some agencies have jurisdiction over so many universities and colleges that, while it might be possible for representatives from each to attend and listen, chaos would result if all attended and spoke. Second, some agencies have such a heavy workload that much of the real decision making takes place in committees meeting prior to the agency meeting and often simultaneously with one another. Finally, as was mentioned in chapter 4, some agencies prefer to discuss the really sensitive issues in informal premeetings or intermeetings to which neither press nor presidents are usually welcome.

We found a few board members and staff unenthusiastic about the idea of regular presidential attendance at all agency meetings because they felt that one or a few dissenting presidents might take advantage of the presence of the mass media and turn the public meetings into arenas for last-minute opposition to some policy decisions. But the obvious way to avoid such unpleasant situations is to offer to institutions—through informal bilateral contacts, through formal multilateral advisory structures, or through both—the opportunity to react to proposed policies at an *early* stage. Each of these methods has its own advantages and drawbacks, and we will examine these in turn.

Informal bilateral contacts

Since agency staff must work closely with institutional personnel in obtaining the base data out of which agency policies are ultimately formed, this method of tapping academic opinion has the virtues of frequency, simplicity, and flexibility. It is as easy as picking up a telephone, and as effective as good interpersonal relations. But since interpersonal relations are sometimes not smooth, bilateral exchanges may not produce either confidence or candor. Moreover, in such contacts, the institutions respond in isolation of each other, thereby losing an opportunity for learning to understand the problems of other institutions or the growing pains of the entire statewide system.

To elaborate on these points: It is no secret that, in some states, institutions are uneasy over the prospect of the agency staff's having too much influence on the lay membership. If the values and preferences of the staff overlap sufficiently with those of the institutions, or if the staff shows itself ready to transmit to the agency even those academic opinions which differ markedly from its own, then informal bilateral contacts may work well. But if, for example, an executive director is a dynamic and forceful leader, he may intimidate the institutional spokesmen in a one-to-one relationship; even if he does not, university and college personnel may not know whether their dissenting opinions are shared by the other institutions and whether these dissenting opinions, expressed informally and individually, are reported accurately to the lay membership of the agency. A staff member who necessarily has his own view of the world, is only human if occasionally, in reporting to the board, he plays down institutional objections to a policy proposal or reports only those criticisms that *he* considers relevant.

In such a sensitive relationship, not only must justice *be* done, but also it must be *seen* to be done. One way to provide greater assurance that criticism will reach the ears of the board members undistorted (and, incidentally, one way to strengthen the spine of those too easily intimidated in a person-to-person relationship) is to create formal advisory structures for a multilateral exchange of opinions and the ultimate transmission of these opinions to the board.

Formal structures for collective advice

Formal advisory structures encourage candor if, through these structures, institutional spokesmen learn that their opinions are shared by others and therefore speak out more freely. They should promote confidence, too, since collective opinions formally rendered are usually reported with greater care (although many such structures are advisory to the executive director rather than to the agency itself).

But there are reasons even more important than increased candor and confidence that justify the considerable "costs" and dangers which an elaborate system of formal advisory committees involves. In the first place, the advice that comes out of a collective sounding is usually much higher in quality than advice gleaned from three, six, or nine separate exchanges. One's thinking is undoubtedly stimulated by hearing others speaking cogently to a well-prepared agenda. If the agenda and background papers are circulated early enough to give institutional spokesmen a chance to do their homework (including intrainstitutional consultation), if adequate time is allowed for discussion, and if the participants believe that their deliberations will be taken seriously, then it is possible to draw from the institutions wisdom that neither the agency's members nor its staff possess. Illinois and Florida provide examples of this favorable situation.

Understandably, some agency staff to whom we spoke felt that their position at the center of things—commanding a statewide perspective and having the institutional data at their fingertips—gave them not only a breadth of approach denied to most college administrators, but also, in some instances, a greater knowledge of the institutions than the institutional officers themselves had. Though we felt that such claims might be justified in cases where the agency was extraordinarily well staffed, nonetheless we were troubled by the implied impatience with the partial perspectives of institutional officers. No matter how wise the central staff, the institutions can still provide valuable knowledge and experience.

Even if the central staff were omniscient, it would still be prudent to involve institutional personnel in advisory procedures for at least two reasons. First, an agency that, through a meaningful advisory process, has made the effort to win institutional support for its policy recommendations may find it easier to obtain state support. Providing that it does not seem as though the advisory tail has wagged the dog (a danger which will be discussed later in this section), the coordinating agency must benefit from having widespread institutional backing for its proposals. And, in cases where one or more institutions feel they cannot offer such backing, an advisory system will preclude their complaining that they had no opportunity to criticize the policies being instituted.

Second, when the time comes to implement the policies approved and funded by the state, university and college personnel who were conscientiously consulted during the formulation period will be much more likely to comply readily with the spirit as well as the letter of the resulting policies.

In addition, it is often argued that a good advisory system will give institutional personnel a wider appreciation of statewide priorities—though whether this is indeed possible or even desirable is a matter of dispute. Those who see it as an advantage contend that a person, asked to respond *in vacuo* to some proposed policy, will normally react solely in terms of the perceived interests of his own institution; but if he must sit and listen to widely different reactions to the same issue, he will better appreciate the difficult task of coordination. In particular, if he observes firsthand the large gap between the cumulative demands of all institutions and the relatively limited state resources available to higher education, he will recognize the crucial need to try to establish priorities on a rational basis and may even accept cuts in his own favored programs, if not without pain, at least without anger.

We spoke to some coordinating agency staff members, however, who were quite pessimistic about the possibility of educating institutional personnel to a statewide point of view. Moreover, some university and college personnel felt strongly that they should not be asked to perform as statesmen making compromises in the name of the public interest. It was healthier and more normal, they maintained, to present the institutional points of view as forcefully as possible and then to allow the coordinating agency and the state to decide what was in the public interest.

Whatever the reasons for instituting a formal system of consultation with the institutions, such a system imposes heavy burdens on a coordinating agency and leaves it open to certain dangers. It was clear from the many complaints we heard—about pro forma consultation by agency staff, about one-way communications, and about poor institutional response—that a meaningful advisory system requires both a firm commitment from the agency leadership and the investment of literally hundreds of hours of staff time. Most agency staffs are so overworked that they are reluctant to devote much time to what seems a marginal priority, particularly if the state legislature is impatient for results and somewhat dubious about the agency's justification for being.

Furthermore, an extensive advisory network not only slows things down but also can as easily result in serious dissent as in cozy consensus.

It has been said, "If one consults a sufficiently large number of people for a long enough time, one can develop insurmountable opposition to the most innocuous idea." And the consensus that may emerge from the process is likely to reflect institutional logrolling, not a genuine meeting of the minds regarding the state interest. To handle this problem, the agency and the staff must make it clear from the outset that all advice, even that unanimously tendered, is subject to review by the central agency. One would not expect unanimous advice to be rejected often, but that possibility must remain open; otherwise a state legislature may come to feel that its coordinating agency has been captured by the interests it was created to coordinate. This was alleged to have been the case with the presidential advisory committee to the Texas Commission on Higher Education; when the latter was abolished and replaced by the Texas Coordinating Board in 1962, all mention of the presidents' advisory group was omitted from the new statute.

Types of advisory relationships

Ideally, a coordinating agency would have a two-way communications network established with all major constituencies of universities and colleges: presidents and administrative officers; faculty; students; and, in states with coordinating boards or voluntary associations, trustees. In practice, both limited staff time and presidential sensitivities make it difficult to forge agency links with the three last-named groups. We will examine these relationships one level at a time.

Presidents' Advisory Councils: In a few states (e.g., Connecticut, Massachusetts, and Missouri), advisory councils composed of institutional presidents are mentioned in the enabling legislation for the coordinating boards, but in most cases they have been established by agency or staff initiative. In the states included in our study, they varied markedly in nature and function, from informal bodies which met only occasionally to discuss such items as athletic tickets all the way to formal structures which operated under tight staff supervision and had heavy agenda paralleling the agency's own workload.

In cases where these councils were accused of ineptitude, the "blame" might lie in several directions. Sometimes it seemed attributable to staff shortcomings: e.g., calling meetings at only a few days' notice, failing to prepare adequately for meetings, lecturing to the presidents rather than inviting discussion (one university executive reported that his group was treated like a seminar of not very bright graduate students). Sometimes, it seemed due to the presidents' attitudes: e.g., unwillingness to discuss issues of substance in front of each other. (One agency member reported that when they are together, the presidents are polite and deferential to one another, but when seen individually, some are ready to cut the others' throats.) Sometimes, the difficulties are caused by size and diversity: i.e., the advisory council has too many members representing too many different types of institutions.

Given favorable attitudes on the part of both agency staff members and institutional presidents, the problems of size and complexity can be met in several ways. A presidents' council that is too large to permit worthwhile discussion can be reduced in size by having only a moderate number serve as the formal advisory committee; although in some instances (e.g., Texas), the agency staff makes the selections, it seems more satisfactory for the institutions to choose their own representatives (as in Virginia). The Texas board is faced with the problem of diversity—since its jurisdiction extends to community colleges—as well as size. It meets both these difficulties by establishing one representative advisory committee for the senior institutions and another for the community colleges. We were told that this division was the price exacted by the community colleges before they would agree to come under board jurisdiction in 1962. Whatever the reason for the creation of the two advisory bodies, the operational results are interesting.

The advantage of having separate advisory groups for junior and senior institutions is that the agenda can be more immediately related to the interests of the group and may thereby elicit more conscientious participation. Moreover, the resulting recommendations of each group are probably more satisfactory to its members since they have not been compromised with those of the other body.

To illustrate this point: In Oklahoma, where the advisory group includes presidents from the state universities, the state colleges, and the junior colleges, university personnel expressed some resentment because although the universities represented approximately 50 percent of the total enrollment and all of the doctoral students, they constituted only two voices out of eighteen and found much of their time taken up with the specialized problems of agricultural junior colleges. Of course, we also heard complaints about the few large institutions dominating the many small ones. In short, the difficulties attendant upon combining diverse types of institutions into one committee cut both ways.

It is equally obvious, however, that separate advisory committees may offer conflicting recommendations which will then have to be resolved in some way. If the presidents prefer the relative purity of separate advisory groups, they may be throwing important priority decisions to the staff or to the lay membership.

Recognizing this fact, one institutional president in Georgia felt that, notwithstanding the obvious problems, all chief executives should meet together and endure until some kind of academic consensus was reached on statewide priorities. The notes from our interview with him read:

> X thinks the presidents' advisory council is so big and diverse that many of the chief executives are willing to let the staff turn it into a one-way information session. He feels rather that it should meet regularly and, if necessary, on its own; that any president should have the opportunity to get an item on the agenda; and that the council should have guaranteed access to the Regents. He realizes that with presidents free to add to the agenda, there will be a lot of garbage to wade through, but this is obviously the price one pays for free opportunity to discuss the important questions. X is a real believer in "creative tension," and what he wants is the chance for everyone intimately concerned with the government of the Georgia institutions to fight out problems when that is necessary—including problems between the segments of the higher education community.

X's comments about having the presidents' council meet on its own raises a question that came up in other states: Should the executive director of the agency chair the meeting of the presidents? Ideally, a sensitive executive director would probably conduct the meeting with a light gavel, see that agenda papers were circulated properly, provide otherwise unavailable information for the discussions, and report faithfully to the agency the consensus of opinions which emerged. But since real situations rarely approximate this ideal, serious thought should be given to the possibility that the presidents' group would operate better with someone else as chairman or even with agency staff absent altogether. If this were done, greater freedom of discussion might result, although in some cases it could be more apparent than real: Some presidents in one state complained to us that their "candid comments" had a way of being leaked back to the executive director. Moreover, the expertise and statewide perspective of the central staff would be lacking. Yet another draw-back is that the original function of the group might be obscured, as in one state we visited, where some institutional presidents tried to turn the advisory council into a force to get rid of the executive director.

In cases where the executive director does not chair the meetings, our observations made it clear that no major university head should occupy the chair; pecking-order sensitivities are too strong to allow that. On the other hand, if the presidents' group is reduced in size to make discussions more meaningful, it is imperative that the presidents of major universities be included on it, no matter what other slots are rotated. To exclude them would be an invitation to turn the presidential advisory council into a paper organization, with the real consultation channels flowing informally elsewhere.

Technical Advisory Committees: Much of the institutions' partici-pation in the data-collecting activities of the coordinating agencies takes place below the level of the presidents, among the so-called technical advisory committees. These committees—usually composed of vice-presidents, deans, registrars, other administrative officers, and, less often, faculty members—may deal with types of educational programs (e.g., graduate programs, continuing education), aspects of agency and college operations (e.g., budget formulas, space utilization), statewide matters (e.g., transfer of credit), or, as in the Georgia system, areas of instruction (e.g., mathematics).

The advantages and disadvantages of technical advisory committees are similar to those of presidents' councils. These committees also per-form the down-to-earth function of helping to relieve the heavy workload of the agency staff. Moreover, they may benefit the entire operation of the coordinating agency by directly involving the institutions in data collection. Since the agency and the institutions often disagree on basic facts about the system, as well as on the conclusions to be drawn from them, institutional participation may smooth out such roughness con-siderably:

> If the data are derived cooperatively, . . . they tend to create a common ground for educational planning. Policy formation, based upon the same facts, is less subject to misunderstanding by the parties involved.[1]

1. Arthur Browne, "The Institution and the System: Autonomy and Coordination," *Long-Range Planning in Higher Education,* ed. Owen Knorr (Boulder, Colo.: Western Interstate Commission for Higher Education, 1965), p. 47.

If technical committees are to work well, they usually need staff assistance from the agency. In some states we visited, the committees, while looking impressive on paper, seldom met and had no separate secretariat. On the other hand, several members of one advisory committee on graduate programs told us that the group had begun to function effectively only after they had requested that the agency executive director not be present at their meetings. Apparently, his informal style of conducting the meetings—where no votes were taken and he himself interpreted the consensus—was unsatisfactory to the group. On its own, it developed an explicit set of ground rules, and most of the institutions seemed to react favorably to this change.

An interesting question arose in one state about whether technical advisory committees should confine themselves to collecting data and recommending policy or whether they should also recommend in the area of actual operations. In this instance, the advisory committee on continuing education had intervened in a controversy between the state land-grant university and a state college and had recommended in favor of the latter. Spokesmen for the state university later complained to us that the committee had misused its power, or rather that the executive director of the coordinating board had tried to stay free of the controversy by hiding behind the committee. Our view was that the committee had made an honest effort to evaluate the situation and that the more tough issues the academics tackle by themselves, the better. The final decision, of course, was made by the statewide agency, but it backed the advisory committee's recommendation and urged the committee to develop statewide policies that might keep these occasional squabbles to a minimum.

Agency Contacts with Trustees, Faculty, and Students: As the following discussion will indicate, few coordinating agencies now have many meaningful contacts with trustees, faculty, or students, chiefly because the agencies themselves seem relatively indifferent to that prospect. Even those staff members who are aware of the desirability of such contacts are too limited by the sheer weight of their workload to translate their awareness into action. A few executive directors stated that, in any case, their efforts to establish relationships with other institutional constituencies would be greatly hampered by the insistence of some presidents that they determine the mode and degree of consultation with the other groups. This insistence seems to be based partly on the concept of autonomy—a conviction that forces outside the institution should not have dealings with internal parties, except through the office of the president—and partly on the feeling that, in the interests of effective communications, the president's office should be aware of the flow of recommendations coming into and going out of the institution.

This lack of contact means that when the presidents are asked to give institutional responses to a proposed policy, the responses of some may reflect thoroughgoing internal consultations whereas those of others may represent nothing more than the reactions of the very top administrators. It also means that when the statewide agency seeks university persons other than administrators to serve on an advisory committee, some presidents may want to make the selections themselves. Of course, not all presidents will be of this mind; but if a few are intransigent on this point, and particularly if they happen to be the most powerful presidents, the coordinating agency will find it awkward to act against their wishes. Moreover, as we were told by two executive directors, occasionally a university president is not above trying to restrict direct agency contact with other institutional groups as much as possible so that he can depict the outside forces as villains when dealing with the inside, and vice versa. One frustrated agency executive said that when he left it to university and college presidents to transmit his explanation of statewide problems, it inevitably got filtered through heavy local interests.

Trustee Participation: The statute creating the Colorado all-lay coordinating board called for an advisory council that would include legislators and trustees. This stipulation may reflect the judgment of the director of the earlier voluntary system that trustee involvement is crucial to statewide planning and coordination:

> Proposals were made throughout the early organizing days of the Association [of State Institutions of Higher Education] to more directly involve the Board members. . . . There was considerable reluctance on the part of two or three of the institutions to have any direct involvement of the Boards in the work of the Association and the balance of the presidents bowed to the wishes of their colleagues in this respect. . . . At a time when Board participation on basic policy became extremely important, the long festering resentment of many Board members, stemming from what they felt was virtual exclusion from the work of the Association, could not be overcome.[2]

2. Harry S. Allen, "Voluntary Coordination of Higher Education in Colorado" (MS, Office of Institutional Research, University of Nebraska, 1967), pp. 51–53.

In some cases, contact between trustees and agencies is achieved by having trustees serve as institutional representatives. Here and there, trustees are included as individuals on technical advisory committees, but the closest that some agencies come to regular communication with trustees is to mail them the minutes of agency meetings, and not all of them even do this. Some agency directors recognized that this lack of contact made for some problems but claimed that they just had to rely on the institutional presidents to educate their respective boards to statewide problems. Judging from our conversations with trustees in several states, not all presidents undertook this task successfully.

Faculty Participation: Specialized faculty talents can be utilized through technical advisory committees; but most faculty members participate as experts rather than as spokesmen for the faculty point of view. Further, the appointment usually comes from above: It is made by the central agency—as with the Texas Coordinating Board, which used faculty in its master planning—or, more frequently, by institutional presidents. Under these conditions, real grass-roots faculty participation is negligible.

Much more meaningful but also extremely rare (Illinois is the only example known to us) is the practice of creating a statewide advisory committee composed of faculty chosen by the academic senates of the participating public and private institutions. This group is asked to react to major planning recommendations and, according to Glenny, former director of the Illinois Board of Higher Education, the faculty group has shown more imagination and less institutional rigidity than has the presidents' advisory group. The charge that institutional autonomies are violated by direct contacts between faculty and coordinating agency is without sound basis, since the agenda are confined to statewide issues, and intrainstitutional affairs are not discussed. Some Illinois observers note that getting faculty leaders out of the institutional environment and letting them see the state's dilemma in trying to meet unlimited demands and ambitions with limited resources has been a healthy development.

Some agency directors to whom we talked shied away from the thought of opening the Pandora's box of direct agency relations with faculties. Others were more favorable to the possibility but said that presidential antipathy to such contacts was strong; as with trustees, they just had to rely on the university and college presidents to educate their teaching staffs to statewide problems. Sometimes, however, confrontations seem unavoidable. For example, in California, where the agency has no official link with representatives of academic senates around the state, professional faculty organizations are being drawn into the picture over such explosive issues as faculty salaries and year-round operations of public campuses. In the final chapter, we will suggest that growing faculty militancy may force coordinating agencies to establish direct contacts with faculty either through academic senates or through professional associations.

Student Participation: The matter of present student participation in statewide coordination can be easily dealt with: Georgia is the only state in our survey which expressly created (in 1968) a statewide student council for formal liaison with the governing board. We heard some students in a few other states complain about statewide policies, but their views were expressed almost exclusively through institutional rather than statewide channels. In Florida, for example, several student body officers protested to the consolidated governing board about tuition increases, year-round operation policies, and compulsory ROTC, but there was no regular channel of communication. Although agitation for greater student power is still focused primarily on the local level, it may soon follow the power trail to the state capitals and ultimately seek some type of formal liaison with the statewide agencies.

Relations with State Government

If we grant that close agency relations with higher educational institutions are desirable in the interests of incorporating academic insights into agency policies and of soothing academic anxieties about agency procedures, a question arises: Should the agency seek also to establish close relations with state offices? Those answering in the affirmative argue that the agency, to be really effective, needs political insights to balance the academic ones and that it must reassure state officials of its credibility as a guardian of the public interest.

But can an agency gain these insights and this credibility without paying too high a price? Ideally, an agency would identify closely enough with each side to partake of the benefits but not so closely as to suffer the disadvantages. One coordinating board director described his agency as follows:

We are neither a direct agent for the governor or legislature, nor a front for colleges and universities. We take an independent position, much as would a federal regulatory agency. We gather facts and attempt to arrive at proposals rationally and objectively. We have no close friends, but we always have a defensible position.

However, our field work left us with the distinct impression that few agencies have in fact obtained such a position of equilibrium between higher education and state government, and that none has been able to maintain it for any length of time.

Lacking this balance, some agencies—particularly the consolidated governing boards, the voluntary associations, and the coordinating boards that have institutional majorities and advisory powers—tend to identify more closely with the institutions; others—particularly coordinating boards with all public members and regulatory powers—tend to identify more with the state government. Coordinating boards with mixed memberships and varying powers sometimes fall on one side of the line and sometimes on the other.

These facts have great bearing on various attitudes about what relationships between coordinating agencies and state governments are desirable. For example, persons who favor an agency that leans toward the institutions generally want to postpone the political inputs until agency recommendations are presented to state governments. Representative of this view is the following statement from a letter:

no agency which exercises substantial powers over higher education should be so constituted as to come under direct control of either the administrative or legislative branch of state government, or to invite direct involvement in the heat of a partisan political campaign.

Any board charged with responsibility for higher education ought to make its recommendations on the basis of its best judgment about the "needs" of higher education. It is the responsibility of the governor and the legislature to determine how these needs must be balanced against others. If the board, however, is dominated by or involves high officials of either the administrative or legislative branch of state government, it is placed in an almost impossible position. It must either on the one hand adjust its recommendations to what the governor and/ or the legislature wants, or on the other be identified as making recommendations under one "hat" and rejecting them [under] the other.

Those who feel that the agency should be more an organ of state government would regard this desire to keep the state at arm's length as highly unsatisfactory. At the very least, they point out, an agency must compete effectively with many other groups for public funds; at best, it should have the enthusiastic support of both the legislative and executive branches for all its many programs. But the agency will gain neither substantial appropriations nor enthusiastic support, they continue, if it fails to work closely with those in power, if it presents publicly a budget request that is politically unrealistic, and if it forces someone in state government to adopt the unpopular position of "negative realism." It would be far more constructive, then—the argument goes—to establish formal or informal links, or both, with persons in state government, to educate them early to the problems and needs of higher education and to receive from them advice about how to proceed effectively in the political world.

On this issue, as on so many others in the field of planning and coordination, there are good arguments on both sides. In chapter 11, we shall offer our brief judgments on the matter, bearing in mind that the specific relationships will, and perhaps should, differ markedly from state to state. In the remainder of this chapter, we shall review the various types of advisory relationships between agencies and persons in state government. We shall discuss also the special problems that arise in these relationships, particularly in the agency's dealings with the legislature and with the governor's office.

The question of whether a coordinating agency and the state government should have contacts with each other is, to some degree, meaningless. Obviously, they in fact do. For one thing, the state government is formally responsible for establishing the statutory agencies. Moreover, at their inception, all but four agencies[3] of the forty-eight had at least a majority of their members appointed by state government officials (usually, of course, the governor); and all agencies must, of necessity, end up by approaching the organs of state government for both funds and supporting legislation. Even if the government appointees serve for staggered terms and have a sturdy sense of independence, the moment of fiscal truth at the end of the process ensures that state governments will not be left out of the picture.

3. The two voluntary associations (Indiana and Nebraska) have no governmental appointees, and the two coordinating boards with institutional majorities (California and Minnesota) have only minority representation from gubernatorial appointees.

It is pertinent to recall also that, in four states, the governor himself or some legislators or both sit on the agency as members, and obviously the governmental voice can be heard loud and clear in agency deliberations. In other states, however, the agency must acquaint itself with governmental thinking, and state officials must be made to understand agency activities and recommendations, through the same three channels as are available for agency-institution contacts (though they are dealt with here in slightly different order):

1. Governmental personnel—from legislators and budget officers through committee research staff—may attend agency meetings to observe and, on occasion, to ask questions or express opinions;

2. Through specially created formal structures, state government personnel can be drawn together periodically to render collective advice and to hear agency explanations on given subjects; and

3. Persons in state government and agency staff members can make contact with one another informally and frequently, and the staff can incorporate governmental opinion in papers and in verbal reports to the agency.

Again, these alternatives are not mutually exclusive; states can and do use all three channels. And again, each of these types of contact presents certain problems which require further comment.

Attendance at agency meetings

This issue differs in many ways from the superficially analogous issue of having institutional personnel attend agency meetings. Short of going into executive session, an agency is in no position to suggest to persons from state government that their presence would be unwelcome; one does not bite the hand that feeds. In any case, laws have been passed in several states explicitly requiring that public bodies, such as coordinating agencies, have open meetings. Legislators and state budget officials were present at several of the meetings which we witnessed, the latter evidently to observe and the former obviously to pursue some constituent interest. Constituent interests are as likely to clash with statewide interests as are institutional ones; and there can be some awkward moments when a highly vocal legislator presses hard for some cherished project (e.g., creating a new institution, or changing the basic role of an existing one, in his district). Last-minute criticisms from state sources are even more distressing than those from the institutions, and they probably indicate a similar breakdown in earlier formal and informal contacts.

Formal structures for collective advice

To our knowledge, Colorado is the only state that has a formal advisory committee upon which legislators sit. This committee comprises two senators and two representatives, divided evenly by party, who, along with five institutional representatives, help to advise the seven-member, all-public coordinating board. Since Colorado was not included in our study, we can but pass on secondhand opinion that the advisory committee seems to be working well.

Most state legislatures, of course, have standing committees on education to which the coordinating agency can turn, if it so desires, to give or receive advice; but we found few of these committees adequately staffed to play a major role. In marked contrast is the practice of a few states whereby a joint legislative committee devoted exclusively to higher education is established and provided with competent help. These committees, which usually generate numerous reports and recommendations, may overlap and even conflict with established coordinating agencies. In California, for example, the Joint Legislative Committee on Higher Education bypassed the Coordinating Council and had its own staff, aided by a consulting firm, undertake a basic reexamination of the Master Plan. The Illinois General Assembly, reacting against the ability of its coordinating agency to overwhelm the legislature with facts and recommendations, passed a bill in 1967 to create a Legislative Commission of Higher Education, which was intended to aid the legislature in evaluating coordinating board proposals. In response to the coordinating board's request that a second channel not be created, the governor vetoed the bill, however, and the legislature ended up merely strengthening the staffing of its regular education committees.

In Washington, where the coordinating council created in 1969 included four legislators as nonvoting members, concern was expressed that "legislative overview would be usurped or subverted by the limited legislative participation."[4] A companion bill was therefore developed to establish a Joint Committee of Higher Education, and two legislators were

4. Washington Temporary Advisory Council on Public Higher Education, *Higher Education in Washington* (Olympia, 1969), p. 11.

made members of both the coordinating council and the joint committee to provide liaison between them. Time will tell if the two groups work successfully together.

Other agency contacts with state government

Most agency-government contacts occur outside the context of agency meetings or advisory committees, when agency members and staff meet with executive and legislative personnel in the normal course of seeking and giving information and advice.

Not surprisingly, financial matters seem to be a major topic of discourse when agency and state government meet. Twenty-eight out of thirty-two agencies responding to the Smart questionnaire reported that direct informal contacts were the rule between the state chief fiscal officer and the agency staff director.[5] Access to the governor himself varied more widely. In response to the question of how many times, over the first ten months of the year, the agency director had met with the governor to discuss matters of education, the thirty-two agencies gave the following information:

	Coordinating Board	Governing Board
Never	1	–
1–2 occasions	4	–
3–5 occasions	4	6
6–10 occasions	7	4
More than 11	6	–

Access to the governor is by no means automatic; in one state we heard that only the threat of mass resignations by members of the coordinating board could overcome the reluctance of a new governor's assistant to let them see the governor before the legislative session was over.

The pattern of agency-state executive contact varies with the size of the agency and of the state. In the smaller agencies, the executive director makes most of the contacts on his own, though frequently the chairman of the board accompanies him. In the larger agencies, and particularly in the larger states, more of the liaison work is conducted at the staff level. In North Carolina, for example, a member of the staff goes with the state Advisory Budget Commission on visits to the various institutions.

Agency personnel have widespread contact with legislators too; only one of the thirty-two agencies responding to the Smart questionnaire

5. Smart's questionnaire, though several years old, provides considerable factual data on agency contacts with state government.

indicated that its director, staff, or board members were seldom in touch with the legislature. Most agencies drew a sharp distinction between furnishing factual information, which they would do for any legislator who requested it, and actively lobbying for bills, which they would do only if the agency had formally taken a position on the issue.

When asked about the numbers of persons involved in legislative-executive liaison, the twenty-seven agencies responding to the Smart questionnaire reported as follows:

No. of Staff Who Participate	Coordinating Board	Governing Board
1	4	1
2	4	1
3	4	2
4	4	0
5-10	3	4

Problems in agency-state relations

If the potential dangers of too heavy an agency involvement with the institutions are inordinate delays and the reputation of being a holding company for the institutions, then the corollary dangers of excessive agency involvement with state offices are pressures for premature decisions, the reputation of being a whipcracker for the state, and the possibility of getting caught in the cross fire when state officials oppose one another. We will comment on each of these dangers in turn.

The state officials who create the coordinating agency usually do so in the interests of greater efficiency and economy and are therefore impatient to see results. In some quarters of state government, there is little appreciation of the more compelling and prior need for careful planning and of the crucial importance of involving the institutions in such planning, even at the cost of some delay; or of the possibility that the coordinating board may end by recommending that the state spend *more* funds on higher education in order to have a better system. Like any other state institution operating on public funds, a coordinating agency is very vulnerable to criticism at appropriations time; consequently, it will sometimes distort its own priorities and will make premature decisions in order to produce quick results.

If it does so very often, not only will its decisions be of poorer quality, but also it will lose the confidence of the institutions, whose cooperation (as explained in the first half of this chapter) is, in the long haul, essential for successful agency functioning. This cooperation cannot be coerced by an agency's cracking the whip for the state; academics belong to a stubborn tribe, difficult to lead under the best of circumstances. Therefore, an agency must be careful that, in carrying out its necessary liaison with the organs of state government, it does not irreparably damage its relations with the institutions.

The danger of the agency's getting caught in political cross fire is probably the greatest of all, although some agencies seem unaware of it. For instance, in many states (e.g., Georgia, Illinois, North Carolina, Ohio, Texas, Virginia), we were told that, over the past ten years, public higher education made its greatest advances when a strong governor managed to persuade the legislature and the public of the value of supporting higher education. But even if the coordinating agency can win the confidence of a vigorous and effective governor, it still has the prospect of being confronted later by a successor to that office who is less favorably disposed. An agency that becomes too closely identified with a given political personality or office may suffer when state politics shuffles the deck. It is no coincidence that incoming governors sometimes procure the right to appoint a whole new slate of coordinating agency members nor that several agency executive directors have resigned following the election of a new state governor.

Relations with the legislature

In two states included in our study, circumstances were such that the legislature played an unusually strong role in higher education. One was New Mexico, which had a long succession of one-term, two-year governors. In the absence of executive continuity, the legislature turned to the coordinating board for advice on higher education policies; and consequently, the board became more or less identified with the legislature. The second was North Carolina, the only state in the Union where the governor lacks veto power. At the time of our visit, the rebellious legislature was choosing to disregard the joint recommendation of the coordinating board and the governor that a regional universities bill not be passed. (In 1969, the governor and six powerful legislators were added to the coordinating board, but it is too early to tell whether this will lead to the governor's taking a stronger leadership role in higher education.)

In most cases, certain characteristics of the legislature preclude its forming close ties with the agency and thereby more or less force the agency to identify with the executive branch instead. For one thing, some legislatures are in formal session for only sixty days every two years, and even some of those that meet annually are restricted to a thirty-day budget session during the second year. As mentioned earlier, standing committees and interim committees, even if they do exist, are often poorly staffed, leaving busy legislators to oversee as best they can a huge range of state activities and proposed new programs. And the rapid turnover in legislators (accelerated in the 1960s by the effects of reapportionment in many states) add to the problem. Fairly typical was the complaint of a senior California senator that it is almost impossible to keep every new wave of solons educated to the nuances of problems in planning and coordinating higher education.

In addition to the structural arrangements that constitute a barrier between the agency and the legislature, there are, according to one recent study,[6] more basic reasons why legislators do not concern themselves more with higher education. First, public opinion has not seemed to demand detailed legislative oversight of higher education, except in the area of taxes going to higher education and student unrest, both of which will probably arouse even more public interest in the future. Second, given this freedom from public pressure, most legislators will not take the time to master the technical details of governing and coordinating a statewide system of higher education, being content to rely on their power of the purse for control. Finally, many recognize that the governor, with a statewide constituency and an executive staff operating continuously, is in a better position to foster relations between the state and higher education. Eulau and Quinley quote a New York assemblyman as saying:

> When you ask if I'm satisfied with the amount of control the Legislature has, I'm putting it in the frame of reference with a governor who is sensitive to the needs of higher education. If you had a governor who didn't have that sensitivity, who came in with budgets that were inadequate, and we raised them, and he vetoed them, under those circumstances then I would say we haven't enough control.[7]

Occasionally, relations are strained not so much by legislative reluctance to consider agency data and recommendations as by the agency's unwillingness to take a public stand on some controversial issue. In Okla-

6. Heinz Eulau and Harold Quinley, *State Officials and Higher Education* (New York: McGraw-Hill Book Co., 1970).
7. Ibid., p. 59.

homa, for example, Central State College, with powerful legislative backing, sought in 1967 to change its name to Central State University. Despite the pleas both of some legislators opposed to the bill and of others who were genuinely neutral and sought guidance on the issue, the board confined its response to quoting its definition of a university and refused to take a stand on the issue as such. The possibility of a gubernatorial veto may have influenced it to avoid an "unnecessary fight"; but we did hear some grumbling about the board's "default of its responsibilities."

We also came across some legislators in Pennsylvania who criticized their coordinating board for not taking a stronger leadership role on a bill to change Indiana State College to Indiana University. Our notes read as follows:

> X voted for the bill and is now ashamed of that vote. X thinks that the legislators are only now becoming aware of what they did, and that they will take a longer look at any similar bills for other state colleges. No one had thought it through, and X thinks it is up to the State Board to provide this kind of anticipatory thought.

The coordinating board took a stand against the bill, but it was a rather timorous one. A possible reason for its excessive caution is discussed in the following section.

Relations with the governor's office

In citing instances of gubernatorial actions which tended to strengthen or weaken the coordinating agencies in their states, it is not our purpose to debate the merits of the issues involved but to point out how the agency's relationship with the governor can influence the agency.

For example, we heard complaints from members of the Pennsylvania coordinating board (the Council of Higher Education of the State Board of Education) that the governor in office at the time of its creation had not really acted to enhance its prestige and authority. Apparently, he submitted an education budget, signed the bill giving university status to Indiana State College, and even appointed a Superintendent of Public Instruction without consulting the State Board.

In Florida, the old Board of Control (now the Board of Regents) suffered considerable embarrassment when a governor, indignant at not being consulted over the choice of a new president for the University of

Florida, threatened to withhold his signature from the man's paycheck; the name was subsequently withdrawn. Since the Florida structure lends itself readily to gubernatorial intervention in higher education,[8] it is no coincidence that we heard several reports there of gubernatorial maneuvers to obtain early resignations of board members and even wholesale changes in board membership.

As a final example of problems arising from gubernatorial actions, we cite the dilemma of the California coordinating board. An incoming governor wanted the state university to impose tuition fees. If the board had been consulted and had recommended against tuition fees, it would have found itself colliding head-on with the chief executive. If, on the other hand, the governor were to ignore the board (as, in fact, he did), its prestige was bound to suffer, since its very reason for being was to consider just such matters.

Frequently, gubernatorial actions reinforce the agency's role. In Virginia, for instance, where the coordinating board operates as a confidential advisory body to the governor, one recent occupant of the office made his support of the board clear in a variety of ways. He first asked the board to recommend to him just how a special $1 million enrichment fund for graduate programs should be distributed; he later transferred several state programs in higher education and their budgets from his office to the board; and he emphasized in numerous meetings with institutional officers that he would move on certain requested matters only after he had heard the advice of his coordinating board. As long as he remained in office, the board's position was fairly secure.

A similar sequence of events occurred in Texas. The governor created a citizens' commission on higher education which recommended a complete revamping of the coordinating system thus giving the governor a whole slate of appointments. He thereupon backed up the board not only financially but also by taking the politically delicate step of vetoing a bill to grant East Texas State University the right to grant the doctorate. (The coordinating board had asked the institution to terminate its doctoral programs.) But again, the governorship later changed hands, a critic of the coordinating board came to power, the executive director of the board resigned, and the future of the agency remains to be determined.

In Ohio, a member of the governor's staff pointed out to us that

8. The Board of Regents is ultimately responsible to the Board of Education, which is composed of the six elected statewide officers (who also constitute the cabinet, the Budget Commission, and other executive bodies).

public expenditures for higher education had increased dramatically as a direct result of the governor's selling higher education to the people; the governor would never, he added, have accepted this responsibility if he had not been assured that, through the coordinating board, he could inject his own ideas into the system. The earlier voluntary system, continued this observer, could never have elicited this much leadership from the governor because he would have no way of knowing whether the recommendations forthcoming were genuinely in the public interest or merely self-serving. Since the board is all public and has a strong executive director, the governor can be more certain on these points, and therefore he works hard to see the board's recommendations implemented. It should be pointed out that the governor in question had appointed the entire board and, in effect, chosen the executive director. It is speculated that, if his successor is of the same party, the board and the executive director may continue to prosper.

Agency relations with the governor are, then, a mixed bag. In one state, we were told that a good governor, sympathetic to higher education, was "worth all the studies and research in the world"; in another we heard the warning that a coordinating board "should not invest all its chips in one color": i.e., should not associate itself too closely with any one political personality. In chapter 11, we will discuss how future developments in state government practices may affect the functioning of coordinating boards.

PART THREE

PROBLEMS AND ISSUES

NINE

Private higher education and state governments

Except for some scattered programs and certain state scholarship plans, few state actions have been directly relevant to private higher education. In his assessment of statewide planning, Lewis B. Mayhew points out that while "lip service is usually given to the need for both public and private higher education, . . . the fundamental problems of private education, with few exceptions, are left untouched."[1] Recently, however, the push of several Federal programs that require public-private cooperation and the pull of increasing economic distress in some private institutions have combined to make state relations with private higher education an issue of emerging importance. This issue was the subject of a rapid succession of reports published in Illinois, Missouri, New York, and Texas, and of chapters in larger studies carried out in California and Washington. This chapter is essentially an overview based on these state studies and on relevant works by Allan Cartter, Richard Knoller, Fred Nelson, and William Valente.

Historical precedent

A historical fact not always appreciated is that during the colonial period and the first century or so of independence, most New England and Middle Atlantic states gave substantial subsidies to their so-called private institutions of higher education. Harvard, for example, had received over a half-million dollars and 46,000 acres of land by 1874. Yale, William and Mary, Dartmouth, Columbia, Williams, Bowdoin, Bates, Colby, Middlebury, Union, Hamilton, Rochester, and Cornell are just a few of the

1. *Long Range Planning for Higher Education* (Washington: Academy for Educational Development, 1969), pp. 154–55.

other institutions which received some form of public assistance during these periods.[2]

As the rest of the country was settled, however, the tradition of public higher education became stronger, augmented in no small measure by the Morrill Act of 1862. In addition, most state constitutions came to include prohibitions against state aid to sectarian institutions—a reflection of the increasing divisiveness of religious differences—and, in some cases, this prohibition was extended to all private institutions.

By the early 20th century, the private sector still enrolled over two-thirds of all college and university students, but the public sector's share had begun to increase slowly but steadily, rising to about 50 percent by the 1930s. After World War II, as a result of the GI Bill, the war baby "bulge," and the trend in demographic factors, college and university enrollments expanded considerably and were absorbed for the most part by the public sector (Table 7).

TABLE 7

PUBLIC AND PRIVATE COLLEGE AND UNIVERSITY ENROLLMENTS, 1940–70

YEAR	APPROXIMATE ENROLLMENTS	PRIVATE		PUBLIC	
		Number	Percentage	Number	Percentage
1940	1,500,000	700,000	47	800,000	53
1950	2,300,000	1,100,000	48	1,200,000	52
1960	3,600,000	1,500,000	42	2,100,000	58
1965	5,600,000	1,900,000	34	3,700,000	66
1970	7,600,000	2,100,000	28	5,500,000	72

Figures compiled by Nelson showed that in 1965 private institutions outnumbered public ones in thirty-three states but that private *enrollments* were larger in only five northeastern states: Connecticut, Massachusetts, New York, Pennsylvania, and Vermont. Projections of future enrollments invariably indicate that as the public community college expansion cuts more drastically into first-time freshman enrollments, the private sector's share will dwindle even further.

Figures for 1970, compiled by the U.S. Office of Education, showed that private institutions outnumbered public ones in twenty-nine states

2. Fred Nelson, "State Aid to Private Colleges and Universities" (MS, School of Education, Stanford University, 1969); Frank W. Blackmar, *The History of Federal and State Aid to Higher Education in the United States* (Washington: Bureau of Education, 1890).

but that private enrollments were larger in only two, Massachusetts and Pennsylvania.

Need for state aid

Cartter, a leading spokesman for the private sector,[3] has estimated that if present trends go unchecked, "only a handful of extremely well endowed private institutions will remain as viable quality institutions." He cites as evidence the growing gap between costs at public and private institutions, noting that "you cannot give away on one corner what you are trying to sell at near-cost further down the block." According to Cartter, the ratio of major college costs in private institutions to those in public institutions—which had remained remarkably stable at around 1.6:1 since 1928—changed in the last decade to 2:1 and threatens to climb to 2.5:1. This change is partly due to rapidly increasing costs in the private sector (attributable in some measure to the delayed escalation of academic salaries at approximately 7 percent annually), but more to the "artificial restriction" of price increases in the public sector because of the "emotional and political appeal of zero or low tuition in publicly supported institutions." Cartter offers Table 8 as evidence that cost increases in the public sector have not paralleled the rise in incomes and prices.

TABLE 8

INDEXES OF MAJOR COLLEGE COSTS AND INCOME, 1928–64

| YEAR | PUBLIC COSTS | | PRIVATE COSTS | PER CAPITA DISPOSABLE INCOME | AVERAGE FAMILY INCOME | |
	In-State	Out-of-State			Before Taxes	After Taxes
1928	100	100	100	100	100	100
1932	108	112	111	58	n.a.	n.a.
1936	102	112	109	77	73	72
1940	112	121	115	86	80	79
1948	152	170	159	193	187	171
1952	180	205	185	226	228	205
1956	200	233	218	260	265	240
1960	238	286	279	287	303	276
1964	268	333	346	336	356	322

SOURCE: Allan M. Cartter, "Some Financial Implications of an Enlarged Federal Student Aid Program" (MS, Chancellor's Office, New York University, 1969).

3. "The Responsibility of States for Private Colleges and Universities," *The Organization of Higher Education* (Proceedings of the Sixteenth Annual Legislative Work Conference, Southern Regional Education Board, White Sulphur Springs, W. Va., August 27–29, 1967).

Cartter points out that low tuition charges in effect subsidize many families that could afford to pay (or could borrow to pay) higher costs but do not really accomplish the ostensible goal of helping students from underprivileged families. Realistically, the disadvantaged student needs not only free or subsidized tuition and grants for transportation, food, and books, but also money to compensate partially for the income that his family must forego because he attends college rather than taking a job. Few public scholarship schemes offer anything approaching this kind of coverage, but more could, observes Cartter, if higher tuition rates were charged. This, in turn, would help private institutions to stay viable.

Reasons other than economic have been advanced to support the concept of state aid to the private sector. In Texas, for example, the Liaison Committee on Texas Private Colleges and Universities, asked by the coordinating board to study the future of private higher education in that state, not too surprisingly stated as its major premise:

> We believe in the value, viability and necessity of a dual system of higher education so that there can be freedom of choice, diversity, pluralism and maintenance of quality for both the public and private sectors.[4]

Other advocates of aid to private institutions have pointed out that, given our present concern over impersonal mass institutions and student alienation, the private colleges' freedom to remain small and intimate if they so desire takes on a special value. Still others stress the desirability of having at least some institutions operate from an explicit religious or ethical base in today's permissive society. Others emphasize that the private sector's greater freedom to experiment and innovate in curricular matters represents a gain to society. Finally, it is argued that the very existence of free private institutions can strengthen freedom in the public sector, for if oppression occurs in the latter, the best professors can leave for greener pastures.

Of course, not everyone agrees that state aid to private institutions is desirable. Some base their opposition on definitions of the separation of church and state that preclude the channeling of *any* public funds to church-related institutions. Others resist any move that would raise tuition charges in the public sector. Probably the largest group would state that they do not oppose state aid to private higher education in principle

4. *Pluralism and Partnership* (Austin: Coordinating Board, Texas College and University System, 1968).

but would endorse it only *after* the public sector has received "adequate" state support—which, by their interpretation, may well mean "never."

Recent state studies

Obviously, Cartter and the members of the Texas Liaison Committee are not disinterested when they urge state action to strengthen the private sector. Their views are to some extent reinforced, however, by the reports of two state committees, both composed of out-of-state educators, from public as well as from private institutions. The New York (Bundy) and Illinois (McConnell) Commissions seemed to agree that

> the value to society of strong private institutions of higher learning is clear and great . . . any deterioration in the established quality of these private institutions—whether in terms of faculty, curriculum, academic standards or physical plant—would be harmful not only to the institutions themselves but also to the public good.[5]

and that

> [state] assistance can be given without endangering in any way the financial support and educational development of the public institutions.[6]

In addition, both studies found "evidence of serious need, but not of impending catastrophe," and they concluded that "a combination of improved management, strong private support, and a modest amount of public aid should assure their vigorous health for the foreseeable future."[7] Both praised existing state scholarship plans but suggested that aid be given directly to institutions on the grounds that "aid *via* the student turns out essentially to be aid *to* the student."

The Bundy Commission urged direct institutional grants, apportioned on the basis of degrees awarded, and suggested a ratio of B.A. and M.A.:n ($400) and Ph.D.:6n ($2,400). The McConnell Commis-

5. New York Select Commission on the Future of Private and Independent Higher Education in New York State [Bundy Commission], *New York State and Private Higher Education* (Albany: State Education Department, 1968), p. 13.
6. Illinois Commission to Study Non-Public Higher Education in Illinois [McConnell Commission], *Strengthening Private Higher Education in Illinois* (Springfield, 1969), p. 46.
7. *New York State and Private Higher Education*, p. 15.

sion recommended a $500 grant for each state scholarship recipient enrolled, $100 for all other full-time-equivalent freshmen and sophomores, and $200 for all other full-time-equivalent juniors and seniors. In each case, the recommended state subsidies would amount to about 5 percent of the current operating expenditures. The institutions were urged to pay careful attention to problems of deferred maintenance in their capital plant and, especially in Illinois, to the need for improving libraries and increasing faculty salaries. Both reports also emphasized that, in the interests of avoiding parochialism and homogeneous student bodies, *all* students, in-state and out-of-state, should be counted for purposes of computing state aid. Pointing out that the state "exported" more students to other states than it received from them, each commission advised a policy of national leadership in encouraging reciprocity between states.

Although both studies in effect validated Cartter's basic justification of state aid to private institutions, neither was prepared to accept his rather large estimates of the savings that would accrue from subsidizing the expansion of private institutions rather than taking them over as in Houston, Youngstown, Akron, Toledo, Cincinnati, Louisville, Omaha, Wichita, Kansas City, and several other cities.[8] Regarding the state takeover of the University of Buffalo, the Bundy Commission said,

> This case . . . is frequently cited as an instance in which the state could have preserved a private institution by supplying a few million dollars annually, while instead, by incorporating it into the State University system, the burden on the public purse was unnecessarily magnified. Our study of the situation . . . has led us to conclude that the quality of that institution has been markedly improved by its new public status; that only infusions on the scale applied by the State University could have brought it to its present level; that if public funds of that magnitude had been injected into a private institution its ability to continue to attract private support would probably have sharply diminished; and that independence of operation would probably have been impossible given such a scale of public aid. In other words, there are conditions under which acquisition by a public institution is preferable to continued private operation, and Buffalo is such a case.[9]

8. "The Responsibility of States for Private Colleges and Universities," p. 5.
9. *New York State and Private Higher Education*, p. 53.

The McConnell Commission observed:

The argument is often heard . . . that enrollments can be increased substantially at private institutions if financed by public
subsidies for facilities and operating budgets, and that such subsidies would be smaller than the cost of expanding public institutions or developing new ones . . . [it] is not easy to develop
unit costs information which will permit precise comparisons
among different types of institutions. . . . It is sufficient to suggest, however, that the public sector's costs are no higher than,
and may be somewhat below, the costs in the private sector.[10]

Church-related institutions

Both the Bundy and the McConnell Commissions rejected the concept
of giving state aid to institutions "whose central purpose is the teaching
of religious belief," but both also cautioned against assuming that
"church relationship or affiliation in and of itself should preclude state
assistance, since such relationship need not per se involve or presuppose
a sectarian purpose." In addition, they endorsed the relatively loose interpretation of separation of church and state which has emerged with
respect to the First Amendment of the U.S. Constitution and urged that
it be adopted as the state guideline (a step which would, in New York,
necessitate an amendment to the state constitution, which the New York
Commission favors).

In higher education, the issue of church-state relations is perhaps
less charged with volatile public emotion than it is in elementary and
secondary education, but it suffers from a lack of judicial guidelines.[11]
Although a test case from Connecticut is finally making its way through
the appeals channels, there have been as yet no Federal cases involving
national programs in higher education; thus the practice has been to
extrapolate from the "child benefit" criteria of the *Everson* case for lower
education and to assume that most programs in higher education that
have as their primary purpose something other than the advancement of
religious instruction as such are acceptable. In 1966, however, a Maryland
court, after hearing the *Horace Mann League* case, decided that the de-

10. *Strengthening Private Higher Education in Illinois*, pp. 41–42.
11. Ann Van Wynen Thomas and A. J. Thomas, Jr., *Constitutionality of Aid by the
State of Texas to Church-Related Institutions of Higher Education* (Austin: Coordinating Board, Texas College and University System, 1969).

gree of religiosity of the recipient colleges should be the major determinant of constitutionality. Thus, only one of four church-related colleges was judged sufficiently nonsectarian to qualify for state grants for the construction of dormitories, cafeterias, and science buildings. Since the U.S. Supreme Court did not grant certiorari to review the *Horace Mann League* case, it is still uncertain which will ultimately be the main criterion of constitutionality: the primary purpose of the aid in question or the religiosity of the recipient institutions.

The Bundy and McConnell Commissions suggested that the coordinating agency in the state undertake an examination to determine the institutions eligible for state aid; each anticipated that the recommended programs would fall well within whichever of the Federal guidelines is ultimately established.

According to William D. Valente, a Villanova law professor who analyzed the situation in Pennsylvania, if there is a political will to render state aid to private higher education, sophisticated constitutional lawyers can find many ways of arranging for state funds to go even to church-related institutions. Although Valente's major purpose is to argue the merits of state nontax aid via a building authority for facilities assistance, he theorizes:

> [If state tax] funds are raised by special statutory collections under an act which dedicates such collections to a special purpose fund, without passing through the state treasury, then such revenues, if expended for a primary secular purpose, even at church-related institutions, with restriction against the use of such facilities for religious activities or sectarian purposes, would not be [unconstitutional] under the prevailing Pennsylvania decisions.[12]

A study for the state of Washington by a consulting firm suggested another answer to the problem of the constitutionality of state aid to church-related institutions: the restructuring of such institutions into public and private components. Under such an arrangement, the governing board would be composed predominantly of laymen, and all but a few (e.g., religion, philosophy) departments would become secularized and state supported. The part played directly by the church and its

12. *An Analysis of the Proposed Master Plan for Higher Education for the Commonwealth of Pennsylvania* (Villanova, Pa.: Villanova University, 1967), p. 18.

members would be limited to minority membership on the governing board and control over the sectarian academic departments.[13]

Types of state aid

In considering the Bundy and McConnell recommendations and the practices and proposals of other states,[14] one should not overlook the most basic of all state aids to private higher education: tax exemption. John Dale Russell has estimated that exemption from property taxes is equal to approximately 15 percent of the total current income of private institutions.[15] Since the revenue forgone must obviously be made up by higher rates for the taxpayers, the gesture is not insignificant.

Direct Grants: As noted earlier, the practice of giving direct grants to private institutions was widespread in the early colonial and post-Revolutionary days. In recent years, Pennsylvania has given more public funds to a wider variety of private institutions than any other state. In fact, it has never founded a "state university," preferring instead to grant heavy subsidies to Pennsylvania State University (a private university designated as the land-grant institution). State grants went also to a number of other institutions—including the University of Pennsylvania (also private) and many denominational colleges—until 1921, when a state court decision blocked direct aid to church-related institutions. In the 1960s, Pittsburgh and Temple Universities joined Penn State as "state-related" institutions, receiving, for example, $25 million in 1967-68 in exchange for holding down tuition charges to Pennsylvania residents. The Master Plan of 1965 suggested the rationalization of state aid to other institutions by creating a "state-aided" category which would allow for a $5,000-per-doctoral-student subsidy.

Facilities Assistance: Maryland has long aided its private institutions by giving financial assistance for the construction of facilities, the only requirements being that the recipient colleges match the construction grants dollar for dollar and that they indicate in advance for what (secu-

13. Washington Temporary Advisory Council on Public Higher Education, *Higher Education in Washington* (Olympia, 1969), chapter 2.
14. Our discussion here makes no pretense of being comprehensive. For a detailed report on various programs relevant to higher education in thirty-six states, see the appendix of the Missouri report: Alan Pfnister and Gary Quehl, *Private Higher Education in the State of Missouri* (Jefferson City: Missouri Commission on Higher Education, 1967).
15. "The Finance of Higher Education," *Partnership for Higher Education*, eds. R. H. Kroepsch and D. P. Buck (Boulder, Colo.: Western Interstate Commission for Higher Education, 1967), p. 13.

lar) purpose the money is to be used. In 1965, some $6 million was appropriated for this program. The *Horace Mann League* decision has now restricted this assistance to those institutions judged to be at least de facto nonsectarian.

Probably the best known form of facilities assistance is that given by the New York Dormitory Authority, which (despite its name) finances all types of capital facilities in both public and private institutions. The Authority issues long-term, tax-exempt bonds to finance buildings and then leases them to private institutions, which must have pledged tuition revenues as guarantees of payment. The Illinois Commission recommended that this model be followed but stipulated that, to avoid excessive commitment of tuition revenues, institutions should be required to furnish one-third of the projected costs from their own funds or from Federal grants. In 1967, Pennsylvania passed a similar law, and it exists also (with some variations) in New Jersey and Connecticut.

Contractual Relations: Lacking a land-grant university, the state of New York contracted with Cornell to provide higher education in agriculture, industrial and labor relations, home economics, and veterinary medicine. A public administration program offered jointly by Syracuse and New York University is also administered under state contract, as is a school of forestry at Syracuse and a school of ceramics at Alfred University. Cartter cites a more recent New York experience:

> Faced with the alternative of beginning another new college of medicine, which would take perhaps five years to become operational, nearly ten years to begin granting degrees, and perhaps 20 years to become well established, the state offered to subsidize expansion at eight existing private institutions. . . . Each of these schools will expand their entering classes, receiving $6,000 per additional student annually plus some capital funds for facilities, and within four years a distinguished class of graduates will emerge. The cost to the state was less than the cost of new medical facilities of their own, and in effect, this program created a new "instant medical school."[16]

Since 1962, Florida has contracted to pay the University of Miami a per-student subsidy for state residents enrolled in the medical school. By 1967, the subsidy was $4,500 per student, and the university was re-

16. "The Responsibility of States for Private Colleges and Universities," p. 5.

ceiving over $1 million annually. Alabama has contracted with Tuskegee Institute for a wide variety of services, and New Jersey has entered into an agreement with the Newark College of Engineering. The Illinois Commission recommended a state appropriation of $1 million to contract with private institutions, individually or in consortia, for such special services as programs for disadvantaged youth, including counseling and tutoring.

Intrastate and Interstate Associations: One may safely predict that increasing cooperation among institutions—public-public, private-private, public-private; both intrastate and interstate—will be a dominant theme of the 1970s. Such arrangements not only will permit more effective educational planning but also may offer a solution to the thorny problems connected with constitutionality of direct state aid to denominational institutions. For example, if state funds were to be given to a Kansas City Regional Council for Higher Education (fourteen institutions, both public and private), a North Carolina Learning Institute (University of North Carolina, Duke University, the State Board of Education, and the North Carolina Fund), a Connecticut Research Commission, and a Southern Regional Education Board, and if such funds were subsequently distributed to a variety of public and private institutions, some legal objections might be overcome.

Quite apart from considerations of law, the formation of consortia is widely encouraged as desirable in itself. The McConnell Commission, for example, suggested that a modest amount of state "seed money" ($400,000 per year) be used to stimulate cooperation in such areas as academic programs, business procedures, library coordination, and the use of specialized facilities such as computer installations, audiovisual services, and educational television facilities.[17]

The Texas Liaison Committee stressed strongly the desirability of developing cooperative arrangements among public and private institutions in various regions of the state and, in a detailed analysis of the North Central Texas area, indicated some of the possibilities for such cooperation. In California and Ohio, there was some discussion of adopting a regional pattern for the system of governance for public colleges and universities to facilitate collaboration across institutional boundaries. Even if the formal system of governance was not altered, state grants to regional associations would make it possible to promote interinstitutional

17. *Strengthening Private Higher Education in Illinois*, p. 54.

cooperation and to include the private sector as well. At the interstate level, as an example, private institutions in five southern states received $680,000 from state governments through Southern Regional Education Board contracts in 1964–65, and these grants evidently raised no constitutional problems.

Management Advisory Service: Both the Bundy and McConnell Commissions were struck by the inadequacy of management practices in many private institutions with respect to such matters as financial and accounting procedures, portfolio management, academic planning, physical plant and maintenance, space utilization, allocation of general administrative overheads to auxiliary enterprises (e.g., dormitories, food services, bookstores, athletic programs), and purchasing procedures. Consequently, the McConnell Commission recommended a state appropriation of $200,000 to make professional consulting services available to smaller institutions, with the expectation that savings far greater than that amount would result.

Income Tax Credit: In at least one state, Indiana, provision is made for allowing a tax credit (not a deduction, but a credit from the final amount due) for contributions to institutions of higher education, public and private. Half the amount donated (up to a maximum of $50 for individuals and $500 for corporations) can be claimed. The California report [18] recommended that the state permit a tax credit for donations to private higher education.

State Scholarships: The term *state scholarships* is used here to mean state funds awarded to students on the basis of academic excellence, although the amounts given may vary according to the recipients' financial need. The Missouri report survey indicated that at least twenty-two states have scholarship programs of one sort or another, and that ten of these were initiated during the past decade.[19] Under such programs, the award is given to the student rather than to the institution and the student may attend the college of his choice, public or private. (In all but five states, he must stay within the state.) Since the awards, which usually range up to $1,000, are restricted in all but six cases to payment of tuition and fees, they tend to be applied at private institutions where these charges are higher. No constitutional problems have arisen over using these awards

18. California Staff of the Joint Legislative Committee on Higher Education, *The Challenge of Achievement* (Staff report to the Committee. Sacramento, 1969).
19. Pfnister and Quehl, *Private Higher Education in the State of Missouri.*

at church-related colleges. New York, the state with the largest program, awarded some 20,000 Regents' Scholarships in 1965–66.

Scholar Incentive Awards: In addition, New York and Illinois offer grants of up to $800 and $1,000 respectively, awarded purely on the basis of need. In 1965–66, some 154,000 students were aided through the New York program.

Tuition Equalization Grants: A few other states (Michigan, New Jersey, and Wisconsin, to our knowledge) have stopped short of scholar incentive awards to *all* students able to demonstrate financial need but do offer grants of up to $500 to help those attending private institutions pay the higher tuition charges involved. The California report recommended that some variation of a tuition equalization grant be instituted and that the state constitution be amended, if necessary, to overcome a prohibition against state aid to any institution "not under the exclusive management and control of the State as a state institution."

Special Awards: Many states offer other special types of student awards: to persons preparing for careers in teaching or medicine, to the disadvantaged, etc. These awards can usually be used at private as well as public institutions.

Loans: Finally, some states (e.g., New Jersey, New Mexico, Texas) supplement Federal student loan programs with state loans which can be used at either public or private colleges.

Institutional accountability

The question of what conditions are attached to state aid is a sensitive one, since it is fear of governmental encroachment on institutional autonomy which makes some spokesmen for the private sector hostile to either Federal or state aid. But, clearly, public monies cannot be granted without some regard for protection of the public interest. So the real question becomes: What constitutes adequate protection of that interest?

The Bundy and McConnell Commissions recommended that all recipient institutions render regular and full financial reports, including a certified audit, and provide evidence of sound management. They suggested that aid should go only to colleges and universities that are nondiscriminatory (racially and religiously) with respect to both faculty and students. They urge participation in statewide planning. Finally, each commission stresses adherence to standards of quality and proposes a way to check on it:

State aid should be available only for the support of education which is at least equal in quality to that provided in the public institutions of the state. The Regents should require of institutions receiving state aid an adherence to standards higher than those currently required for holding charters. . . . Public funds must not be used to sustain at a subsistence level institutions which would better be dissolved or merged.[20]

. . . after five years . . . an outside board of evaluators [should] be appointed and charged with the responsibility of studying what has been accomplished in improving and upgrading the institutions as a consequence of the investment of public funds. . . .
. . . a set of criteria [should] be devised for appraising the purposes to which the State's subventions have been put. . . . [e.g.,] strengthening of faculty; enrollment of disadvantaged youth; improved management practices; . . . success in securing increased private gifts. . . . State funds used only or in large part to expand enrollments or to proliferate programs [should] be deemed not to have been expended judiciously.[21] (Order transposed.)

Both the study by the Texas Liaison Committee and the Washington study suggested that regional accreditation be the minimum qualification for eligibility to receive state funds. But some groups in the public sector would demand considerably more stringent conditions. The American Association of State Colleges and Universities, for example, has urged that, in addition to the standards of fiscal accountability and nondiscrimination already discussed, private institutions receiving state funds should be subject to the same criteria concerning space utilization and faculty-student ratios as apply to the public sector.[22]

In Pennsylvania, commonwealth funds are awarded to the state-related universities in exchange for a substantial reduction in the tuition charged to state residents and for the appointment by the state of one-third of their trustees. At the state-aided University of Pennsylvania, concern was expressed about the possibility that some control over tuition

20. Bundy Commission, *New York State and Private Higher Education*, p. 52.
21. McConnell Commission, *Strengthening Private Higher Education in Illinois*, p. 60.
22. Reported in *Chronicle of Higher Education*, November 25, 1968.

levels, or over percentage of in-state enrollments, would be extended to their category, which is currently subsidized on a more permissive basis.

Politics and state aid

Separation of church and state is the issue that generates the most intense political feeling with respect to state aid to private institutions. Because the situation in higher education is inevitably linked to the more explosive one in the elementary and secondary schools (where attendance is compulsory and younger minds are more vulnerable to "indoctrination"), it suffers from guilt by association. Yet the Bundy Commission, at least, argued that the state of affairs in higher education is qualitatively different, that private colleges and universities—"if they are good—serve the public interest in a wider and deeper way than most private elementary and secondary schools." Furthermore, continued the commission, most church-related institutions, particularly Catholic ones, are now undergoing an evolutionary process which may parallel that experienced by Harvard, Columbia, and Cornell, all of which started life as explicitly Christian institutions and became secular over time. On the basis of this reasoning, the Bundy Commission concluded that "in its application to higher education the state Constitution should be amended," [23] but a revision of the state constitution, which cut out the restrictive Blaine Amendment (applying to church-related education at all levels), has since been defeated by the voters of New York. This outcome, plus intense struggles in other states (e.g., Ohio) over so-called fair busing (for elementary and secondary education) and over tuition equalization grants, indicates that the church-state issue is still divisive.

Another possible danger is outright conflict between the public and private sectors over access to limited financial resources. The traditional "peace formula"—that public institutions get public money and private institutions seek private funds—has been inaccurate for some time; many public universities go far beyond their alumni in tapping private sources of wealth, and many private universities and colleges get significant sums of public money from the Federal government. Notwithstanding this fact, Knoller found several persons whom he interviewed on the issue to be distinctly uneasy about a further blurring of the boundaries.[24] By put-

23. *New York State and Private Higher Education*, p. 52.
24. "An Overview of Issues and Ideas Relating to State Aid to Non-Public Institutions of Higher Education" (MS, Office of Institutional Studies, University of Vermont, 1969).

ting state aid on a grant-formula basis, the Bundy Commission hoped to make it "evident to college administrators that no individual advantage is to be gained from direct appeals to the legislature," and thus to minimize the likelihood of an open battle over state appropriations to higher education.

In the South, the issue of racial integration in the schools introduces further political complications. The provision in some states of grants-in-aid that allow parents to send their children to segregated private schools has, in the words of one private college administrator, "muddied the moral waters of a state scholarship scheme."

Finally, the observations of one state executive officer, harassed by questions of state aid to private higher education, bear repeating:

> X preferred state subsidies for buildings to those for operations. For the latter you have to go back to the legislature every two years; for buildings, you don't. They're permanent; they're visible; they may even be beautiful. For tuition equalization grants which would go mainly to church-related schools, there would be a host of questions such as: which students are chosen and how are they chosen (angry disappointed parents!); what are they studying (something useful?); do they engage in panty raids or Communist front activities? etc. etc. The whole question of helping the student is a very emotional one, particularly when religion is involved.

Role of the coordinating agency

Scrutiny of the relevant reports from California, Illinois, Missouri, New York, Texas, and Washington makes it obvious that coordinating agencies will come to play a central role in most state programs relating to private higher education. The very first recommendation of the Bundy Commission, for example, was that the coordinating effectiveness of the Board of Regents and its staff in the Department of Education be strengthened substantially and that the regents then assume the major role in evaluating institutional eligibility for state aid, in promoting interinstitutional cooperation, in making contracts with private institutions for state services, and—most important—in undertaking the overall master planning of both the public and the private sectors.[25]

25. *New York State and Private Higher Education*, pp. 42–45.

The McConnell Commission praised the coordinating board for its past efforts to involve private institutions in master planning and, for future programs, gave it a broad charge similar to that given to the New York board.

The Texas Liaison Committee was even more emphatic: "We believe the role of the Coordinating Board . . . is absolutely central and crucial for the future and development of all higher education—public and private." [26] The board was asked to examine carefully two items which will probably be on the public-private agenda in many states: the location of new public institutions, especially low-cost community colleges, in areas where private colleges already exist; and the effect of salary increases in the public sector upon the private institutions (an issue which has already caused friction in California).

The Bundy Commission and the Texas Liaison Committee recommended that the association of independent colleges in the state act as the formal spokesman for the private sector and, in that capacity, take far more energetic steps in planning and coordinating. Such associations now exist in over twenty-three states, and many are for the first time recruiting aggressive leaders, acquiring adequate operating funds, and initiating vigorous programs. Representatives from private institutions already sit on eight coordinating boards, as was indicated in chapter 2, Table 1. In several states (e.g., Texas and Illinois), a committee from the private sector has been established to advise the board; and more such advisory committees will undoubtedly be formed if state programs for private institutions increase.

To the question of whether any particular type of coordinating agency is more effective than others in guiding state programs for private institutions, no answer is possible at this stage. From certain perspectives, one might speculate that the coordinating board would be superior to the consolidated governing board, since it seems likely that private institutions, nervous at becoming linked more closely with the state government, would prefer the looser coordinating board arrangement to the consolidated governing board with its emphasis (at least until now) on administration. In two states with governing boards, Georgia and Oregon, there have been created loose planning agencies with jurisdiction over both the consolidated governing boards and the state boards of education, and these agencies may facilitate the integration of private sector planning and development.

26. *Pluralism and Partnership*, p. 84.

But such speculation must defer to the hard facts about present experience. According to the Cox and Harrell study of Federal programs, private-sector spokesmen in states with governing boards seem as ready as those in states with coordinating boards to give the central agency a stronger role in administering those Federal programs that are channeled through the state government.[27] If so, then the type of coordinating agency may be irrelevant to the purpose of setting up acceptable policies and initiating efficient practices with respect to state aid to private institutions.

27. Lanier Cox and Lester E. Harrell, Jr., *The Impact of Federal Programs on State Planning and Coordination of Higher Education* (Atlanta: Southern Regional Education Board, 1969).

TEN

Other problems in statewide coordination

This chapter touches briefly on several other problems which we did not ourselves investigate but which deserve some mention. They are: (1) the impact of Federal programs on statewide coordination and planning; (2) relations between higher education and the public schools; and (3) institutional accreditation and statewide coordination.

The Impact of Federal Programs

Up until World War II, the Federal government's interest in higher education was expressed mainly through the Morrill Land-Grant Act of 1862 and various acts dealing with agricultural research, and the rural extension movement. But the postwar years saw a succession of Federal programs which, taken together, had a considerable impact: They include, among others, the Atomic Energy Commission, the GI Bill, the National Science Foundation, and the National Defense Education Act. In all these programs, the Federal government dealt directly with the individual institutions, faculty members, or students. The Higher Education Facilities Act of 1963 introduced a new pattern: In certain cases, agencies of the state were given responsibility for administering parts of the programs. The question that concerns us is how such state-administered Federal programs affect statewide coordination and planning.

Cox and Harrell studied this matter for the Southern Regional Education Board, and the following observations are taken almost entirely from their very thorough report.[1] By means of interviews in eleven states and questionnaires in all fifty, these investigators examined the reactions

1. Lanier Cox and Lester E. Harrell, Jr., *The Impact of Federal Programs on State Planning and Coordination of Higher Education* (Atlanta: Southern Regional Education Board, 1969).

of three different categories of respondents—governors, state agencies administering Federal programs in higher education, and presidents of both public and private institutions—to three major issues:

1. The impact on coordination and planning of present Federal programs, both those administered by state agencies and those handled directly by the Federal government;

2. The possible effects of consolidating some or all state-administered programs into one state agency; or of converting some of the directly administered Federal programs to state-coordinated ones under the coordinating agency; and

3. The desirability of several new proposed Federal programs' in higher education.

Present Federal programs

The four higher education programs currently being administered by one or more state agencies are: Title I of the Higher Education Facilities Act of 1963 (HEFA), which pertains to undergraduate facilities; Title IVᴀ of the Higher Education Act of 1965 (HEA), which pertains to equipment grants for the improvement of undergraduate instruction; Title I of the 1965 HEA, which pertains to community service and continuing education programs; and the State Technical Services Act of 1965, which pertains to technical services to industry and commerce.

The state is required to designate an agency that will administer each program. In the case of the undergraduate facilities and equipment programs, the agency chosen must be representative of all the institutions of higher education, public and private, within the state. Thus, in all fifty states, the same agency administers the two programs; but in only twenty of the forty-six states with statutory coordinating agencies have these agencies been the ones designated for this responsibility. In only sixteen states do they administer the community service program, and in only five, the technical service program. Only in Ohio and Texas do the coordinating agencies administer all four Federal programs.

The majority of all three groups of respondents—the governors, the administering agencies, and the institutional presidents—expressed general satisfaction with the present operation. In cases where coordinating agencies (especially coordinating boards) were charged with administering one or more of the Federal programs, they named the following benefits as resulting from such programs:

—provided the opportunity to integrate state programs and goals with federal programs and goals;

—provided some specific bases for role assignment through the necessity for deciding priorities;

—aided and focused on planning programs for facilities and program development;

—complemented their existing functions and activities and provided added importance to these activities;

—brought about closer involvement of the private institutions and made the agency more acceptable to them by the help it provides;

—resulted in participation of all public and private institutions in statewide planning; and

—provided additional staff for planning and coordination.[2]

The governors and the administering state agencies were asked whether comparable programs going directly from the Federal government to the state (e.g., Titles II and III, HEFA 1963, pertaining, respectively, to graduate facilities and to facilities loans) were adversely affecting the state's coordinating activities. Most of the governors and most of the consolidated governing boards said that undesirable effects were few; but some of the governors and most of the coordinating boards said that, to some extent, direct Federal programs made state planning and coordination more difficult; they named three problem areas:

—the existence of substantial funds in the hands of institutions for which they are not directly accountable to state government;

—institutional initiation of programs which commit the state to provide matching funds, or to maintain with state funds increased support levels established by federal funds; and

—federal support of institutions' programs or facilities which may not be consistent with state planning.[3]

Consolidation and conversion of Federal programs

The term *consolidation* is used here to mean the combining of three or four state-administered Federal programs under the authority of the

2. Ibid., pp. 171–72.
3. Ibid., p. 170.

state coordinating agency; *conversion* denotes the transfer of some direct Federal programs to state administration under the supervision of the state coordinating agency.

According to Cox and Harrell, consolidation as an issue provoked a wide variety of responses.[4] A majority of coordinating boards and governors favored it; consolidated governing boards were relatively indifferent; and the specialized agencies and institutions that administer some of the Federal programs were understandably opposed to it, since it would mean an end to their role. An "appreciable number" of institutional presidents had no particular feelings on the matter one way or the other; but of those expressing opinions, a slight majority opposed consolidation. Broken down further:

> The presidents in governing board states, especially the private institution presidents, either generally favor consolidation or are not opposed to it. In contrast, the presidents in coordinating board states generally oppose the concentration of administrative responsibility for the four programs in that agency.[5]

The three groups of respondents were reluctant to commit themselves on the issue of whether some programs currently administered directly by the Federal government should be converted to state-administered programs. The opinions that *were* expressed were divided along the same lines as those drawn on the consolidation issue, except that some institutional presidents expressed stronger negative reactions.

> —most state governors favored the extension of state coordination of federal aid to other programs but several mentioned the need to create adequate safeguards for the interests of the private institutions.
> —of the *minority* of statewide governing and coordinating boards which took definite positions, almost all believed that state planning and coordination would be enhanced by state administration of one or more of the following presently "direct" programs: graduate facilities; facility loans; nonsponsored research; library improvement grants; and the developing institutions programs.
> —only 60% of the institutional presidents expressed an opinion on this issue, but a substantial majority of this number was nega-

4. Ibid., p. 172.
5. Ibid., p. 173.

tive. More private than public presidents took positions, and their percentage of negative opinions was higher.[6]

On some issues, an institution's doctorate-granting status seemed a more significant factor in its response than did its public or private status. For example, a majority of presidents of both public and private institutions without doctoral programs favored state coordination of the graduate facilities program; but in the case of doctorate-granting institutions, a majority of the presidents of public universities and 90 percent of the presidents of private universities opposed the idea. Among the arguments offered in opposition were:

—graduate education is regional and national in nature and should be evaluated and supported at the national level;

—greater sophistication in evaluating graduate needs exists in Washington;

—criteria for decisions on graduate facilities should be completely different from the purely objective criteria used in the undergraduate facilities program;

—out-of-state judgments are needed to avoid political decisions on expansion of in-state graduate programs;

—the limited number of graduate institutions in many states makes state administration unnecessary; and

—the limited funds under the . . . program would be ineffectively utilized if allocated on a state basis.[7]

Along still another line of analysis, Cox and Harrell found that, in general, presidents in governing board states were more favorable to both consolidation and conversion than were presidents in coordinating board states. The explanation is not too difficult to find. With few exceptions, the consolidated governing boards have been in existence for thirty years or more. Many "were established in times of relative educational tranquility and their relationships with the institutions and the state were fully developed prior to the era of academic turbulence following World War II." Their governing power over the institutions is direct and complete, and their image is definitely tied to higher education rather than to the state. In contrast, most coordinating boards were established during the past fifteen years, when change was rampant; their authority ranges from purely advisory to heavily regulatory and their image varies accord-

6. Ibid., p. 177.
7. Ibid., p. 176.

ingly from lobbyist for higher education to arm of state government. This uneasy role as intermediary has often cost them the full confidence of both sides; one can understand, then, the reluctance of many institutional presidents to strengthen an agency whose status is still so much in doubt. One can see also why coordinating boards reacted more enthusiastically than did governing boards to the idea of having their often shaky authority enhanced by being given responsibility for administering one or more Federal programs; and why they, more than the governing boards, would welcome the consolidation of existing state-administered programs under their direction and the conversion of one or more direct Federal programs to their administration.

New Federal programs

The three groups of respondents were asked to give their opinions on three possible Federal programs. Federal support for institutional and state planning was the least controversial; tax remissions to the states raised the most questions; and general institutional grants were the most popular.

Federal Planning Grants: Most governors, administering state agencies, and institutional presidents endorsed the value of Federal support for planning. But they gave higher priority to noncategorical Federal grants to institutions. Moreover, it was pointed out that planning aid had already been forthcoming under the 1966 amendment to HEFA; all that is needed, they felt, is that the U.S. Office of Education remain flexible in relating program planning to facility planning and that funds be increased. Most of the respondents agreed that, if a direct Federal program were initiated, it should be on a continuing basis, rather than for a three- to five-year period. The governors and the state agencies split on the question of how best to implement the program, but not, perhaps, as much as one might suppose. About half of the coordinating agencies and over half of the governors felt that Federal planning grants should go to the institutions as well as to the state rather than to the state alone, whereas about 40 percent of the presidents favored grants to the state as well as to the institutions rather than to the institution alone.

Federal Tax Remissions to the States: If new Federal planning grants were made, they would probably be relatively small and categorical; but if Federal tax remissions to the states were instituted on any scale at all, they would probably constitute relatively large block grants. It is precisely their indeterminacy which attracted the support of most governors and aroused the opposition of most institutional presidents. Any prospective increase in the state's fiscal discretion stirs many different fears and uncertainties in the world of higher education. Would the block grant be tied to education as distinct from other fields? To higher education as distinct from elementary-secondary? Would Congress build in safeguards to ensure that these funds for higher education would be over and above continuing reasonable levels of state support? Would private higher education in general, and church-related colleges in particular, qualify as easily under (often) tighter state constitutions? Would care be taken to see that such additional funds did not act to dry up private sources of support? How would the principle of equalization among states be applied? Would the largest remissions go to the largest states? The wealthiest? The most needy? Those making the biggest proportionate effort in higher education?

Even if it were possible to formulate a tax remission program which would relieve these anxieties, the question of how to administer it would remain. Most governors and coordinating agencies welcomed the strengthening of state planning and coordination of higher education that would result from state administration; but half of the presidents of public institutions and a substantial majority of the presidents of private ones indicated that they were opposed, undoubtedly because they felt it desirable to maintain pluralistic bases of support and to prevent the state role from being magnified at the expense of the Federal. Even half of the coordinating agency directors reported that they would join the presidents in opposing any move to create a tax remission program in lieu of all other Federal support for education, a move favored by half of the governors.

General Institutional Grants: The three groups were much more in accord about the desirability of a general institutional grant program. Again different parties expressed different qualifications, depending on which particular interests they felt needed protecting. Many public and private institutional presidents wanted the grants to be structured in such a way as not to diminish their current support from state governments and private sources respectively. The more prestigious, research-oriented universities (public and private) would prescribe criteria based on institutional quality, whereas less affluent institutions would insist on criteria of need.

After reviewing these and other complexities, Cox and Harrell endorse a general institutional grant "as a supplement to existing categorical support but not as a replacement for it," such a grant to be pegged to a formula based in part on enrollments and in part on productivity at different academic levels. "The quality of an institution, its faculty, or its programs," they add, "should continue to be a factor in appropriate categorical federal programs supporting research and graduate or professional education essential to the national interest." [8]

Given this conceptualization of Federal institutional grants, it is understandable that most presidents would prefer that the program be directly administered by the Federal government. Most governors and state agencies, however, viewed the program as one which would allocate funds to the states to be used for general institutional development under state plans developed in accordance with broad Congressional and agency guidelines and procedures. Only in this way, they urged, could the integrity and coherence of state planning be maintained.

Many presidents of private institutions indicated that such a state role would constitute a substantial infringement on their autonomy. (They held this view even though they had had no complaints about the state administration of the Federal facilities program. But the general institutional grants would, of course, have a greater impact on their academic programs.)

Cox and Harrell point out that channels would be open whereby states could protect their interests in Federal higher education programs without demanding that the state agencies administer such programs. The state would seem to have two central concerns: to ensure that the public institutions' participation in Federal programs not interfere with their carrying out the role and scope missions assigned to them in state planning; and to have some check on the future commitment of state funds implicit in the acceptance of some Federal programs. But these concerns can be protected solely by *state* legislation requiring that the coordinating agency approve institutional participation. Congress, then, would be left free to decide, on the merits of the issues themselves, whether to channel the funds through state agencies (thereby bringing private institutions under closer state scrutiny) or to have Federal agencies administer them directly to the institutions.

Relations between Higher Education and the Public Schools

To analyze this topic requires a knowledge not only of higher education but also of the functioning of the public school systems in the various

8. Ibid., p. 196.

states. Professors Usdan, Minar, and Hurwitz—who have such expertise—conducted a study of this subject under the joint sponsorship of the American Council on Education and the Education Commission of the States. This brief summary is based chiefly on their report.[9]

The authors, while finding little evidence of overt conflict between the two levels, nevertheless felt that several emerging issues, if ignored, could produce serious crises in the future. Though not endorsing any particular structure for interlevel coordination, they urged that states give this matter serious attention in the near future; its relevance to statewide coordination will be obvious.

Changing power bases

Usdan found the power base of the elementary-secondary sector to be declining somewhat, and that of higher education to be increasing. Previously, the various interest groups concerned with the public schools—classroom teachers, school administrators, school board associations, and parent-teacher organizations—were able to form an effective coalition that would press for programs and financing acceptable to the "educational establishment." But more recently, increasing unionization and militancy have split the ranks of the classroom teachers and, in some instances, have repelled previous allies in the coalition. In addition, since the days of Sputnik, public and legislative criticism of the accepted values of progressive education has increased markedly. Thus, controversy and dissent now exist, where before, harmony prevailed.

In former days, higher education embraced a much smaller percentage of the population than did the public schools and was offered through a limited number of institutions. While many colleges and universities could whip up considerable support from alumni and clientele groups (e.g., agricultural interests, state bar and medical associations), such support more often than not was squandered in rivalries that raged in the state capital as well as in the football stadium. But more recently, these conditions have given way to mass higher education and to interinstitutional cooperation, both of which mean increased power. The immense expansion of higher education—involving vast increases in enrollments and the proliferation of new institutions—has created problems of orderly

9. Michael D. Usdan, David W. Minar, and Emanuel Hurwitz, Jr., *Education and State Politics* (New York: Teachers College Press, Columbia University, 1969). For brevity, only Usdan's name will be used hereafter in referring to this book.

development and soaring costs. And many states, to meet these problems, have established coordinating agencies which have tended, in some cases, to lessen institutional budgetary rivalries and, in many cases, to make the state's higher educational system more coherent.

Issues relevant to both sectors

Usdan found a great deal of fragmentation on the present educational scene; there is little interaction, whether of conflict or of cooperation, between the higher education and the public school levels. But, he notes: "One thing seems certain: the pressures toward political interaction of elementary-secondary and higher education will increase in the years ahead . . . [and] can be ignored only at considerable peril to education." [10] The two levels share a number of common problems.

Fiscal Questions: Not surprisingly, the fiscal issue was considered to be potentially the most explosive.

> Typically, the two sectors have drawn on somewhat different sources of support, the public schools having been heavily dependent on local real property taxes and the colleges and universities drawing their monies directly from the state, from student fees, and from federal grants and contracts. As costs have risen, however, and particularly as the tax burden on real estate has come to seem unreasonable, the schools and colleges have increasingly turned for aid to the same source: general state revenues. They have come into competition, sometimes overt but more often unspoken, for larger shares out of a common but limited pot of money.[11]

Traditionally, state support to local school districts is given through a foundation program that provides a fixed amount of funds based on a formula involving criteria to equalize rich and poor districts. This kind of support has the virtue of certainty but the defect of rigidity; complaints were voiced to us in several states (e.g., Florida and Ohio) that state appropriations to the public schools were not keeping pace with those to higher education. Noting the taxpayers' revolt over local property taxes, Usdan predicts that "most states will have to make extensive revisions in their school support and revenue systems in the near future." [12]

10. Ibid., p. 9.
11. Ibid., p. 7.
12. Ibid., p. 179.

One state legislator at a WICHE Legislative Workshop Conference in 1967 summed up the situation as follows:

> Primary and secondary education people, community college people, and higher education people are all competing for a limited number of dollars that are available to the legislature. . . . To consider higher education's problem alone is to ignore some of the other major problems that do exist. What we have to do in solving higher education's problem is to set our whole educational program in order.[13]

Education in the 13th and 14th Grades: Several issues connected with the so-called 13th and 14th grades may constitute sources of friction between the higher education and public school sectors.

The most fundamental question is: What should be the basic orientation of the institutions offering this education? In some states, "the 13th and 14th grade programs have been grafted onto the public schools and chiefly promoted and dominated by the public school interests. In others, the major initiative has come from higher education."[14] This basic orientation tends to determine the type of faculty recruited, the kind of curriculum stressed, relations with both high schools and colleges, and other features. In some nine states, the junior colleges have retained close ties with the local school districts from which they emerged, sometimes even continuing to use a local board of education as their parent board. In such cases, the state board of education normally acts as an overall coordinating agency. In some nine other states, at least part of the junior college functions have been assumed by branch campuses of universities, which act in a governing capacity, subject to whatever statewide coordination exists. Finally, in some twenty-five states, the trend has been to establish a separate statewide comprehensive community college system, with either the state board of education or a coordinating agency for higher education being the final planning authority.

Occasionally, a mild tug of war over control of the community college system has taken place, as when the Texas community college system was transferred from the Education Agency to the Coordinating Board, when the North Carolina community colleges made the reverse trip, and when

---

13. L. W. Newbry, "Commentary on 'The Finance of Higher Education,' by John Dale Russell," *Partnership for Progress*, eds. R. H. Kroepsch and D. P. Buck (Boulder, Colo.: Western Interstate Commission for Higher Education, 1967), p. 15.
14. Usdan, Minar, and Hurwitz, *Education and State Politics*, p. 7.

the California community colleges were placed under the jurisdiction of a special statewide board. But Usdan reports (and our own research in those three states confirms) that, so far, most such transitions, and the subsequent maintenance of liaison with both sides, have been accomplished fairly smoothly. To avoid the possibility of future discord, Usdan says, it may be necessary to create some mechanism for bringing together on a more regular basis the relevant views of higher education and of the public school system.

As community colleges become more completely identified with higher education (as most seem to be doing), then two other issues will probably emerge. For one thing, community colleges—unlike four-year colleges or universities—derive a considerable part of their financing from local sources. This means that higher education (or, rather, a segment of it) is competing with public schools for local property taxes as well as for general state revenues, and this fact must be remembered. For another thing, the problem of coordinating vocational-technical education will probably grow more difficult if the community colleges move from the public school systems to become part of higher education. Usdan found vocational-technical education to be suffering from "lack of direction, lack of commitment, underemphasis, and general confusion. . . . the problem is less conflict over an issue than the absence of issue substance around which conflict might revolve." [15]

Teacher Education and Certification: Except for California, where most college and university personnel opposed the public school establishment by backing the Fisher Bill to demand more subject-matter mastery in teacher training, Usdan found this issue to be relatively quiet. Indeed, in New York and Indiana, it evidently served as a vehicle for interlevel rapport.

Structural arrangements for interlevel coordination

There exist a number of structural arrangements designed to set the "whole educational program in order": that is, to plan and coordinate elementary-secondary education along with higher education on a statewide basis.

State Board of Education as Coordinating Agency: As noted in chapter 2, the state board of education serves as the consolidated governing

15. Ibid., p. 182.

board for higher education in Idaho, Montana, and, according to late information, Rhode Island; and as the coordinating board for higher education in Michigan, New York, and Pennsylvania. (For the special case of Florida, see chapter 2, Table 1, footnote 6.) The report by Usdan, Minar, and Hurwitz covered only Michigan, New York, and Pennsylvania; and of this group, our study included only Pennsylvania, so the following comments are based on these states.

In theory, giving one agency responsibility for the integration of all education, from kindergarten to postdoctoral work, is the simplest and most direct way of handling problems of interlevel coordination. But this mechanism is too new for definitive evaluation yet: The Michigan and Pennsylvania boards were given planning jurisdiction over higher education only in the early 1960s, and the New York board began to take its responsibilities in this area seriously at about the same time. Usdan says tentatively, "where there are overall coordinating agencies there tends to be less conflict between educational levels." [16] But the gains in interlevel relations may be losses insofar as effective integration of the higher education system is concerned. We found that the Pennsylvania board was burdened with too many problems to make a good job of coordinating higher education; judging from the Usdan report, the same is true in Michigan;[17] and, according to the Bundy Commission, in New York.[18] We will make a more extended critique of the state board of education as a coordinating agency in the final chapter; here the point is that, notwithstanding its possible merits as a vehicle for interlevel cooperation, the state board of education's apparent defects as regards higher education suggest that other means of achieving interlevel collaboration should be sought.

Interlevel Liaison Groups: In at least four states, special bodies have been created to provide formal liaison between the coordinating agency for higher education and the state board of education. These four liaison groups, and the dates of their establishment, are: the Georgia Education Improvement Council, 1964; the Massachusetts Advisory Council on Education, 1966; the New Jersey Coordinating Council, 1967; and the Oregon Education Coordinating Council, 1965. The Georgia and Massachusetts groups have been assigned planning missions, especially with

16. Ibid., p. 174.
17. Ibid., p. 99.
18. New York Select Commission on the Future of Private and Independent Higher Education in New York State [Bundy Commission], *New York State and Private Higher Education* (Albany: State Education Department, 1968), p. 13.

respect to problems overlapping elementary-secondary and higher education. The New Jersey group is oriented more toward coordinating the actions of the two boards (of education and of higher education) and reviewing their budgets. In addition to a strong planning charge, the Oregon agency must perform a coordinating function *within* higher education, since the community colleges in that state fall under the jurisdiction of the state board of education; it has also been designated as the state agency to administer some of the Federal programs in higher education.

The planning charge to the Oregon liaison group is impressive. It is supposed to:

1. Coordinate planning and evaluative efforts of related agencies to ensure that planning terminology and procedures are such that the various planning efforts of related agencies may be effectively integrated.
2. Ensure that all of the State's educational needs are identified and planned for by some agency.
3. Establish with related agencies procedures for planning that will, whenever feasible, provide for the simultaneous development of data and information necessary to planning at the agency and statewide level.
4. Develop cooperatively with the related agencies a statewide master plan for presentation to the Governor and the legislature.
5. Establish regulatory procedures for evaluation and periodic revision of the master plan.
6. Evaluate the progress of the various educational programs of the state in light of the adopted master plan and make recommendations to ensure that each level and element of education receives appropriate emphasis.   .
7. Make periodic progress reports to the Governor's office on the status of comprehensive planning.[19]

Though the planning mandates of the four groups are similar, their membership differs considerably. The Georgia agency is composed predominantly of persons from the two boards and from state government. The New Jersey group is made up exclusively of officers and members

19. Quoted in Lewis B. Mayhew, *Long Range Planning for Higher Education* (Washington: Academy for Educational Development, 1969), pp. 66–67.

of the two boards. The nine members of the Massachusetts agency are prohibited from being associated in any way with the institutions; though the original proposal to include four Massachusetts legislators was eliminated, a legislative advisory group was immediately formed. Finally, and uniquely, the law creating the Oregon body permits the governor to appoint "such number of members as he deems appropriate to serve at his pleasure." The nine members actually chosen represented the two boards in question, the executive office, and the private institutions, among others.

Usdan (whose report covered Georgia, Massachusetts, and New Jersey, but not Oregon) commented on the difficulties that these liaison groups have in trying to justify their existence in between two jealous giants:

> The leadership [of the Georgia group], contend the critics, cannot afford to be dynamic or aggressive. Both the Regents and the State Board are much more powerful and entrenched agencies, and a weak fledgling like the GEIC cannot afford to offend either of the established state education boards.[20]

On the other hand, Usdan notes that meetings of such bodies tend to bring the executive officers together on a regular basis, a useful end in itself, but one that could be accomplished without a formal agency (whose annual budget ranges from $100,000 in Georgia to $300,000 in Massachusetts). Moreover, earlier evidence in Georgia indicates that executive officers who do not want to cooperate cannot be made to do so merely through the liaison group's existence.

Usdan judged the interlevel conflict to be low in Georgia and Massachusetts but hesitated to ascribe the "cause" to the existence of the liaison group: "It may be the case that such institutions are formed only where the climate of relationships is fairly good."[21] In fact, in New Jersey, where interlevel conflict was high, the liaison group was created as part of the price exacted by the public school sector, which objected bitterly to the creation of a coordinating agency for higher education and to the removal of all postsecondary institutions from the jurisdiction of the board of education. Clearly, more time and experience are needed before these relatively new groups can be judged fairly.

20. *Education and State Politics*, p. 36.
21. Ibid., p. 174.

State Political Channels: Another approach to the problem of planning and coordinating across levels is to use the existing structures of the state government itself:

Coordination between levels might be effected in the legislative-gubernatorial sphere. . . . If true initiative in educational policy-making comes to reside in the interaction of governors and legislators, it may lose some of the parochial and piecemeal characteristics it has heretofore displayed.[22]

Usdan is doubtful, however, that such cooperative interaction can be achieved, seeing "massive and perhaps insurmountable obstacles . . . in many states." The traditions of separation of powers, mutual suspicions and jealousies, and widespread fragmentation of interest in education all constitute problems. Although higher education has generally moved closer to the orbit of the governor's office, the public school system has usually identified more closely with the legislature, partly, perhaps, as a reflection of past attempts to keep public education free of gubernatorial politics: hence, the separate election of the state superintendent of public instruction (in twenty-six states) and even of the state board of education (in ten states). Beyond this, there exist other reasons for public education's ties with the legislature:

Both the system of finance and the actual appropriation of funds have generally been questions in whose disposition legislatures have taken initiative. In addition, they have helped in the development of that body of law that has enouraged the professionalization of the field and limited the discretion of the local school authorities. Thus, they are accustomed to dealing with public school problems, often in some detail.[23]

Recently, some states have proposed or actually taken steps that would strengthen the governor's power to integrate the planning and financing of all public education. In some cases, this means merely that the governor has designated an executive assistant as "program coordinator" for education and has asked all the various agencies to work with him. On Smart's questionnaire, seven of the thirty-two agencies responding to the question reported that the equivalent of a cabinet secretary for education existed in the state.

22. Ibid., p. 177.
23. Ibid., p. 176.

In other cases, the governor has proposed the formal merger of the state board of education and the coordinating agency for higher education, with the combined department headed by an appointed superintendent of public instruction who would sit on the governor's cabinet and be responsible for all phases of education. Governor Hatfield of Oregon urged this course in the early 1960s arguing:

> In several respects [the two boards] overlap. In others they duplicate. In relation to still other responsibilities the assignments are unclear. . . . I am also concerned about the competitiveness between the two constituencies which these boards represent.[24]

Legislation to make the suggested changes failed to gain approval, and the Educational Coordinating Council (mentioned in the previous section) was established instead. When it studied this subject, among others, it concluded (perhaps not too surprisingly) that "a continuation of the two existing state boards . . . and an educational coordinating council . . . is the most effective means of producing the coordinated governance of education in Oregon." [25]

Finally, fuller integration of educational policy making may occur as a result of efforts to reform the executive establishment wholesale. Massachusetts, for example, has passed legislation which by mid-1971 will place all 170 existing state agencies in one of nine state executive offices, headed by an appointed secretary with the following powers:

1. To review, approve or amend budget requests of agencies within his office.
2. To have access to all records and documents legally available to him within any agency in his office.
3. To conduct studies of the operations of said agencies to improve efficiency and manageability, and to recommend to the governor changes in the laws affecting those operations.
4. To conduct comprehensive planning with respect to the functional fields for which his office is responsible.[26]

Within two years, each secretary must submit plans for the further reorganization of the agencies under his jurisdiction. Some twenty-seven state

24. Samuel Gove, "The Oregon State System of Higher Education" (MS, Department of Political Science, University of Illinois, 1967), p. 3.
25. Ibid.
26. Massachusetts Office of Planning and Program Coordination, *Modernization of the Government of the Commonwealth of Massachusetts as Enacted 1969* (Boston: Commonwealth of Massachusetts, 1969), pp. 4–5.

agencies in education and the arts are to be included in the executive office of educational affairs.

Chapter 11 will comment on how such state executive moves affect the coordination of higher education. The subject is mentioned here as simply another way in which public school systems and higher education can be brought together.

Institutional Accreditation and Statewide Coordination

Although we did not, in our field work, formally cover the subject of institutional accreditation, we came across one situation which, in our opinion, merits attention and reflection.

In the particular state involved, a recently arrived president at a state institution found himself in disagreement with the statewide coordinating board; he had, in fact, led a movement in the committee of institutional presidents to seek the ouster of the board's executive director.

An accrediting team—whose head was, by pure chance, a dean from the president's former institution—then visited the campus in question. During its long and thorough inspection, the team heard in detail the various grievances that the campus entertained against the coordinating board. Subsequently, the team arranged to visit the executive director of the board for one hour, during a stopover in the state capital; at that time, they discussed some of the issues.

When the report of the accrediting team appeared, it charged that higher education in the state was overcentralized; the report was given wide circulation by the institution in question.

Without attempting to judge the rights and wrongs of this disagreement, we do ask whether (1) such accrediting teams operate under explicit guidelines regarding acceptable and unacceptable degrees of "centralization" in higher education resulting from statewide coordination; and (2) careful provision is made to include on each accrediting team which wishes to pass judgments on such issues at least one member who has some relevant experience.

We see no objection in principle to accrediting teams attempting such judgments. (Leverage like this could be useful against a coordinating agency which works poorly.) But they should do so only after guidelines have been openly developed (preferably in cooperation with state coordinating agencies) and after qualified persons have been included on the visiting team.

PART FOUR

EVALUATION

ELEVEN

The appropriate machinery: Conclusions and recommendations

Up to this point, the aim has been to present the material in a descriptive and analytic manner and to refrain from editorial comment. In this chapter, I will give a synthesis and evaluation of the preceding material, bearing well in mind that there is probably no correct solution and that even if there were, it would probably vary from place to place and even from time to time in the same place. Nevertheless, some generalizations and recommendations are called for. They will be enumerated in the first part of this chapter and followed by longer sections elaborating on certain major points.

The States and Higher Education: An Uneasy Partnership

1. Although the Federal government, through its enormous fiscal powers, may ultimately come to play the dominant role in higher education, state financing will continue to be indispensable for the indefinite future. In any case, universities and colleges will always have to function in the context of state law and thus will be subject to statewide coordination and planning.

2. It is important to distinguish between a state's role vis-à-vis academic freedom and its role vis-à-vis university autonomy. The two concepts are related but not synonymous. The former usually involves some controversial speech or action by faculty members, students, or administrators to which the state objects. The problems here, though obviously important, are not discussed in this study since they have already been thoroughly investigated by others and the issues have not, in essence, changed. University autonomy, by way of contrast, involves the institution's attempt to govern itself in the face of state efforts to plan and coordinate higher education on a multilateral basis. The problems here have

not been thoroughly studied, and in any case change over time and therefore require redefinition.

3. As a first step in this redefinition, a further distinction must be made between procedural autonomy and substantive autonomy. The former refers to state controls over how institutions go about pursuing their goals (e.g., preaudits, line-item budgets, central purchasing); the latter concerns what program goals the institutions are pursuing and how they mesh with the goals of other institutions in the context of state needs and resources. Of course, procedural controls can affect an institution's ability to achieve substantive goals, but for reasons explained in Chapter 1, this study has chosen to concentrate on issues relating to substantive autonomy.

4. In the realm of substantive autonomy, the state has a legitimate but delicate role to play, ensuring that the public interest is adequately protected as institutional development takes place. Notwithstanding the impressive diversity and vitality of American higher education that has emerged in the absence of a centralized system, the need for the function of coordination to be performed on a statewide level has become inescapable.

5. There is no such thing as "no coordination." Where neither voluntary nor statutory agencies have existed, normal state organs—governor's office, budget office, legislature, state auditor, etc.—made the decisions, usually on an ad hoc basis, which implicitly performed this function.

6. Institutions which, because of strong political influence, have been "winning" under this piecemeal sort of coordination are understandably reluctant to change the ground rules. But the haphazard approach is definitely losing ground in higher education as in other areas of public affairs. Soon the only choice will probably be whether the comprehensive planning is done by an agency specializing in higher education,[1] by a state executive office responsible for all education, or by a state planning office which uses program budgeting and the newest tools of management information systems to try to integrate the development of all state activities.

7. In my view, if set up and supported in accordance with the recommendations below, a specialized agency will be the most effective of these three alternatives. Such an agency will serve the public interest in

---

1. The reader is reminded that *coordinating agency* is used for the general category; *voluntary association, coordinating board,* and *consolidated governing board* are the subtypes.

that only an agency specializing in higher education knows how to plan for it effectively. University autonomy will be better protected because the agency will be able to gauge the extent to which the new management tools can appropriately be applied to higher education.

The Nature of the Specialized Agency

8. Each state must determine for itself, on the basis of its own traditions, needs, and resources, whether the specialized agency should be a voluntary one established by the institutions themselves or a statutory one created by the state. While each alternative has its advantages and drawbacks, the evidence strongly indicates that states with more than a few institutions will find it necessary to create a statutory agency.

9. Whether the statutory agency should be a consolidated governing board, a division of the state board of education, or a coordinating board is again a matter that each state must decide for itself; again very real advantages and disadvantages attach to each choice.

a) The consolidated governing board, with no institutional subboards to oppose it, has the strongest powers for implementing planning; but paradoxically, it has generally tended to stress administration rather than planning. In addition, some question arises as to whether a single board should try to administer more than a small number of institutions or institutions of different types.

b) Using the state board of education as the coordinating agency would seem to have the advantage of integrating all educational planning from kindergarten to the doctorate, but these advantages may be more apparent than real, whereas the problems involved in stretching board attentions to include higher education and in recruiting the special kinds of staff needed to coordinate higher education are very real indeed.

c) Coordinating boards of one sort or another now constitute the most numerous type of agency and will probably continue to be the model relevant to most states. They have the greatest potential for success, but if it is to be realized, many complex factors must fall into line.

10. Coordination at its best requires that both state government and higher education make concessions and give of their resources, but such cooperation has been rare. Yet coordination poorly done may be a positive evil, intruding yet another party into the state higher education rela-

tionship, soaking up additional state funds, and consuming the time and energy of busy people, without improving the quality of higher education. If it is going to be done at all, it must be done well. The parties involved must agree to make the necessary concessions and to provide the necessary resources.

Requirements for Agency Structure and Functions

In this section, I will outline my recommendations about the requirements of an effective coordinating agency.

11. *A Strong, Independent Staff*: A staff which combines experience in both the academic world and the sphere of state government is the first requirement. The salary, powers, and prestige of the chief executive officer are the most important considerations, since even if the pay scale drops off at the intermediate and junior levels, good men will usually agree to work for an outstanding leader in whom they have confidence and from whom they can learn. The status and salary of the chief executive officer should at least equal those of the senior public university president in the state. This means that the state must be willing to pay agency staff more than the normal civil service rates and that the universities and colleges must recognize that they are better off in the long run working with a strong and effective coordinating staff. On occasion, they may "lose" battles which they would have won had the staff been a weak one; but their willingness to subordinate short-run losses to long-run gains and to suppress their fears and accept leadership is crucial.

    a) Voluntary agencies tend to use staff from the institutions themselves. The agency staff must be independent, free from the fear that the first time a staff report offends a powerful institution, their job tenure is in danger.

    b) The problem is different for consolidated governing boards: Here the question is whether the institutional presidents want the executive officer of the board to be a powerful educational leader or merely a secretary to the board.

    c) Coordinating boards have more trouble paying high salaries than do voluntary associations or consolidated governing boards, which normally operate outside the purview of state civil service controls. It is sometimes awkward to pay the chief of a coordinating board almost as much as the governor and more than the superintendent of public instruction.

d) Similarly, when the state board of education acts as the agency, it is often difficult to get a first-rate coordinating director, since he must operate under the chief executive officer of the state board of education and thus will be inferior to him in both pay and prestige.

The problem of acquiring and retaining high-quality staff is so crucial that I venture to offer some additional suggestions which might prove to be helpful. First, in order to make the somewhat perilous position of executive director of a coordinating agency more attractive to men of top stature from the academic world, they should be offered three-year contracts. Then, if an earlier departure proved to be desirable, the remaining time on their contracts would have to be "bought up," as is done in the case of the equally valuable and perilous position of football coach. Second, after two such three-year contracts had been fulfilled, the top executive should be given a sabbatical leave; the need to recharge one's battery is just as great here is in the academic world. Finally, more capable persons from state government offices and institutions of higher education might welcome being seconded to the coordinating agency if they were permitted to retain their employment perquisites (e.g., retirement system, health insurance, eligibility for leave) while on leave of absence.

12. *A Strong Membership*: A first-class staff that wins the confidence of both state government and higher education can go a long way toward accomplishing effective coordination. But it is not infallible; it should be controlled by a board whose members are wise enough to know when to give the staff their head and strong enough to check them when they need it. A majority of good public members can assure the state that the public interest is being safeguarded; a minority of good institutional members (or strong academic advisory committees; see #13) can assure the universities and colleges that the decisions being made reflect a concern for institutional autonomy.

Although I am in general sympathy with the "strong governor" movement in the states and can therefore understand why governors are reluctant to have important activities taken out of their hands and placed under the supervision of multimember boards with staggered terms, I also believe that a legitimate case can be made for treating higher education in this manner. I believe that a board should have enough members, whose terms are sufficiently long, that it becomes impossible for any governor in a single four-year term to appoint a majority of the members. I also believe that some kind of legislative confirmation is desirable, so that the board is not viewed as an exclusively guber- natorial concern. Ideally, the governor would appoint members from a roster of names screened by a well-qualified and heterogeneous body. (Educators certainly should not dominate this screening group.) Prece- dents for such a procedure now exist in Massachusetts, North Dakota, and Rhode Island.

a) In the interests of making their deliberations seem less self-serv- ing, voluntary agencies should consider adding public members to their (at present) exclusively institutional membership.

b) Consolidated governing boards should consider adding some in- stitutional members or creating very strong academic advisory committees (see #13) or doing both.

c) Coordinating boards should have a minority of institutional mem- bers or very strong academic advisory committees or both.

d) With respect to including state legislators or executive officers on coordinating agencies, the (admittedly slight) evidence in- clines me to feel that they should be included either as nonvoting members (e.g., Washington) or on a separate advisory commit- tee (e.g., Colorado).

13. *Strong Academic Advisory Committees:* As a vital, if time-con- suming, quid pro quo for institutional readiness to accept a coordinating agency with a strong staff and strong powers (see #14-17), a network of academic committees should be set up to give advice on both the plan- ning and the operations of coordinating agencies. Although most agency staff are so overworked that they may be reluctant to give time to educat- ing the various institutional members to a statewide point of view, there are at least three good reasons why this effort should be made. First, no matter how academically sensitive the staff may be, it is a basic protec- tion for the institutions that their views be heard early in the process of decision making. Second, wisdom is there, waiting to be tapped. Third, the very act of participating in a forum where all institutions present their claims may demonstrate vividly the extent to which aspirations exceed state resources and thus help to convince educators of the need to coop- erate in setting statewide priorities.

These advisory committees may range from technical ad hoc bodies, through standing committees on special subjects, to (at the very top) a council of presidents, the last being particularly important. (Administra- tors, faculty members, students, trustees, legislators, and the lay public may also be used where appropriate.) The coordinating staff should aid these committees by preparing papers, circulating agenda well in advance, and so forth. The council of presidents, in particular, should be a body where members can speak their minds freely, assured that their views will reach the ears of coordinating agency members undistorted. To this end, I recommend that the agency chief *not* act as chairman but that this office be elected; that the agency chief *not* act as "interpreter" of the presidents' thinking but have the right to make personal comments on their formal recommendations; and that the presidents be encouraged to attend board meetings and speak out when they so desire. Of course, a powerful council of presidents could become a runaway body, bypassing the agency chief and making a direct bid to the state government, but a strong agency director must accept this risk, recognizing that it is preferable to institutional distrust of the decision-making process. It should be possible to persuade state officers to discourage end runs by the council of presidents.

But the interests of the universities and colleges may still be inadequately protected (in the sense of getting their views, right or wrong, effectively presented at the crucial moments of decision making) if the board is composed entirely of public members and if it succumbs to the understandable temptation to handle the more controversial items in private, informal premeetings or intermeetings. A chief executive officer of the caliber recommended in #7 would probably not abuse his position in these private meetings by misrepresenting the institutional points of view; but nonetheless, I recommend that institutions be given minority board membership as insurance that their ideas are being fairly considered at all times: *Justice must not only be done; it must be seen to be done.* In addition—and granting that the evidence is mixed, with gains and losses either way—I recommend that lay trustees rather than presidents represent institutional interests on the agency. The latter are too directly and materially involved in the well-being of their institutions to have the flexibility required to make mutual concessions in the interest of statewide priorities. Furthermore, there is a very strong fear among many legislators that even a minority of college presidents will dominate any board they are on. (Britain and some provinces in Canada include faculty members on their coordinating agencies, not as representatives of the institutions to which they are attached, but as persons usually more conversant with academic values and problems than are lay trustees and probably more flexible than are institutional presidents.)

14. *Strong Powers in Planning*: At the least, any coordinating agency should be mandated to engage in comprehensive and continuous long-range planning for *both* public and private higher education. To this end, it must have power to establish, in consultation with the institutions, categories for reporting data and to require such information as is demonstrably necessary for good planning. If there is no master plan, or if the existing one requires updating, the coordinating agency should undertake the task. Each state will have to decide which particular pattern is most appropriate for itself (see chapter 5); but other things being equal, the mixed in-state/out-of-state pattern is recommended. Under this method, the bulk of the work is done by committees of in-state persons (primarily institutional representatives but also, in some cases, lay members, legislators, or others) and out-of-state experts are brought in for certain specialized tasks. Although heavy institutional participation will probably slow the planning down a bit and may occasionally create problems which could otherwise have been avoided, it is, on balance, recommended for the same two reasons adduced in connection with advisory committees: the protection of institutional interests and the invaluable opportunity to educate the educators to the statewide point of view. Finally the agency should be charged with overseeing the implementation of the planning.

15. *Strong Powers in Program Review*: All agencies—whether voluntary, coordinating, or governing boards—must have the power to approve "new programs," as defined in chapter 7. If it has already been decided, in earlier planning, what new institutions should be created and what role and scope assignments should be made, then the agency must see that the goals are implemented; if it has not, then the agency must make such decisions and revise them as needed. Within the role and scope allocated, the agency should have power to approve all new doctoral programs as well as master's and baccalaurate programs in (1) general fields not previously offered and (2) high-cost fields. Agency approval should *not*, however, be required for new courses; the danger that some new programs will be constructed piecemeal and presented to the state as faits accomplis is less threatening than the difficulties attendant upon getting the agency involved in approving individual courses. The agency should also have the power to *recommend* the elimination of existing programs; the institutions in question would thereby be obligated to report to the state within three to six months, giving any reasons they might have for noncompliance with such recommendations. Finally, legislatures should

not designate institutions "universities" or alter institutional roles without agency approval.

In the crucial area of program review, as in that of planning, the agency should lean over backwards to involve the institutions in the decision-making process. Out-of-state experts may be brought in, as required, for highly specialized fields, but the painful work of determining priorities should be carried out chiefly by internally constituted committees, under the direction and with the help of agency staff.

16. *Strong Powers in Budget Review*: Although advocates of strong co-coordination insist that, if an agency is to engage in effective planning, implementation, and program review, it must undertake detailed budget review, my own feeling is that each state and each type of agency must decide on this matter for itself. In states with coordinated governing boards, no question arises, since the board must by definition perform this function. In states with voluntary coordinating associations, by way of contrast, the participating institutions have never gone beyond the point of presenting joint budget requests and, occasionally, exchanging data. (In Indiana, these data tended to be comprehensive but still did not cover such important areas as institutional foundation funds.) The historical facts do not mean that voluntary agencies could not or should not engage in serious and detailed budget review; they mean simply that it is unlikely that they will choose to do so.

It seems to me that what is vital is not so much separate budget review by the agency as detailed information about institutional budgets. If a state has a primitive budget process which would be markedly improved were the coordinating agency to perform a detailed review, then it is probably worth the cost in time, energy, and possible tension between the agency and the institutions. Alternatively, if a state whose budget process is fairly sophisticated will agree to defer an important part of that process to the agency, then separate agency review is appropriate. But it seems more likely that states will increasingly use both an executive budget and a legislative budget and that politicians hypersensitive to matters of taxation and public expenditures will refuse to defer to the coordinating agency. In such a situation, it seems unfair and wasteful to ask institutions to submit explanations to a third party. It makes more sense to invite the agency staff to sit in on executive budget hearings and to put questions. Though the budget cuts will ultimately be made by the governor's staff, the agency will have had the opportunity to hear detailed information and to make sure that the right questions are put at the budget hearings.

In particular, the agency should be informed about institutional sources of income other than state funds so that appropriate program coordination can be maintained. The state should not, however, reduce normal appropriations by an amount equal to nonstate funds or institutions will lose all incentive to seek such support. Furthermore, not only should the state (and the coordinating agency) do nothing to discourage the pursuit of excellence with nonstate funds, but also the budgeting process should include some means of encouraging and rewarding *differentially* excellence and special needs. This means that if formula budgeting is used (and, for all of its problems, it represents a net improvement over the old system of giving differential rewards on political grounds), extreme care must be taken to make room for innovation and experimentation and to recognize the special needs and achievements of different institutions. It is, for instance, unreasonable to apply the formula ratios established for normal, ongoing programs to new or emerging institutions or to institutions with special programs for the urban disadvantaged. Planning-programming-budgeting systems (PPBS) are as yet virtually untested in higher education; should they be found feasible, the coordinating agency must play a central role in advising the state government as to which alternative programs in higher education are in the best public interest.

17. *Strong Powers in Capital Outlay Review and Federal Programs*: Although this study did not examine capital outlay review, my recommendations that the agency have strong powers in planning and program review imply the further opinion that the agency should be empowered at least to recommend, and perhaps even to approve, long-range capital construction priority lists on a statewide basis, consistent with established program priorities. Basing these views of Federal programs on the study undertaken by Cox and Harrell,[2] I welcome the emphasis on long-range planning and on cooperation between the public and private sectors in current Federal programs administered by state agencies. I recommend that, to promote maximum coherence between Federal programs and state planning, the coordinating agency be designated as the body to handle most or all state-administered Federal programs. (In some states, this is done already, of course.) At the same time, I recognize the value of maintaining direct Federal-institutional links and therefore do not

2. Lanier Cox and Lester E. Harrell, Jr., *The Impact of Federal Programs on State Planning and Coordination of Higher Education* (Atlanta: Southern Regional Education Board, 1969).

recommend converting such programs to state-administered status. But if such conversions do take place, or if Federal tax-sharing schemes are introduced into higher education, I suggest that a coordinating agency operating along lines suggested above is the proper body to act for the state.

Special Problems in Coordination

18. *Relations with Private Higher Education:* Present trends indicate that interaction between the states and private institutions of higher education will increase. The Federal government's Higher Education Facilities Act and other programs now require the participation of the private sector. But beyond that, as long-range planning becomes more sophisticated, it will necessarily involve the private sector. Moreover, the deepening financial crisis in many private institutions will impel them to seek state aid through student scholarships, tuition equalization grants, facilities assistance, state tax credits for gifts, and per-student or per-degree subsidies. Indeed, in some cases, the state may have to take over a private institution. Without endorsing one type of state aid over others, I would emphasize the urgency of setting up careful procedures for making these important decisions. In particular, statewide councils of independent universities and colleges should be created (or existing ones improved) and provided with a modest secretariat to aid in lateral communication, cooperation, and political articulation. Further, private institutions should be drawn into the coordinating agency's planning and operations; they should perhaps be given a seat on the statewide board, and they should certainly be represented on the major advisory committees.

The extent of state control should be proportionate to the amount and type of state aid rendered; if such aid is modest and indirect, intervention should be minimal. But if the state grants substantial sums directly to its private institutions, state controls must inevitably be rather elaborate. First, the recipient colleges and universities would have to cooperate fully in furnishing data for planning purposes, using the same management information system as does the public sector in order to facilitate studies in cost effectiveness, space utilization, and so forth. Second, they would probably have to check with the coordinating agency before embarking on high-cost new programs. Finally, they could certainly expect a yearly post-audit of expenditures and perhaps a periodic review of the academic worth of the programs supported through state aid.

The delicate issue of state control would seem to be better handled by voluntary bodies and coordinating boards than by governing boards, whose strong administrative powers may alarm private institutions, although Cox and Harrell did not find any such difficulty arising in cases where Federal programs were administered by governing boards. In two governing board states in our sample, a broader and looser planning mechanism had been set up over the governing board and the state department of higher education (see #19), and private institutions may find this alternative more attractive.

19. *Relations between Higher Education and the Public School System*: On the basis of the Usdan study,[3] we conclude that relations between the two sectors of public education have not as yet become a source of major friction. As competition for public funds grows more fierce, however, state officials may come to demand professional help in planning priorities for all public education. Some kind of formal liaison between the coordinating agency for higher education and the state board of education may become necessary, particularly when the junior college system is operated by the state board of education.

The most obvious way of accomplishing this liaison is to vest responsibility for all public education in the state board of education itself; but as pointed out in #9 above, the integrating potential of such a structure seems to be outweighed by its immediate disadvantages in such areas as staffing and operations in higher education. At least four states (Georgia, Massachusetts, New Jersey, and Oregon) have created loose planning organizations that operate over their coordinating agencies and their state boards of education, but it is too early to evaluate their performance. For the present, and bearing in mind that state governors and legislators may ultimately demand a more formal structure, I would recommend that liaison be accomplished by exchange of membership: the chief executive officer and some board member from each group sitting with the other. Staff interchange and cooperation should also be encouraged.

20. *Accreditation and Coordination*: Without having studied the issue thoroughly, I recommend that any accrediting team that wishes to pass judgment about the degree of centralization of state systems do so only after formulating explicit guidelines and including on the team a person with experience in this area.

---

3. Michael D. Usdan, David W. Minar, and Emanuel Hurwitz, Jr., *Education and State Politics* (New York: Teachers College Press, Columbia University, 1969).

Institutional Autonomy and the Public Interest

21. In the past, institutions were free (at least, from external controls) to embark on whatever educational programs they chose to; the result has been the remarkable diversity and vitality that are the hallmarks of American higher education. But by the nature of things, this free market can no longer obtain. Since the state must, perforce, enter this sensitive field, it is crucial that it do so by means which will protect the public interest while holding to a minimum the inevitable intrusions into university autonomy. To quote President Claude Bissell of the University of Toronto:

> Autonomy does not depend upon financial independence, for in these days, no university, not even the mighty private foundations in the U.S., is financially independent. Nor does it depend upon isolation from politics, which at best is nervous and unreal, for every university these days must engage in constant conversations with those who have been elected to public office. Academic autonomy really depends on a broad social assumption that, despite the exigencies of the moment, we must not make decisions on inadequate information.[4]

If the recommendations listed above are followed, the coordinating agency should be in a position to see that important substantive decisions are based on adequate information. The institutions, weighing net gains and losses, should recognize that if they cooperate in the creation of a coordinating agency with a strong staff, membership, and powers, these substantive decisions will be better than those arrived at by normal state political processes. The state government, likewise weighing net gains and losses, should recognize that a strong coordinating agency which has the institutions' confidence will bring more effective institutional response to the public interest than will normal state organs which try to compel such results.

The Coming of System to Higher Education

It is easy to be either too sentimental or too cynical about the good old days in higher education. Certainly the fantastic growth in numbers and types of institutions responding to—and in turn further increasing—the

4. Quoted in *University Affairs,* Association of Universities and Colleges in Canada (Ottawa), April 1967.

demand for higher education is a major phenomenon of the 20th century. We are witnessing what can be accomplished when imagination and energy are unfettered and encouraged.

But no one pretends that this growth has been without undesirable results. In particular, much unnecessary duplication has occurred as institutions have tried to emulate the elite model of the university. With the wisdom of hindsight, one can attempt to make a net assessment of the situation, taking into account the conditions of the times.

With respect to past developments in higher education, my judgment is that the country has gained much more from the vitality of a free market than it has lost and that such gains could probably not have come about had an attempt been made to control spontaneous development and so to avoid undesirable results. One thinks, by way of analogy, of the development of this continent's natural resources since the Civil War. If this development had been carried out through several layers of bureaucracy operating to prevent any and all waste, our present standard of living would probably be much lower.

Nevertheless, the moment has come with higher education—just as it has come in the area of environmental exploitation—when the frantic pace of expansion must be slowed down and plans must be made for the wise use of resources. Happily, in higher education at least, we now have planning and coordinating techniques which go beyond the mere avoidance of waste and look to the larger purpose of meeting the state's needs. Moreover, planning has grown much more flexible as institutions have become more willing to participate in the process. Persons in higher education can still exercise energy and imagination, but in order to find support, these must normally find expression within the established guidelines. As William Fels has remarked, unlimited freedom of action must give way to the right to choose within a structure that limits but sustains choice.[5] In the place of unplanned diversity and unnecessary duplication, we must now substitute planning for diversity and necessary duplication.

The closing of the frontier should prove no more traumatic for higher education than it has for other aspects of American life which have gradually yielded to the coming of system. The rugged individualist who once took delight in driving freely over empty country lanes has ultimately come to accept the necessity, in the face of increasingly heavy

5. Quoted in Logan Wilson, "Form and Function in American Higher Education," *Emerging Patterns in Higher Education*, ed. Logan Wilson (Washington: American Council on Education, 1965), p. 33.

traffic, of having traffic signals and traffic rules and has found that his essential freedoms have not suffered unduly thereby. The crucial word here, of course, is *essential*, since we all recognize that some freedoms are inevitably curtailed by the coming of system. In the case of higher education, the essential freedoms have never been properly sorted out from the marginal ones, so academics are more than normally nervous about the imposition of a state system. Professionals who head various special interest groups (e.g., highways, mental health, public schools) often urge that their activities are too important to be left to politicians; in some cases, this may be true, in others, not. But college and university personnel can point to sensitive issues of academic freedom which do, in fact, give higher education a status different from other activities.

Nevertheless, if it can be shown that academic freedom and university autonomy, though related, are not identical; that statewide systems of higher education can be established without inhibiting academic freedom; and that the essential features of autonomy can be retained within such statewide systems, then the grounds for continued academic resistance are gone. Frederick Rudolph has pointed out that the "historic policy of the American college and university" has traditionally been "drift, reluctant accommodation, [and] belated recognition that while no one was looking, change had in fact taken place."[6] Wilson has noted that one unfortunate consequence of this resistance to change is that it often "places educators in the role of passive observers rather than active participants in shaping the larger destinies of their institutions."[7]

Surely, then, it is time for administrators, trustees, faculty, students, and alumni to acknowledge that the state has a legitimate role to play in helping to determine policies in higher education; and, accordingly, to cooperate in establishing a system that will protect the public interest and at the same time preserve the essential ingredients of autonomy.

Just what are these essential ingredients? In this country, no one so far seems to have given this matter much thought. But in Britain—where a national "system" of higher education has been slowly evolving since 1919 when the government set up a coordinating agency, the University Grants Committee (UGC), to advise on the distribution of grants to universities[8]—the question has received considerable attention. The

6. *The American College and University* (New York: Vintage Books, 1962), p. 491.
7. "Form and Function in American Higher Education," p. 33.
8. Robert O. Berdahl, *British Universities and the State* (Berkeley: University of California, 1959).

various parties who have looked at this issue (and they include Sir Eric Ashby,[9] the Robbins Committee,[10] Sir Hector Hetherington,[11] Sir James Mountford,[12] and the University Grants Committee[13]) have reached something of a consensus. These authorities agree that any self-respecting university, no matter how willing it is to be responsive to systematic planning based on the public interest, must retain control in the following areas:

- *a*) the appointment, promotion, and tenure of academic and administrative staff;
- *b*) selection of students;
- *c*) curriculum content and degree standards;
- *d*) the balance between teaching and research (and, in the U.S., one would add public service); and
- *e*) allocation of income among different categories of expenditure.

One must stretch this list to fit the current situation in Britain, where the government now sets faculty salary scales and imposes a maximum percentage quota for the upper academic ranks, influences by state scholarships the flow of students, affects by its grants the amount and type of research undertaken, and through its coordinating agency allocates funds to the universities in block form, but only after having examined a detailed breakdown of the budget request and having obtained a moral commitment that government funds will not be used for unapproved new programs. Nevertheless, without question, British universities operate with a considerably higher degree of autonomy than do most American public institutions.

One good reason for their greater autonomy is that, until recently at least, all the British institutions under the UGC had full university status and were similar in basic orientation. In the past ten years, the Colleges of Advanced Technology have been given university status and transferred from the immediate supervision of the Department of Education and Science to the UGC (the rest of the technical sector remained under

9. "Self Government in Modern British Universities," *Science and Freedom*, December 1956, pp. 1-6.
10. [Robbins] Committee on Higher Education, *Higher Education* (London: Her Majesty's Stationery Office, 1963).
11. "On University Autonomy," *University Autonomy: Its Meaning Today* (Paris: International Association of Universities, 1965).
12. *British Universities* (London: Oxford University Press, 1966).
13. *University Development, 1962-67*, Cmnd. 3820 (London: Her Majesty's Stationery Office, 1968).

Department of Education and Science jurisdiction). A problem soon arose in that the Colleges of Advanced Technology used this greater freedom to jettison some of their special and highly valued features (e.g., work-study programs, applied research) and began to move toward the traditional university model. If the UGC is to maintain diversity within the enlarged university system, then, it may have to intervene even further than it has in the past.

Since, in the United States, nearly every state has decided that it wants a diversified system of higher education, and since most institutions try to emulate the university model, this diversity can be maintained only by explicitly differentiating functions and enforcing this differentiation through time. (Earlier chapters have already made clear the importance of institutional involvement in such basic planning and the need to make changes in assigned role and scope from time to time.)

If one grants the American need for diversity, and if one grants also that planned change is preferable to a free-for-all, then it follows that the state coordinating agencies are going to have to make many decisions involving the five areas which the British deem crucial to substantive autonomy. For example, implicit in the concept of differentiation of function are differential faculty salary levels, differential admission standards, restrictions on numbers of lower division students at university centers, transfer standards, differential teaching loads and opportunities for research, and approval of new programs on the basis of their consistency with assigned role and scope.

In the face of so much intervention in university policy, does it make sense at all to speak of autonomy? I think it does, as long as at least two conditions are observed: first, that the policies in question are determined only after the *close* participation of the institutions; and second, that such policies be set forth as *general* guidelines rather than as controls over an institution's actions with respect to appointing a specific professor, admitting a specific student, creating a specific course or research project. If these safeguards are observed, then in our opinion the coming of system to higher education will prove tolerable.

The Search for Principles and the Dilemma of Evaluation

Ideally, one should, at this point, offer a set of criteria which could be used in making judgments about the relative strengths and weaknesses of the various modes of coordination. Unfortunately, as mentioned in chapter 3, no guiding principles for the coordination of higher education have yet emerged, and decisions about coordinating procedures continue to be handled in an ad hoc manner.

As Lewis B. Mayhew has noted, "There have been no studies to indicate that elaborate coordination does or does not affect levels of state expenditure for higher education, percentage of a population attending college, cost of instruction or increased productivity of higher education."[14] We did, in fact, give serious thought to attempting such measurements in this study, but because of the multiplicity of intervening variables between type of coordinating agency and outcomes, we decided that the effort was impractical.

In the absence of objective criteria, each writer on coordination must perforce fall back on his own private assessments. The surprising thing is that, with the significant and eloquent exception of M. M. Chambers, most authorities seem to agree on certain items of "conventional wisdom": the overriding importance of high-quality staff; the need for at least a majority of noninstitutional members; the ineffectiveness of voluntary coordination; the primary importance of data gathering and continuous planning; and the desirability of making a clear distinction between coordinating functions and governing functions.[15]

There would also be widespread agreement with James L. Miller's principle that the coordinating agency should concern itself exclusively with education beyond high school and should be organizationally separate from the state-level agency which oversees elementary and secondary education:

14. *Long Range Planning for Higher Education* (Washington: Academy for Educational Development, 1969), p. 32. George H. Brooks, of Colorado State University, has recently (1969) completed a study, "The Relationship Between Governmental Structure and the Financing of Higher Education." Dr. Brooks found that the "overall ratio of allocation to request, year by year, and institution by institution, has not increased as a result of the change to the [coordinating] Commission."

15. See, for example, John Dale Russell, *Control and Coordination of Higher Education in Michigan* (Staff study no. 12, prepared for the Michigan Legislative Study Committee on Higher Education, Lansing, July 1958); Lyman A. Glenny, *Autonomy of Public Colleges* (New York: McGraw-Hill Book Co., 1959); Glenny, "State Systems and Plans for Higher Education," *Emerging Patterns in American Higher Education*, ed. Logan Wilson; A. J. Brumbaugh, *State-Wide Planning and Coordination of Higher Education* (Atlanta: Southern Regional Education Board, 1963); Arthur Browne, "The Institution and the System: Autonomy and Coordination," *Long-Range Planning in Higher Education*, ed. Owen Knorr (Boulder, Colo.: Western Interstate Commission for Higher Education, 1965); T. R. McConnell, "State Systems of Higher Education," *Universal Higher Education*, ed. Earl J. McGrath (New York: McGraw-Hill Book Co., 1966); James G. Paltridge, "Toward a Systems Model for State Coordination," *Educational Record*, Winter 1969.

The major questions facing elementary and secondary education on the one hand and education beyond the high school on the other are significantly different. Furthermore, the sheer magnitude of the elementary-secondary job almost inevitably creates a situation in which higher education has to receive less attention than it deserves if a single agency is trying to do the whole job.[16]

Though a state board of education may be able to accomplish the task of coordinating all levels of education in states like Idaho, Montana, and Rhode Island, the evidence indicates that in states with larger and more complex systems (Michigan, New York, and Pennsylvania), higher education has suffered as a result of such attempts.

There would probably also be widespread—but not unanimous[17]—agreement with T. R. McConnell's ultimate position on voluntary coordination:

I have long been an advocate of . . . voluntary coordination . . . but have now concluded that purely voluntary methods, at a certain stage of a state's development of facilities and resources for higher education, are almost certain to be ineffective. . . . they are unlikely to produce the continuing and impartial planning on which a comprehensive and diversified system of higher education must be built.[18]

Finally, if we accept the arguments that a coordinating agency should concern itself exclusively with higher education and that it should not be voluntary, there remains the issue of coordinating board versus consolidated governing board. The proper choice between these alternatives probably depends very heavily on a state's particular circumstances: the size and complexity of its system of higher education; its political traditions; its needs and resources. A look at Table 1, in chapter 2, will show that most states which use a consolidated governing board have relatively few institutions to coordinate (community colleges are sometimes not under agency jurisdiction) and that many are among the less affluent. States with many institutions are probably better off with a coordinating

16. Letter to President James Cole, Bowdoin College, Brunswick, Maine, January 30, 1967, p. 1.
17. For a dissenting view, see M. M. Chambers, *Voluntary Statewide Coordination in Public Higher Education* (Ann Arbor: University of Michigan Press, 1961).
18. "The Coordination of State Systems," *Emerging Patterns in American Higher Education*, ed. Logan Wilson, p. 136.

board. Indeed, most experts seem to favor the coordinating board over the consolidated governing board, partly because in states where institutions are already governed by local or segmental boards, the coordinating board allows them more autonomy and is politically easier to insert into the structure than is a consolidated governing board, which must supersede existing boards. Miller, in his letter to President Cole of Bowdoin, gives an even more important reason:

Assigning to the statewide board *only* planning and coordinating responsibilities has the advantage of organizationally precluding the possibility that the statewide board will concentrate upon day-to-day administration and neglect its responsibility for long-range statewide planning.[19]

Nevertheless, Miller continues, "either [type of board] can be made to function effectively if it is well staffed and administered. . . . organizational *structure* is less important than adherence to certain organizational and administrative principles."

Maine and West Virginia, neither of which had previously had a coordinating agency, have recently moved into the ranks of states with a consolidated governing board, the former after accepting the recommendation of a study by the Academy for Educational Development and the latter after rejecting the recommendation of a state study commission report that it adopt a coordinating agency. Utah has just switched from a coordinating board to a consolidated governing board that will oversee all its nine or so public institutions. Evidently the appeal in these cases was that statewide planning could be more effectively implemented by a board with strong governing powers. These changes may also reflect increasing state impatience with the complexities of achieving successful coordination through a coordinating board.

As mentioned earlier, California is currently in the throes of reexamining its whole basic structure of higher education. The staff report of the Joint Legislative Committee on Higher Education recommended, among other things, that the present university regents and state college trustees be merged into one consolidated board, thus eliminating the existing Coordinating Council. The statewide community college board would also come under the jurisdiction of the consolidated board. Subboards would coordinate the university and state college campuses and the local community colleges in each region of the state. From our perspective, these

19. P. 3.

proposals represent a kind of overkill: Integration and coordination would be puchased at an unnecessarily high price, in that the commendable goals of flexibility and interinstitutional cooperation which the staff report seeks could be obtained using a coordinating board with different membership and leadership (a public majority and a nationally recognized educator as executive director) and with certain regulatory powers in place of the present advisory ones. The report is surprisingly casual about this whole middle range of possibilities between voluntary coordination and total integration, saying only that "some form of 'mandatory' coordination, with powers and duties of the council carefully spelled out, is unlikely to be any more effective [than voluntary coordination has been]."[20]

In any case, the search for effective coordination continues, and some would insist that Algo D. Henderson's 1966 verdict is still valid: "No sufficient solution to the problem of planning and coordinating higher education at the state level has, as yet, been found."[21]

Confronted by this uncertainty (and, in some measure, contributing to it), many university and college presidents and trustees have mixed —and often contradictory—feelings about coordination. A particular group tends to welcome or reject the process not for itself but for the specific "answers" it proposes. (One is reminded of the dramatic liberal and conservative reversal of attitudes on judicial review between the 1930s and the 1960s, depending on the kinds of decisions being reached.) The state universities—particularly if they are of high caliber and have built impressive reputations on the strength of their teaching, research, and public service—are usually the most outspoken critics of coordination, and their hostility is understandable. They see themselves as institutions with national and even international horizons for whom narrow statewide planning boundaries are inappropriate. Furthermore, these universities—particularly if they have influential law schools or emphasize land-grant agricultural functions—have often won for themselves strong political support in the state capital and are reluctant to surrender this advantage to an untried middleman. Small wonder, then, that persons from these institutions frequently (though not invariably) labor to keep coordinating board powers weak and its leadership modest or that

20. California Staff of the Joint Legislative Committee on Higher Education, *The Challenge of Achievement* (Staff report to the Committee. Sacramento, 1969), p. 48.
21. "State Planning and Coordination of Public and Private Higher Education," *Educational Record*, Fall 1966, p. 507.

they use their political clout to teach a lesson in humility to the coordinating board the first time it comes up with a "wrong" answer. (Of course, when it comes up with a "right" answer—by opposing the bid of a state college to become a university, for instance—then university opposition is not so fierce!)

Anyone who appreciates the need to protect the qualitative elements of a system whose predominant tone seems to be quantitative will not lightly endorse altered state structures which might threaten that quality. But it is my considered judgment that, since state coordination is both legitimate and inevitable, the most prestigious universities and colleges would in the long run be wiser to cooperate in creating effective boards with outstanding leadership and in encouraging maximum institutional participation. After all, to rely on superior political power for success is to run at least two risks. First, power relationships can alter through time; already in several states the fast-growing state college sector has measurably increased its political base, and the community college movement, which promises to grow even faster, may well do the same. Those that live by the sword may perish by the sword. What is more, *force majeure* is hardly an effective technique for resolving everyday issues. To shift the metaphor, one can do everything with a bayonet but sit on it.

The second risk is that reliance on traditional modes of political influence may become less helpful as state executive offices turn increasingly to management information services, program and performance budgeting, and long-range state planning. (These changes are discussed in the next section.) A prominent state university president, whose relations with the governor's office had been extremely harmonious and fiscally rewarding, remarked rather wistfully that the governor could no longer protect the university from the efforts of his own staff to systematize all state activities. Surely, in such a case, a university could more effectively plead its national and international responsibilities to an outstanding educator serving as executive director of a coordinating agency than to typical state office personnel.

Occasionally, state colleges and community colleges have also risen up in opposition to statewide coordination, usually because the agency has blocked institutional ambitions, in particular the desire of the state colleges to add doctoral work. But, as Miller points out, to stress only the restrictive aspect of coordination is to present a false picture of how such agencies should operate:

The essential core function. . . is the development of a comprehensive state system of education beyond the high school which will adequately serve the needs of all of the people. This is a constructive mission, not a negative one. It involves the identification of needs and the development of plans to meet those needs, and there is not a state in this union in which this does not mean markedly increased state appropriations, a steady increase in the number and quality of programs offered, and in many states. . . the establishment of new institutions. . . . There is a negative aspect to this only in the sense that every institution probably cannot have everything it would like to have. . . . [Good coordination] does not stifle institutional growth; it assists institutions to grow in an orderly fashion.[22]

Not all agencies have lived up to this ideal, of course. But sometimes the attitudes and actions of persons in higher education have been partly responsible for the failures. If, in their desire to avoid negative controls, they labor to keep agency powers minimal and agency leadership weak, they should not be surprised when the results are indifferent rather than positive. Indifferent results, in turn, often arouse legislative hostility and may even result in the selection of a new agency director more attuned to survival. In fact, several agencies have gone through (or are still in the midst of) periods when politically savvy directors were vital in getting them safely past the Scylla of legislative impatience on the one side and the Charybdis of institutional resentment on the other. If, on the state's part, political pressures continue to be rawly applied, or, on the institution's part, presidents insist on having their own way, regardless, then a coordinating agency's period of oversensitivity to extraneous demands will be prolonged. But if the state political leadership begins to accept planning and budgeting techniques appropriate to higher education, and if institutions come to understand what can be gained by strengthening and working with the system, it should be possible for the agency, under the direction of an educational statesman, to move to the next stage and for the state and the institutions to reap the benefits of positive coordination at its best.[23]

22. James L. Miller, "New Directions in the Coordination of Higher Education" (Speech at workshop, Association of Governing Boards of Universities and Colleges Spring Conference, Williamsburg, Va., May 17–18, 1965).
23. That not all educators are likely to accept the logic of this argument is indicated by the fact that two members of the Advisory Committee to this study still retained major reservations about statewide coordination after reading the manuscript in draft. See Appendix B for excerpts from their letters of reaction.

Looking Ahead

With so many basic changes having occurred in this field during the past twenty years, it may seem the height of folly to try to look ahead. Yet in both higher education and state government, there are discernible trends which will probably affect statewide coordination in important ways, and this study would be remiss if it did not at least speculate about their possible impact.

By far the most significant developments are those taking place in the realm of state government reforms. We will deal with these in some detail after making a brief survey of other relevant trends.

Further expansion

One major trend in higher education that will undoubtedly be extended into the future is the steady increase in the percentage of college-age youth who attend some kind of postsecondary institution. The 50 percent goal set by President Truman's Commission in 1947 has been met, and the talk now is of universal higher education,[24] at least through so-called 14th grade. As a consequence, institutions are having to wrestle with such issues as open admissions and special programs for the disadvantaged; and one can anticipate that both the additional costs of handling larger numbers of students and the special costs of handling a more heterogeneous group of students will draw statewide coordinating agencies more deeply into matters of admissions, financial aid, articulation, and special programs.

Involvement in contemporary problems

Another trend (which is, in a sense, a continuation of an existing trend that will probably intensify so drastically as to constitute a change in kind) is the increasing involvement of universities and colleges in the contemporary problems of the community, region, state, and nation. This involvement will probably have its primary impact on the institutions themselves; but inevitably questions of overlap, interinstitutional cooperation, and financial support and accountability will arise, and here the coordinating agencies may be of some service. A good agency will en-

24. See, for instance, McGrath, ed., *Universal Higher Education*.

courage initiative at the local level but will also help to foster interinstitutional consortia (including the private sector, if it wants to participate).

Relations with the private sector

State relations with the private sector of higher education will probably multiply and, if the Illinois, New York, and Pennsylvania examples are any precedent, the coordinating agency will play a central role. Federal programs administered by the coordinating agency will work in this same direction insofar as they require the participation of both public and private sectors.

Effects of Federal programs

The certainty of more Federal programs in higher education is matched only by the uncertainty of how they will be channeled: to the student as grant or loan, to the faculty member for research, to the institution as block grant or categorical aid, to the state as general grant or grant earmarked for specific purposes, or (most likely) some combination of these. If the state receives any significant portion of Federal money (through tax sharing, as Pechman and Heller proposed some time ago and as President Nixon has suggested in his concept of "Creative Federalism"), the coordinating agency will almost certainly be the means for distributing it in the field of higher education. Even if the institutions themselves are the recipients of Federal funds, a state agency may be asked to administer the program, as was done with Title I of the Higher Education Facilities Act of 1963. Thus, even though new Federal programs will probably mean a strengthening of the relative Federal influence, the influence of the state will not decline in an absolute sense, and the coordinating agency's role will be somewhat increased.

Impact of faculty and student militancy

The trend toward greater faculty and student militancy is an even larger imponderable. So far, neither faculty nor students have paid much attention to the phenomenon of statewide coordination; only recently has the American Association of University Professors, through its Committee R, shown serious interest in the subject. But as coordinating agencies become more actively involved in such issues as faculty salaries, percentage quotas for various academic ranks, teacher-student ratios, year-round operation, admissions policies, transferability of credits and financial aid, it seems inevitable that faculty organizations (particularly unions engaged in collective bargaining) and student groups will take an increased interest in their activities. This means that statewide links will have to be forged between these groups and the coordinating agencies for purposes of communication.

Developments in state government

The probable developments in state government alluded to previously are several: some pertaining to legislative functions, some to executive functions, and some to constitutional revision.

Legislative Functions: Pertinent developments in the legislative branch of state government relate mostly to fiscal oversight. Some twenty states now have joint legislative budget committees which use at least some professional research staff. These committees are increasingly thorough in their examination of executive budgets, and higher education can expect no exemption from their scrutiny. During the past decade, reapportionment has resulted in an abnormally high turnover of personnel and, insofar as it leads to increased two-party competition, may continue to do so in the future. This rapid turnover may mitigate somewhat the closer legislative surveillance of higher education which might otherwise accompany the move to annual sessions and the improvement of staff services to standing committees. In summary, then, these legislative developments mean that the good old days, when higher education received substantial appropriations with few questions asked, are over. Thus, institutions are no longer justified in opposing coordinating agencies on the grounds that they are intruders in Utopia.

Executive Functions: More apposite to this study are developments taking place in the executive branch, where the office of governor is gradually being strengthened to make it the central focus for all state policies, including ultimately those in education. The governor's general powers are in the process of being expanded: prohibitions against a governor's succeeding himself in office are being repealed (only thirteen states now have such a provision); his term of office is being changed from two to four years (all but eleven now have four-year terms); his powers of appointment are being extended; and his veto powers are all but universal (only one state does not grant the governor this power; forty states allow the governor an item veto).

Proponents of the strong governor position are not enthusiastic about multimember independent boards (particularly if those members serve staggered terms). How, they ask, can a governor with a mandate to change things be held responsible if he finds that major segments of public policy spending sizable amounts of state funds are removed from his effective control?

Terry Sanford carried the strong governor theory a step farther: The governor's role with the independent boards should be a powerful one not only so that he can govern in general more coherently but also because his influence is necessary to protect the public interest in particular fields. Sanford criticizes the "self-serving" behavior of some professional leaders in fields like health and education; he is skeptical about the ability of so-called independent boards to resist being captured: "Too often they become 'dependent,' harking to the direction of the professionals."[25] Sanford's thesis is that, the governor, having played a strong role in setting goals for higher education and thus being assured that they are, in fact, in the public interest, will throw his full weight behind efforts to find adequate support for those goals. Previous efforts to hold the governor at arm's length from higher education policy have probably harmed the cause more than they have helped it: "More universities have suffered from political indifference than have ever been upset by political interference."[26] Sanford does not explain, however, just what happens to higher education when a benign strong governor—one who has set precedents for extensive and perhaps welcome gubernatorial intervention—is followed by a less sympathetic governor who may use these channels for unhappy ends.

The strong governor movement will receive even stronger impetus from developments occurring in the governor's planning and financial functions. The Massachusetts example cited in chapter 10 can be taken as illustrative of what may happen in other states over the next twenty years. Under a Housing and Urban Development grant from the Federal government, the Office of Planning and Program Coordination in the Massachusetts Executive Office for Administration and Finance published a study in late 1968 proposing a two-phase reform of all executive agencies. All 170-odd units were to be reorganized initially into one of nine secretariats, each under the supervision of a secretary appointed by and reporting to the governor; each secretary would, within two years,

25. *Storm Over the States* (New York: McGraw-Hill Book Co., 1967).
26. Ibid., p. 199.

propose such further administrative modifications as seemed appropriate. The legislature accepted the basic plan, merely postponing its initiation until April 1971. In the meantime, a unit in the Office of Planning and Program Coordination has been given the following tasks:

> Development and piloting of a program-oriented budgeting system, utilizing cost-identification capabilities of the state's new automated financial information system, and program analysis techniques to be developed within the agencies concerned and within the Bureau of the Budget.
>
> Description and analysis of the state's present information sources, systems and linkages in the health and social service agencies in the "human services" grouping, and development of a rational, workable model of an integrated state-wide information system for this grouping.[27]

If other states pass similar reorganization plans, two consequences are possible. First, yet another layer of review would be added to an already complex system. (In Massachusetts, for instance, the levels would be the local campus of the university, the central headquarters of the university, the board of higher education, the secretary of educational affairs, and the governor and legislature.) Second, program budgeting techniques and management information systems deemed appropriate to other state activities would be applied as well to higher education.

If such reorganizations should indeed occur, then persons in higher education would have to face the fact that their choice is not between having a stronger coordinating agency or retaining the status quo (much less returning to a laissez-faire situation); it is between having a stronger coordinating agency or being ingested into the executive branch of state government. Nor is it at all certain that even a strong coordinating agency can prevent this ingestion; clearly, a governor who has some 170 state activities to administer and coordinate must be very hesitant about granting exemptions from the prescribed structure. But surely, of the many agencies which engage in special pleading for their particular causes, a strong coordinating agency—one which has demonstrated its concern for the public interest by making tough decisions when necessary—is in a good position to argue effectively the case of higher educa-

27. Massachusetts Office of Planning and Program Coordination, *Modernization of the Government of the Commonwealth of Massachusetts as Enacted 1969* (Boston: Commonwealth of Massachusetts, 1969), p. 6.

tion as a unique type of state activity. Only if thus convinced, will state officials be likely to grant higher education a "floating status" outside the organization charts and to defer to the coordinating agency's judgment on the extent to which program budgeting and management information system can be appropriately applied to higher education.[28]

Constitutional Revision: A de jure floating status of sorts has already been obtained by the grant of constitutional autonomy in six states: to the universities in California, Michigan, and Minnesota; to the coordinating board in Oklahoma; to the consolidated governing board in Georgia; to the state department of education acting as the consolidated governing board in Idaho. Under such a grant, the boards usually have general supervision, management, and control over all the institutions under their jurisdictions and in theory are free of normal state operating controls. The constitutional autonomy of the universities in California, Michigan, and Minnesota is often cited as one factor contributing to their high quality, and university spokesmen in other states are anxious to achieve similar status.

Recently there have been movements to revise the constitutions in at least nine states, and the issue of autonomy has naturally arisen. Some state officials have shown reluctance to retain or extend constitutional autonomy, since they fear that such a status might insulate institutions from their proper concern with the public interest. In Maryland, it was agreed instead to continue the statutory autonomy under which the university has operated since 1952. Quite possibly both state legislators and university spokesmen are overestimating the de facto protection which constitutional autonomy gives; events in California and Michigan have revealed the financial vulnerability of even autonomous universities.

Nevertheless, having endorsed in chapter 1 the concept of procedural autonomy for institutions, I would favor constitutional autonomy from state administrative controls for all "mature" institutions or segments of higher education, *with the condition that explicit provision is made for statewide coordination of their program development.* Such a provision is necessary to prevent such situations as the one that arose in Michigan, where the state board of education as coordinating board was given general leadership and planning responsibilities, but each university governing board was granted constitutional autonomy with control over its own

28. Happily, the Western Interstate Commission for Higher Education has just such a study of management information systems currently under way under the direction of Dr. Ben Lawrence.

programs. The New York draft constitution handled this potential problem by making explicit the planning and coordinating role of the Board of Regents and then giving to the governing boards of the State University and City University control of their programs insofar as is "consistent with other provisions of this article."

In summary, then, I believe that substantive developments in higher education should not be put beyond state reach by a grant of constitutional autonomy. Rather, the essential protection of autonomy must come from a coordinating agency which combines effective action with deep sensitivity to academic values. As an incidental value, the operation of an effective coordinating agency will help to reassure the state that its essential interests are being protected and will thereby make it more willing to grant to institutions constitutional autonomy from state procedural controls.

Epilogue

It has been said that the United States, after 250 years as an agricultural society and 90 years as an industrial one, is now moving to a postindustrial age in which innovation and theoretical knowledge will be crucial and universities will replace industries as the dominant institutions. Even if this vision of "the learning society" is exaggerated, higher education is clearly being drawn ever deeper into the political arena.[29]

If, as Henry Adams observed, it is the mark of an educated man to react sensitively to the lines of force that dominate his age, we all—in higher education and government alike—have an obligation to try to understand what is going on and why. In doing so, we will be aided if we can accept Chancellor Gould's advice to dispense with the stereotypes so tempting to each side and strive to achieve mutual respect and trust. Though there may be, as Gould says, "charlatans and hacks" on both sides, much more can be gained by assuming the good faith even of those with whom agreement is difficult.[30]

Such forbearance will be especially important in the future, as the possibilities for conflict increase:

29. Dwight Waldo, "The University in Relation to the Governmental-Political: An Introductory Survey" (Paper presented at the Southern Methodist University Symposium on the American University, Dallas, Texas, July 1969).
30. Samuel B. Gould, "The University and State Government: Fears and Realities," *Campus and Capitol*, ed. W. John Minter (Boulder, Colo.: Western Interstate Commission for Higher Education, 1966), p. 4.

We may expect to see the tension between institutional independence and public accountability grow in intensity. There will be greater stress between the desire for autonomy and the pressure for coordinated effort. It will take all the statesmanship the academic community and the government can muster to enable colleges and universities to serve the broader public interests while preserving the identity, the integrity, the initiative, and the morale of individual institutions and, especially, the intellectual freedom of faculty and students.[31]

Sir Eric Ashby's advice to African universities experiencing troubles with their governments might well apply to emerging relations in this country. He suggests that academics should try to reach agreement amongst themselves on a redefinition of autonomy which will adequately protect the public interest while preserving the essentials of the academic enterprise. "The fewer principles they insist upon, the more united they are likely to be in defending them, and the more uncompromising they can afford to be about them." [32] In addition, he recommends that they approach the state at a time when no crisis in university-state relations exists and request a dispassionate discussion of the principles involved and of the appropriate machinery to handle university-state business in the light of mutually agreed principles.[33]

The "appropriate machinery," I believe, will turn out to be some form of coordinating agency. I am under no illusion, however, that it will be a panacea; as has been emphasized time and again in this report, equilibrium between higher education and state government is difficult to achieve. In fact, when one is confronted with the numerous and inevitable problems posed by the planning and coordination of higher education, one is tempted to conclude that the process is by nature incapable of equilibrium. But few important activities are carried on in an atmosphere of sweetness and light. It might be well to recall here Churchill's defense of the democratic process: It is the worst system of government except any other than has ever been tried. Perhaps it is not too negative to urge that the tensions and disagreements besetting the coordinating process

31. T. R. McConnell, "Governments and the University: A Comparative Analysis," *Governments and the University* (Frank Gersten Lectures, University of York. Toronto: Macmillan of Canada; New York: St. Martin's Press, 1966), p. 92.
32. *Universities: British, Indian, African* (Cambridge, Mass.: Harvard University Press, 1966), p. 342.
33. Ibid., p. 343.

are a lesser evil than either a return to the political jungle, where only the strongest institutions prosper, or a move to direct state administration, which could reduce higher education to mediocrity and uniformity.

Though politicians and the public may find it irritating to be told over and over that higher education is qualitatively a different kind of operation from other state activities, such happens to be the case. With roots that go back for hundreds of years, with a delicate inner rationale that differs markedly from those of government and industry, our universities and colleges are geese that lay golden eggs, and to kill them by improper treatment would rob our society of enormous benefits. The state has every right to assure itself that the institutions within its jurisdiction are operating in the broad public interest, but it must be careful, in interpreting that interest, to recognize the special need of universities and colleges for a high degree of autonomy. It has been said that no one who does not love a university well should be allowed to tamper with it. We must hope that the coordinating and planning agencies, which will have such vital roles to play, will always be characterized not only by their concern for the public interest but also by their genuine affection and respect for our institutions of higher education.

TWO EXAMPLES OF FORMULA BUDGETING APPLIED TO HIGHER EDUCATION

1. *Connecticut:*

   a) Faculty

Level of Instruction	Faculty/ Student Ratio	Credit Hrs. Per F.T.E. Student	Student Credit Hrs. = 1 Faculty Position	Faculty Position	Salary Level: Midpoint A–AA Rating: AAUP
Lower division	19.35 × 15.5 =		300	= 1	Assistant Professor
Upper division	11.60 × 15.5 =		180	= 1	Average: Assistant-Associate
Master's degree	7.5 × 12.0 =		90	= 1	Associate Professor
Doctoral degree	7.5 × 8.0 =		60	= 1	Full Professor
Thesis supervision & independent study	—	—	25	= 1	Full Professor

   b) Nonfaculty — 2 clerical positions for one dean
   1 clerical position for one department chairman
   1 clerical position for four faculty
   1 lab assistant for 50 stations

   c) Library — Clapp–Jordan formula

2. *Oklahoma:*
   After deriving a faculty salary budget along the lines of those given above for Connecticut, the Oklahoma institutional budget formulas are then determined as follows:

   a) Budget Base: Faculty salaries plus 30% of faculty salaries constitute the Budget Base

   b) Organized Activities Related to Instruction: 3% of Budget Base

   c) General Administration: 7% of Budget Base

   d) General Expenses: 8% of Budget Base

   e) Organized Research: 12% of Budget Base

   f) Extension and Public Service: University of Oklahoma: 14%; Oklahoma State University: 11% of Budget Base

   g) Library: 8% of Budget Base

   h) Physical Plant: 16% of Budget Base

SOURCE: Ronald M. Brown, "Formula Budgeting for Higher Education" (Ann Arbor: Center for Higher Education, University of Michigan, October 26, 1968).

TWO DISSENTING OPINIONS

The following comments, dissenting somewhat from the conclusions and recommendations given in chapter 11, came from two members of the Advisory Committee.

You have done well but I must still remain completely unpersuaded. I will not trouble you with a long explanation for my dissent but will drop two propositions in passing:

1) At a recent conference that included primarily university presidents, I heard reluctant acquiescence in the proposition that since move toward coordination was general, it was inevitable and perhaps good. However, those who spoke most positively went on to say that what is required and required desperately is that the coordinating agencies get better staff. Universally it seems assumed that the cause of the shortcoming of the co-ordinating agency is the poor quality of staff. Perhaps one should ask whether it is not the position and the general conception of a coordinating agency which is the cause of the poor staff. The coordinators are expected to think about important educational problems that seem to have eluded the wisdom of university officers who are generally conceded to have good staff. Yet almost anyone in the United States who looks at higher education candidly will say that in a competition for a particular potential university officer, a university can readily win over any coordinating council, with the consequence the University will continue to draw the best staff. Under your accepted and apparently urged solution, we are condemned to try to solve our most rugged educational problems with our least satisfactory educational minds.

2) The premise on which you begin is that while education is good and the people who serve it do have a status which needs to be protected

against the rest of society, nevertheless perhaps the chief value which we should seek now is greater systemization and therefore greater economy in operation. Economies can be directed toward a variety of goods. In my judgment, even in this tight economy, good minds are in shorter supply than dollars and good ideas about education are in shorter supply than dollars. A system of educational organization that excludes or discourages many minds or invites a few minds to think on the problem is less efficient than one which leaves the field for thinking and creativity open, if the objective is more bright ideas instead of the spending of fewer dollars. You acknowledge that at one time the free market was the best environment in which to develop education but announce that the frontier has passed and now order is required. I suspect that the problems that we have to resolve now are more difficult than they were then and that the kinds of bright creative ideas that are required now will be no more congenial to bureaucratic or conservative government agencies or governors than they were then. The cleaner and tidier the blanket of coordination you throw around my shoulders the more oppressed I feel.

I think many of your conclusions are more nearly an expression of the position of people favoring strong statewide coordination than they are completely attractive to those of us charged with the problems of managing a specific institutional system. I guess I would have to say that I feel a good bit of your theory is better than my experience in reality.

I couldn't agree with you more than when you observe "that no one who does not love a university well should be allowed to tamper with it." I would guess that an overwhelming majority of the institutional presidents, who labor under the direction of a governing board, but whose lives are also influenced by statewide coordinating and planning agencies, would say that it is their experience that coordinating agencies are seldom dominated either by staff or members who "love a university." It is a fairly rare occurrence that a governor can be said to love a university either! Isn't the real essence of the trouble that governors and coordinating boards are usually more concerned with holding down costs than with somewhat tenuous concepts of academic quality which the public hardly understands and seldom is anxious to pay for? Governors and coordinating boards are generally so sufficiently removed from the immediate academic scene that they can be fairly calloused about delicate and sensitive subjects. I really am not so much arguing the logic of your conclusions as I am making a plea to recognize the frailties of human nature that so often make a beautifully conceived theoretical design a potentially destructive instrument.

BIBLIOGRAPHY

Abrahams, Louise. *State Planning for Higher Education.* Prepared for U.S. Department of Health, Education, and Welfare, Office of Education, Bureau of Research, under Contract no. OEC 0-8-980767-4634(010). Washington: Academy for Educational Development, 1969.

Allen, Harry S. "Voluntary Coordination of Higher Education in Colorado." MS, Office of Institutional Research, University of Nebraska, 1967.

Ashby, Sir Eric. "Self Government in Modern British Universities." *Science and Freedom*, December 1956, pp. 1–6.

———. *Universities: British, Indian, African.* Cambridge, Mass.: Harvard University Press, 1966.

Baade, Hans W., and Everett, Robinson O., eds. *Academic Freedom: The Scholar's Place in Modern Society.* Dobbs Ferry, N.Y.: Oceana Publications, 1964.

Berdahl, Robert O. *British Universities and the State.* Berkeley: University of California, 1959.

———. "The State Planning and Coordinating Agency for Higher Education." In *The Organization of Higher Education.* Proceedings of the Sixteenth Annual Legislative Work Conference, Southern Regional Education Board, White Sulphur Springs, W. Va., August 27–29, 1967. Pp. 51–65.

Bissell, Claude. In *University Affairs.* Association of Universities and Colleges in Canada, Ottawa, April 1967.

Blackmar, Frank W. *The History of Federal and State Aid to Higher Education in the United States.* Washington: Bureau of Education, 1890.

Brooks, George H. "The Relationship between Governmental Structure and the Financing of Public Higher Education in Colorado, 1960–69." Ph.D. dissertation, Colorado State University, 1969.

Brouillet, Frank B. "An Analysis of State of Washington's Method for Coordinating Higher Education." Ed.D. dissertation, University of Washington, 1968.

277

Browne, Arthur. "The Institution and the System: Autonomy and Coordination." In *Long-Range Planning in Higher Education*, edited by Owen Knorr. Boulder, Colo.: Western Interstate Commission for Higher Education, 1965. Pp. 39–48.

Brumbaugh, A. J. *State-Wide Planning and Coordination of Higher Education*. Atlanta: Southern Regional Education Board, 1963.

Budig, Gene A. *Governors and Higher Education*. Lincoln: University of Nebraska Press, 1969.

Bundy, McGeorge. "In Praise of Candor." *Educational Record*, Winter 1968, pp. 5–8.

California Coordinating Council for Higher Education. *Budget Report to the Legislature, 1968*. Staff report. CCHE no. 3, February 20, 1968.

———. *Budget Review in Public Higher Education*. Sacramento and San Francisco: CCHE no. 1022, December 1965.

———. *The Budget Review Role of the Coordinating Council for Higher Education*. CCHE no. 10, May 23, 1967.

———. *The Master Plan: Five Years Later*. Sacramento and San Francisco: CCHE no. 1024, March 1966.

———. *November Report on the Level of Support for Public Higher Education, 1968–69*. Staff report. CCHE no. 16, December 6, 1967.

———, Committee on Educational Programs. "Council Review of Proposed New Academic Programs," September 25, 1967.

———. "Preliminary Plan for Annual Survey of Educational Offerings, California State Colleges, and University of California," May 20, 1968.

California Master Plan Survey Team. *A Master Plan for Higher Education in California, 1960–75*. Prepared for the Liaison Committee of the State Department of Education and the Regents of the University of California. Sacramento: State Department of Education, 1960.

California Staff of the Joint Legislative Committee on Higher Education. *The Challenge of Achievement*. Staff Report to the Committee. Sacramento, 1969.

Cartter, Allan M. *An Assessment of Quality in Graduate Education*. Washington: American Council on Education, 1966.

———. "The Responsibility of States for Private Colleges and Universities." In *The Organization of Higher Education*. Proceedings of the Sixteenth Annual Legislative Work Conference, Southern Regional Education Board, White Sulphur Springs, W. Va., August 27–29, 1967. Pp. 67–73.

———. "Some Financial Implications of an Enlarged Federal Student Aid Program." MS, Chancellor's Office, New York University, 1969.

Chambers, Merritt M. *The Campus and the People: Organization, Support and Control of Higher Education in the Nineteen-Sixties*. Danville, Ill.: Interstate Printers and Publishers, 1960.

————. *Chance and Choice in Higher Education*. Danville, Ill.: Interstate Printers and Publishers, 1962.

————. *Freedom and Repression in Higher Education*. Bloomington, Ind.: Bloomcraft Press, 1965.

————. *Voluntary Statewide Coordination in Public Higher Education*. Ann Arbor: University of Michigan Press, 1961.

Colorado Commission on Higher Education. *Coordination, Planning, and Governance of Higher Education in Colorado*. Denver: Commission on Higher Education, 1969.

Committee on Government and Higher Education. *The Efficiency of Freedom*. Baltimore: Johns Hopkins Press, 1959.

Conant, James B. *Shaping Educational Policy*. New York: McGraw-Hill Book Co., 1964.

Cox, Lanier, and Harrell, Lester E., Jr. *The Impact of Federal Programs on State Planning and Coordination of Higher Education*. Atlanta: Southern Regional Education Board, 1969.

Education Commission of the States. *Control of Higher Education: Where Is It Heading? Compact* (whole issue), June 1969.

————. *Seven Crucial Issues in Education: Alternatives for State Action*. Denver: Educational Commission of the States, 1967.

Enarson, Harold. "Cooperative Planning to Meet the Needs of Increased Enrollments." In *Current Issues in Higher Education*, edited by G. Kerry Smith. Washington: Association for Higher Education, National Education Association, 1956. Pp. 316–21.

Eulau, Heinz, and Quinley, Harold. *State Officials and Higher Education*. General Report prepared for the Carnegie Commission on Higher Education. New York: McGraw-Hill Book Co., 1970.

Feinstein, Otto; Vann, Carl; Petengill, Robert; Weiss, John; Melman, Seymour; and Bocksteal, Eric. "Economics of Higher Education: Quality and Personalism." MS, Wayne State University, 1967.

Fuchs, Ralph. "Academic Freedom: Its Basic Philosophy, Function, and History." In *Academic Freedom: The Scholar's Place in Modern Society*, edited by Hans Baade and Robinson O. Everett. Dobbs Ferry, N.Y.: Oceana Publications, 1964. Pp. 1–16.

Gardner, John W. "Government and the Universities." In *Emerging Patterns in American Higher Education*, edited by Logan Wilson. Washington: American Council on Education, 1965. Pp. 286–92.

Glenny, Lyman A. *Autonomy of Public Colleges*. New York: McGraw-Hill Book Co., 1959.

————. "Institutional Autonomy for Whom?" In *The Troubled Campus: Current Issues in Higher Education*, edited by G. Kerry Smith. Washington: American Association of Higher Education; San Francisco: Jossey-Bass, 1970. Pp. 153–60.

————. "Long-Range Planning for State Educational Needs." In *Seven Crucial Issues in Education: Alternatives for State Action*. Denver: Education Commission of the States, 1967.

————. "Politics and Current Patterns in Coordinating Higher Education." In *Campus and Capitol*, edited by W. John Minter. Boulder, Colo.: Western Interstate Commission for Higher Education, 1966. Pp. 21–46.

————. "State Systems and Plans for Higher Education." In *Emerging Patterns in American Higher Education*, edited by Logan Wilson. Washington: American Council on Education, 1965. Pp. 86–103.

————. "Trends in Higher Education." In *Financing Higher Education*. Proceedings of the Fifteenth Annual Legislative Work Conference, Southern Regional Education Board, Asheville, N.C., July 27–30, 1966. Pp. 1–13.

Gould, Samuel B. "The University and State Government: Fears and Realities." In *Campus and Capitol*, edited by W. John Minter. Boulder, Colo.: Western Interstate Commission for Higher Education, 1966. Pp. 3–15.

Gove, Samuel. "The Massachusetts System of Higher Education in Transition." MS, Department of Political Science, University of Illinois, 1967.

————. "The Oregon State System of Higher Education." MS, Department of Political Science, University of Illinois, 1967.

Halstead, Kent. *Handbook for Statewide Planning in Higher Education*. Washington: Office of Education, forthcoming.

Heck, James. "Coordination of Higher Education in Illinois." MS, School of Education, University of Delaware, 1968.

Henderson, Algo D. *Policies and Practices in Higher Education*. New York: Harper, 1960.

————. "State Planning and Coordination of Public and Private Higher Education." *Educational Record*, Fall 1966, pp. 503–09.

Hetherington, Sir Hector. "On University Autonomy." In *University Autonomy: Its Meaning Today*. Paris: International Association of Universities, 1965.

Hofstader, Richard, and Metzger, Walter. *The Development of Academic Freedom in the United States*. New York: Columbia University Press, 1955.

Illinois Board of Higher Education. *A Master Plan for Higher Education in Illinois*. Springfield: Board of Higher Education, *Phase I:* 1964; *Phase II:* 1966.

Illinois Commission to Study Non-Public Higher Education in Illinois [McConnell Commission]. *Strengthening Private Higher Education in Illinois: A Report on the State's Role*. Springfield, 1969.

Jencks, Christopher. "Diversity in Higher Education." Consultant paper, White House Conference on Education, July 20–21, 1965.

Kirk, Russell. *Academic Freedom: An Essay in Definition*. Chicago: H. Regnery, 1955.

Knoller, Richard. "An Overview of Issues and Ideas Relating to State Aid to Non-Public Institutions of Higher Education." MS, Office of Institutional Studies, University of Vermont, 1969.

Knorr, Owen A., ed. *Long-Range Planning in Higher Education*. Boulder, Colo.: Western Interstate Commission for Higher Education, 1965.

Kroepsch, R. H., and Buck, D. P., eds. *Partnership for Progress*. Boulder, Colo.: Western Interstate Commission for Higher Education, 1967.

Lee, Eugene C., and Bowen, Frank. *The Governance of the Multicampus University*. Berkeley: Institute of Governmental Studies, University of California, 1971

Livesey, Lionel J., Jr. "Can Higher Education Be Planned?" MS, State University of New York, Albany, 1968.

MacIver, Robert M. *Academic Freedom in Our Time*. New York: Columbia University Press, 1955.

Marsh, Robert O. "Coordination of State Higher Education in Illinois: A Case Study." Ed.D. dissertation, Illinois State University, 1967.

————. "Illinois State Higher Education: Diversity Within Order." *Educational Record*, Summer 1969, pp. 300–04.

Martorana, Sebastian V., and Hollis, Ernest. *State Boards Responsible for Higher Education*. Washington: U.S. Department of Health, Education, and Welfare, Circular no. 619, 1960.

Massachusetts Office of Planning and Program Coordination. *Modernization of the Government of the Commonwealth of Massachusetts as Enacted 1969*. Boston: Commonwealth of Massachusetts, 1969.

Masters, Nicholas A. "The Role of the States." Consultant paper, White House Conference on Education, July 20–21, 1965.

Mayhew, Lewis B. *Long Range Planning for Higher Education*. Prepared for the National Institutes of Health, under Contract no. PH-43-66-1166, as amended under Contract no. PH-43-67-1461. Washington: Academy for Educational Development, 1969.

McConnell, Thomas R. "The Coordination of State Systems." In *Emerging Patterns in American Higher Education*, edited by Logan Wilson. Washington: American Council on Education, 1965. Pp. 129–40.

————. *A General Pattern for American Public Higher Education*. San Francisco: McGraw-Hill Book Co., 1962.

————. "Governments and the University: A Comparative Analysis." In *Governments and the University*. Frank Gersten Lectures, University of York. Toronto: Macmillan of Canada; New York: St. Martin's Press, 1966.

————. *Rationalizing the Development of Higher Education*. Berkeley: Center for Research and Development in Higher Education, University of California, 1966.

————. "State Systems of Higher Education." In *Universal Higher Education*, edited by Earl J. McGrath. New York: McGraw-Hill Book Co., 1966. Pp. 19–39.

————. "The University and the State: A Comparative Study." In *Campus and Capitol*, edited by W. John Minter. Boulder, Colo.: Western Interstate Commission for Higher Education, 1966. Pp. 89–118.

McGown, Wayne F. "How Can States Develop a Good Program-Planning-Budgeting System (PPBS) for Education?" In *Seven Crucial Issues in Education: Alternatives for State Action*. Denver: Education Commission of the States, 1967.

McGrath, Earl J., ed. *Universal Higher Education*. New York: McGraw-Hill Book Co., 1966.

Miller, James L., Jr. "Budgeting Processes." In *Financing Higher Education*. Proceedings of the Fifteenth Annual Legislative Work Conference, Southern Regional Education Board, Asheville, N.C., July 27–30, 1966. Pp. 29–32.

————. Letter to President James Cole, Bowdoin College, Brunswick, Maine, January 30, 1967.

————. "New Directions in the Coordination of Higher Education." Speech at workshop, Association of Governing Board of Universities and Colleges Spring Conference, Williamsburg, Va., May 17–18, 1965.

————. *State Budgeting for Higher Education: The Use of Formulas and Cost Analysis*. Michigan Governmental Studies no. 45, University of Michigan. Ann Arbor: Institute of Public Administration, 1964.

Millett, John D. "The Role of Coordination in Public Higher Education." Address to the Select Council on Post-High School Education, University of Southern Florida, Tampa, September 18, 1968.

————. "State Planning for Higher Education." *Educational Record*, Summer 1965, pp. 223–30.

————. "State-wide Planning and Coordination of Higher Education." In *The Organization of Higher Education*. Proceedings of the Sixteenth Annual Legislative Work Conference, Southern Regional Education Board, White Surphur Springs, W. Va., August 27–29, 1967. Pp. 5–19.

Minter, W. John, ed. *Campus and Capitol*. Boulder, Colo.: Western Interstate Commission for Higher Education, 1966.

Moos, Malcolm, and Rourke, Frank. *The Campus and the State*. Baltimore: Johns Hopkins Press, 1959.

Morrell, L. R. "A Look at Program Budgeting." *Educational Record*, Summer 1969, pp. 286–89.

Mountford, Sir James. *British Universities*. London: Oxford University Press, 1966.

Nelson, Fred. "State Aid to Private Colleges and Universities." MS, School of Education, Stanford University, 1968.

Newbry. L. W. "Commentary on 'The Finance of Higher Education,' by John Dale Russell." In *Partnership for Progress*, edited by R. H. Kroepsch and D. P. Buck. Boulder, Colo.: Western Interstate Commission for Higher Education, 1967. P. 15.

New York Select Commission on the Future of Private and Independent Higher Education in New York State [Bundy Commission]. *New York State and Private Higher Education*. Albany: State Education Department, 1968.

Oettinger, Anthony G. "The Myths of Educational Technology." *Saturday Review*, May 18, 1968, pp. 76–77, 97.

Ohio Board of Regents. *Master Plan for State Policy in Higher Education*. Columbus: The Board, 1966.

Palola, Ernest; Lehmann, Timothy; and Blischke, William R. *Higher Education By Design: The Sociology of Planning*. Berkeley: Center for Research and Development in Higher Education, University of California, 1970.

———. "Qualitative Planning: Beyond the Numbers Game." *Research Reporter*, vol. 3, no. 2. Berkeley: Center for Research and Development in Higher Education, University of California, 1968. Pp. 1–4.

Paltridge, James G. *California's Coordinating Council for Higher Education: A Study of Organizational Growth and Change*. Berkeley: Center for Research and Development in Higher Education, University of California, 1966.

———. *Conflict and Coordination in Higher Education: The Wisconsin Experience*. Berkeley: Center for Research and Development in Higher Education, University of California, 1968.

———. "Organizational Forms Which Characterize Statewide Coordination of Higher Education." MS, Berkeley: Center for Research and Development in Higher Education, University of California, 1965.

———. "Toward a Systems Model for State Coordination." *Educational Record*, Winter 1969. Pp. 71–77.

Perkins, James A. *The University in Transition*. Princeton, N.J.: Princeton University Press, 1966.

Pfnister, Allan, and Quehl, Gary. *Private Higher Education in the State of Missouri*. Jefferson City: Missouri Commission on Higher Education, 1967.

Pliner, Emogene. *Coordination and Planning*. Baton Rouge: Public Affairs Research Council of Louisiana, 1966.

[Robbins] Committee on Higher Education. *Higher Education*. London: Her Majesty's Stationery Office, 1963.

Rourke, Frank, and Brooks, Glen. *Managerial Revolution in Higher Education*. Baltimore: Johns Hopkins Press, 1966.

Rudolph, Frederick. *The American College and University*. New York: Vintage Books, 1962.

Russell, John Dale. *Control and Coordination of Higher Education in Michigan.* Staff study no. 12. Prepared for the Michigan Legislative Study Committee on Higher Education, Lansing, Mich., 1958.

———. "The Finance of Higher Education." In *Partnership for Progress,* edited by R. H. Kroepsch and D. P. Buck. Boulder, Colo.: Western Interstate Commission for Higher Education, 1967. Pp. 5–14.

Sanford, Terry. *Storm Over the States.* New York: McGraw-Hill Book Co., 1967.

Schultz, Raymond, and Stickler, Hugh. "Vertical Extension of Academic Programs in Institutions of Higher Education." *Educational Record,* Summer 1965, pp. 231–41.

Smart, John Marshall. "Political Aspects of State Coordination of Higher Education: The Process of Influence." Ph.D. dissertation, University of Southern California, 1968.

Southern Regional Education Board. *Financing Higher Education.* Proceedings of the Fifteenth Annual Legislative Work Conference, Asheville, N.C., July 27–30, 1966.

———. *The Organization of Higher Education.* Proceedings of the Sixteenth Annual Legislative Work Conference, White Sulphur Springs, W. Va., August 27–29, 1967.

Texas Liaison Committee on Texas Private Colleges and Universities. *Pluralism and Partnership.* Austin: Coordinating Board, Texas College and University System, 1968.

Thomas, Ann Van Wynen, and Thomas, A. J., Jr. *Constitutionality of Aid by the State of Texas to Church Related Institutions of Higher Education.* Austin: Coordinating Board, Texas College and University System, 1969.

Tool, Marc. "The California State Colleges Under the Master Plan." Report to the Academic Senate of the California State Colleges, Sacramento State College, August 1, 1966.

University Grants Committee. *University Development, 1962–67.* Cmnd. 3820. London: Her Majesty's Stationery Office, 1968.

Usdan, Michael D.; Minar, David W.; and Hurwitz, Emanuel, Jr. *Education and State Politics.* New York: Teachers College Press, Columbia University, 1969.

Utah Coordinating Council of Higher Education. *The Importance of Coordination in Higher Education.* Salt Lake City: Coordinating Council of Higher Education, 1968.

Valente, William. *An Analysis of the Proposed Master Plan for Higher Education for the Commonwealth of Pennsylvania.* Villanova, Pa.: Villanova University Press, 1967.

Waldo, Dwight. "The University in Relation to the Governmental-Political: An Introductory Survey." Paper delivered at the Southern Methodist University Symposium on the American University, Dallas, Tex., July 1969.

Washington Temporary Advisory Council on Public Higher Education. *Higher Education in Washington*. Olympia, 1969.

White, Charles H. "The Kentucky Council on Public Higher Education: Analysis of a Change in Structure." Ph.D. dissertation, Ohio State University, 1967.

Wildavsky, Aaron. *The Politics of the Budgetary Process*. Boston: Little, Brown, and Co., 1964.

Williams, Harry. *Planning for Effective Resource Allocation in Universities*. Washington: American Council on Education, 1966.

Williams, Jack K. "Are State Systems of Coordination Antithetical to Institutional Autonomy?" Paper presented at the Twenty-fifth National Conference on Higher Education, American Association of Higher Education, Chicago, March 1–4, 1970.

Williams, Robert L. *Legal Bases for Coordinating Boards in Thirty-Eight States*. Chicago: Council of State Governments, 1967.

Wilson, Logan. "The Abuses of the University." Commencement Address, Michigan State University, March 10, 1968.

———. "Form and Function in American Higher Education." In *Emerging Patterns in American Higher Education*, edited by Logan Wilson. Washington: American Council on Education, 1965. Pp. 29–37.

———. "State Coordination of Higher Education." Speech to the Association for Higher Education of the Washington Education Association, Seattle, December 2, 1966.

———, ed. *Emerging Patterns in American Higher Education*. Washington: American Council on Education, 1965.

American Council on Education
Logan Wilson, *President*

THE AMERICAN COUNCIL ON EDUCATION, founded in 1918, is a *council* of educational organizations and institutions. Its purpose is to advance education and educational methods through comprehensive voluntary and cooperative action on the part of American educational associations, organizations, and institutions.